Fiction's Present

Situating Contemporary Narrative Innovation

Edited by

R. M. Berry
and
Jeffrey R. Di Leo

STATE UNIVERSITY OF NEW YORK PRESS

Published by
State University of New York Press, Albany

For information, contact State University of New York Press, Albany, NY
www.sunypress.edu

Production by Kelli W. LeRoux
Marketing by Anne M. Valentine

Library of Congress Cataloging-in-Publication Data

Fiction's present : situating contemporary narrative innovation / edited by
    R. M. Berry, Jeffrey R. Di Leo.
        p. cm.
    Includes bibliographical references and index.
    ISBN 978-0-7914-7263-7 (hardcover : alk. paper)
    ISBN 978-0-7914-7264-4 (pbk. : alk. paper)
    1. Fiction—History and criticism.   I. Berry, R. M.   II. Di Leo, Jeffrey R.

PN3321.F55 2008
809.3—dc22   2007001679

10 9 8 7 6 5 4 3 2 1

Art lives upon discussion, upon experiment, upon curiosity, upon variety of attempt, upon the exchange of views and the comparison of standpoints; and there is a presumption that those times when no one has anything particular to say about it and has no reason to give for practice or preference, though they may be times of genius, are not times of development—are times, possibly even, a little, of dullness.

—Henry James, "The Art of Fiction"

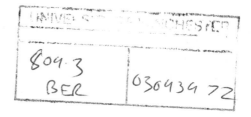

Contents

Contents

Preface

R. M. BERRY AND JEFFREY R. DI LEO

This book is the result of a wonderful conversation its editors had some years back concerning both the current state of literature and its criticism and connections between contemporary philosophy and contemporary fiction. It was our hope then to encourage further discussion of the present inflection of fiction, which we viewed as Janus-faced, looking both forward to the novel's radically changed, political, economic, and technological circumstances and backward to its history of achievements and problems. We decided to begin with a special issue of the journal *symplokē* on the topic "Fiction's Present" (vol. 12, nos. 1–2: 2004), and in the call for papers we asked whether fiction that continued in the tradition of modernist innovation still had any reality for emergent political groups and cultures—a question that seemed to us fundamental. We also asked whether the novel could react to the present demands of global capitalism without abandoning its formal distinctiveness, and we suggested a number of topics ranging from the relation of postcolonialism to the idea of an "avant garde" and the role of value in constituting any present. From the start, it was our aim to juxtapose scholarly articles with essays by practicing novelists.

The creative and critical responses included in the original *symplokē* issue, along with several additional or revised contributions here, seemed to us significant, in part, for the innovative ways in which they simultaneously engaged the aesthetic, political, philosophical, and cultural dimensions of our topic. Much of what we appreciated was their recognition that discussions of fiction's present required adventurous thinking, the most exciting examples of which did not *uncover* spaces hidden from public view but *created* vistas in which the political, aesthetic, and emotional dimensions of contemporary fiction could be performed. Examinations of fiction's present seemed to us most informative not when they were defending philosophical distinctions or developing literary classifications but when they grappled with elusive topics such as the meaning of a narrative present or the relation of fiction's medium to its representations of context. This process, when pursued diligently, seemed to break down traditional divisions of academic and intellectual labor. It compelled, for example, the fiction writers to become more philosophical and the theorists to become more imaginative.

Philosophers in America often pride themselves on their ignorance of works of contemporary fiction, and fiction writers often act as though nothing could be less in tune with their work than contemporary theoretical discourse. Nevertheless, when novelists reflect on philosophical questions and radical thinkers engage with literary texts, remarkable things can occur. The chapters in this book are noteworthy, in large measure, because of their willingness to venture into, and refusal to abandon, topics considered out of bounds, politically suspect, intellectually barren, or otherwise institutionally taboo by academic philosophy or critical theory. Their tendency to move from historicist or sociological perspectives to investigations of linguistic or constitutive conditions, or even to frankly evaluative judgments, suggests an openness not usually found in writing devoted to well-established philosophical problems or literary periods. Obviously much is to be learned when we are encouraged to speak to topics that both engage our interests and push us beyond disciplinary boundaries.

Of course, no intellectual daring can make up for the gaps in the present text. To its editors, the thinkers and writers *missing* from our volume have at times seemed almost as consequential for our aims as those included. We requested essays from numerous individuals whose prior commitments prevented them from contributing, and there were others whom, for one extraneous reason or another, we neglected to contact or contacted too late. Countless social groups and culturally distinctive communities, both in the United States and elsewhere, are omitted or underrepresented, and critics studying formal innovation and writers questioning their medium are privileged at the expense of critics taking a broader culturalist approach or writers representing mainstream publishing. Everywhere the issues raised and topics broached reflect not merely the contributors' local perspectives but the editors' individual, even idiosyncratic, sense of what is fundamental. However, our goal from the outset was provocation rather than inclusiveness, and we proceeded with the conviction that to hesitate for fear of omissions was to postpone fiction's present indefinitely. "Art lives upon discussion," said Henry James in "The Art of Fiction" (1884), ". . . and there is a presumption that those times when no one has anything particular to say about it and has no reason to give for practice or preference . . . are not times of development—are times, possibly even, a little, of dullness." To the editors, the value of this book is not in its coherence or unassailability but in the seriousness of the criticism it incites. The present materializes in quarrels. It is toward such a beginning that these writings work.

Acknowledgments

Chapters by R. M. Berry and Jeffrey R. Di Leo, Samuel R. Delany, Timothy S. Murphy, Leslie Scalapino, Robert L. McLaughlin, Lidia Yuknavitch, Alan Singer, Brian Evenson, Robert L. Caserio, Lance Olsen, Michael Martone, Sue-Im Lee, Percival Everett, Raymond Federman, Ronald Sukenick, Jerome Klinkowitz, and Carole Maso were first published in *symplokē* 12:1–2 (2004). Copyright © *symplokē* 2004. Published by the University of Nebraska Press. Reprinted with permission.

We would like to thank our contributors for sharing their essays and insights with us. We also would like to thank David C. Felts, Brenda Mills and Candice Chovanec Melzow for their assistance in the preparation of this volume. A special note of thanks goes out to David for his assistance in the preparation of the index.

Work on this volume was generously supported by a research grant from the University of Houston-Victoria, Office of the Provost.

Introduction

12 Theses on Fiction's Present

R. M. BERRY AND JEFFREY R. DI LEO

1. Fiction's present is the intersection of everything that fiction has been and everything that it will become. Forms of writing and reading are always already linked to their historical development and traditions, and yet they are being continuously pulled into a future replete with possibilities. We could even say that change and temporality are the only constants in fiction's present, a characterization that leaves us baffled at the word "present" itself. In comparison with fiction's long past and open future, the present seems relatively brief and unstable, with hardly any durability at all, yet this does not diminish its value. On the contrary, value may well exist nowhere else. That is, if fiction still has significance for us, then it necessarily has it now, in the present, all other significance being latent or potential. In other words, the fleeting, unrealizable present may simply name the condition of fiction's continued existence, distinguishing it from whatever, like epic, has only a past or, like justice, only a future. As the elusive space where the past meets our dreams and desires, fiction's present extends the promise of change to all who would undergo it.

  2. The present demands placed upon fiction are unlike any it has experienced previously. Along with its rich history of problems and innovations, fiction at present must confront the suspicion that forms like the novel and story, as well as the framing concepts of literature and art, have exhausted themselves. Many feel that recent military, economic, and environmental threats demand more direct forms of verbal intervention, for example, essays, polemics, autobiographies, journalistic accounts, critiques, and treatises. The war in Iraq, the September 11, 2001, attacks, the rise of globalization, resurgent neoconservatism,

1

and ubiquitous religious conflicts all hold the potential to energize or enervate literary practice, transforming fiction's present from a natural juncture of past and future into a question: To be present, what must fiction now *do*? Should the novel engage the politically and economically pressing issues of the day, in this way hoping to secure its relevance, or will fiction's effort to mirror contemporary history absent itself, dispelling what has made fiction distinctive? That is, is the present something fiction needs to achieve, or is it an inescapable fact, a condition that fiction can, in becoming itself, only acknowledge? Just as literary historians have attributed modernism's early twentieth-century innovations to the horrors of World War I and the scientific advances of relativity theory, the present of fiction may seem in retrospect to have been produced willy-nilly by twenty-first-century forces and events. But it also is possible that fiction's difference from other, putatively more direct, forms may persist through these changes. In fact, one can even wonder whether the second thesis really describes a historically unique situation at all, or whether it merely makes explicit what the adjective "present" means. That is, to the extent that the demands on fiction are present, not past, they remain irreducible to what has come before. The thesis still expresses a predicament, but one having less to do with fiction's contemporary situation than with our difficulty representing it. If presentness is not an object but a limit, then fiction's problem is presentness itself.

3. Economic pressures seriously complicate the task, both critical and practical, of recognizing fiction's present. Many publishing houses are going out of business, cutting back extensively on the publication of new fiction or becoming absorbed into a decreasing number of publishing conglomerates. Within surviving houses, the change is not so much from quality-driven to market-driven decisions as from a business culture where this distinction made sense to a business culture in which it has become unintelligible. "Economic decision making" now sounds redundant, and niche marketing, the once-imagined solution to market consolidation, has proven largely ineffective for the marketing category "literary fiction." Unlike car buyers and clothing shoppers, consumers of aesthetically ambitious novels do not generally presume to know in advance of reading how to identify the commodity they seek, expecting literariness to be defined, at least in part, at the level of production. As a result, this market segment has proven difficult to target. And even though technological innovations such as e-books, e-zines, and on-demand printing have reduced production costs and increased consumers' access to "literary fiction," these innovations have done more to create the material conditions for a richer, more diverse present than to actually establish it. In fact, they may have furthered consolidation. It is estimated that over 150,000 new titles were published in 2003, which would require one to read 411 books a day 365 days a year in order to sample them. If the untested conventional wisdom were accepted that 95 percent of these books are "worthless," then culling the "worthy" 5 percent would require an army of critics and reproduce the earlier problems of homogenization, parochialism, and arbitrariness. And one would still need to read twenty new books a day just to sample the "worthies"! This means that readers are increasingly dependent on selections made by bookstore chains and large-circulation review publications, transferring the economic constraints on fiction's present from the level of production to that of distribution and promotion. The critic who sets out to represent fiction's present based on the books in Borders or the *New York Times Book Review* presupposes a prior constructive activity so vast, systematically organized, and consequential that if it does not render the critic's later construction trivial, it renders it hegemonic.

4. If fiction is to have a present, then writers and critics must exercise leadership. While there are good venues for discussing and reading about fiction's present, we need to generate more and better ones. Not only can such venues introduce readers to work that has proven too heterodox for widespread distribution and mainstream reviews, but they also can provide critical perspective on fiction's present, hosting discussions of the political, aesthetic, and philosophical problems to which contemporary fiction responds. This writing on the present must serve intellectual ends that are more expansive and concrete than those defined by the profession of literary criticism or the academic study of contemporary culture. Its aim must be to organize readers and writers into the producers, not just recipients, of fiction's present. That is, it must address a community that traverses the institutional divisions between publishers, writers, scholars, pleasure readers, marketing directors, teachers, reviewers, editors, theorists, and retailers. The obstacle to achieving this kind of expansive aim is only secondarily that of an alienating critical terminology. It is more fundamentally that of a critical discourse that constitutes itself by its externality. That is, both the intellectual humility that wishes not to prescribe and the intellectual arrogance that speaks about but never to share a vision of criticism's relation to fiction's present as a discourse about another discourse. To accept the collective task not of critiquing an already formed present or of imposing a present on the uninformed but of producing fiction's present is for criticism to accept the participant's position. This is the critical perspective from inside, the viewpoint of one who has been addressed by fiction and for whom productive activity is his or her response. This is the form cultural leadership at present must take.

5. Professional criticism today is much more comfortable examining fiction's past and future than its present. Considerations of fiction's past are enabled by hindsight. Even without critical intervention, history itself widens the fissures in sedimented opinions, providing present consciousness with demystifying insight. And the past has a definiteness that even when attacked is reassuring. If one wishes to assault the canon of nineteenth-century English fiction, then one may feel outgunned and overmatched, but one need not wonder whether there is a canon. Perhaps more significantly, a contemporary critic can regard fiction's past as the trace, material artifact or institutional creation of an alien consciousness, not the critic's own, and discussing fiction's future, because inherently speculative, offers similarly guilt-free pleasures. One need not get things "right." But to accept one's part in producing fiction's present is to accept a degree of complicity and accountability that leaves the critic dangerously exposed. There is rarely an earlier discourse in contrast to which one's own, putatively more advanced consciousness can appear demystifying, and there is little stability or definiteness to one's object. To speak of the present is not normally to speak of a predetermined fact, given condition, or established institution, and yet misrepresenting this unstable object can be fraught with professional, moral, and legal consequences. And in the cruelest irony of all, nothing will count for the critic as confirmation, not even universal agreement. About fiction's present the professional critic speaks as contingently as every other reader. Her or his authority is a posteriori, solely a function of her or his illuminations. There can be no institutional protection. The study of fiction's present lays criticism bare.

6. All worthwhile considerations of fiction's present are limited in scope and value. Given the massive number of fiction writers and fictional texts in the United States alone, a synoptic account of every representative of the present is impossible. One cannot speak of fiction's present as a totality, or not if by "totality" one means all inclusiveness. On the contrary, to speak of fiction's present is necessarily to locate one's own presence, hence to project a limit. That is, the project of determining fiction's present is not that of the social sciences. What is sought does not resemble a description of predominant characteristics, not even one based on a truly representative sampling. What is sought is an account of what has made fiction present for the ones it has located, what establishes its significance for me now—whoever I am determined to be—and in what form it has made its presence known. In other words, the account of fiction's present should not be understood on the model of an empirical survey or anthropological description but rather on the model of personal confession. It necessarily reveals its subject. This remains true even where the account of fiction's present is proffered and accepted, not as the critic's alone but as that of his or her group. It is inescapably an insider's discourse, with all the problems and responsibilities, blindnesses and complicities, of an account of values. The totality demanded of such an account is total candor, total manifestness. What an outsider wants to know is this: What kind of achievement has separated the insider's present from past, set limits on action, and projected its ends, located someone here and now? There will always be a circularity to accounts of fiction's present, to what counts as present example and as present exemplified, but the danger is not that by enclosing the insiders this circle will prevent their seeing all. The danger is that in aiming to see more, the rest of us may fail to see what we see.

7. Totalizing versions of fiction's present must be regarded with skepticism. All efforts to derive generalizable features of fiction from a survey of the most widely circulated novels and stories either will sacrifice difference for identity or erase particularity through abstraction. While such generality in critical discourse is understandable and may be necessary for communication, this search for critical universals is underwritten by an enlightenment and a romantic political vision, not a vision of difference and global diversity. Now, as worldwide communication and trade draw human beings into interdependent proximity, it is hardly the time to retreat into aesthetic provincialism. Fiction's present necessarily exceeds our accounting. However, it may not be universally obvious that the threat to aesthetic diversity today comes from explicitly universalizing theories. That is, even while marveling at the array of distinctive fictions from culturally disparate groups, one may also be struck by marked continuities. In fact, difference and identity may seem at times to have cross-dressed. What appears unmistakably new and important about globally diverse texts is their representation of societies and cultures previously disregarded by the West. Stories are set, partly or entirely, in geographical locales remote from America and Europe. Points of view are those of characters previously marginalized or objectified by Western novels. And plots turn on moral norms, political conflicts, climatic conditions, and local knowledge that, to those whose novelistic paradigms are *Middlemarch*, *Madame Bovary*, and *The Great Gatsby*, seem exotic and enlightening. Although such works also incorporate formal departures related to European modernism or to non-European vernaculars and traditions, fiction's dominant global aesthetic today—to the extent that it is represented by the works most widely available in the United States—is realist. Its marked achievement is the representation of an author's particular world. In accounting for the value of such work, criticism must candidly bring out its own stake in narrative representation, not tacitly assimilate representation to fiction as such. That is, to combine an explicitly anti-universalist, diversifying program with an implicit marginalization of formal innovation and realist critique is to enact criticism's covert wish for totality. What such totalizing represses is the insider's viewpoint, the specific conviction that differences in forms of practice can be as significant for the producer as differences between justice and oppression, freedom and jail. Fiction's present has no outside.

8. All accounts of fiction's present are local and must become so. The limits on our ability to account for the present require that productive criticism acknowledge its own location. This cannot mean limiting its value to its own group, since a critical account distinguishes itself from prejudice only by universal accountability, its openness to questioning by others. Nor can it mean limiting the value of the fictions it studies, since a fiction's limited value marks it as past, no longer of the moment. If the criticism of fiction's present is to localize its object— either literally, by restricting it to a particular geographical region, or metaphorically, by narrowing the critic's focus to race, gender, class, disability, trauma, or some other topos—then criticism must show how this locality produces fiction's present value, not just for locals but for the critic's group as well. In other words, to accept that fiction's present exceeds every accounting is to conceive of the present as multiple, composed of many competing versions, but to concede the absence of any outside, of any accounting for values from without, makes problematic criticism's access to these versions. The present is not bounded like an object. To know fiction's present is to inhabit it, and although criticism may, if sufficiently respectful and open and studious, learn to inhabit more than a single present, attempting to be present in two places at once risks duplicity, the passing off of mere tourism for citizenship. There are urgent reasons today to value fictions that represent locales or topoi underrepresented in Europe and the United States, and utilizing novels to document contemporary history may well be one way criticism produces its own present, but using fiction for ends not its own is appropriation, and when critical appropriation is of another's locale, it becomes conquest. To localize fiction's present is to discover one's own location in another's. All that limits my access are the present limits of fiction for me.

9. All accounts of fiction's present are global and must become so. Although every location projects a limit, the boundary between the local and the global is not, like a mountain range, naturally occurring. Only within the horizon of global change do localities acquire their irreducible significance, and primarily as a local disruption does the global make its presence felt. However, it seems unclear whether these facts describe a new historical phenomenon (i.e., the erosion of geographical divisions through innovative communication technologies and of political divisions through market expansion) or merely make explicit what the words "local" and "global" now mean. Either way, they suggest that political interpretations of fiction's present will be marked by a tension that is difficult to locate. On the one hand, what the criticism of fiction's present discovers at every location is nothing less than the world, global history in its concrete manifestation. Criticism gains access to these presents by overcoming its own limits, the pastness or irrelevance of the critic's global consciousness. On the other hand, criticism's representation of the world beyond its own province, of global history manifest in fiction's distinct versions, is just one more local account. That the critic's account seeks global inclusiveness merely defines its ambition as presentness, as the critic's quest for knowledge that is present, not dated. A synoptic account of fiction's production at various locales, all joined to produce an encompassing picture of global history and change, can provide valuable insight into transcultural forces and help articulate the material obstacles to present achievement, but it cannot represent the conditions that control present consciousness, either for the writer or the critic. The limitations of the present are not presently knowable. If criticism would know the conditions of fiction, then it must know them in the critic's own location, and this makes the encounter with the global a continuous relocation, not only of fiction's present but of criticism itself. Either criticism locates its global consciousness within the present value of fiction or it discovers the global and its own absence together.

10. Fiction and its criticism at present confront a historical divide. If, as some suspect, the forms of the novel and story have exhausted themselves, then their demise is unlikely to mean any decline in the availability of novels and stories—or, more precisely, of books indistinguishable from those formerly called novels and stories. On the contrary, fiction's pastness seems just as likely to mean increased production, a rise in the number of commodities fitting the market category "literature-fiction" coincident with a dwindling readership. Fiction's present, like its absence, is not a sociologically documentable fact. This suggests that one way of recognizing the divide in fiction's history is through changes in the kinds of success, or the markers of it, that will establish fiction's present. A present for fiction is no longer guaranteed,

perhaps not even evidenced, by widespread interest in novels and stories, and commercial success and failure seem similarly ambiguous. It
could even be that recent ethical and political justifications for narrative are themselves not signs of fiction's renewed vitality but responses
to its obsolescence, as though comprising a compensatory effort to
make fiction present. All that will now establish fiction's present is fiction's
unsettling disclosure—to individuals and to groups—of what it has always and everywhere been. That is, the achievement of a present will
be marked by my or our inability to see beyond it, to locate work that
casts the value of this present into the past, coupled with my or our
ability, based on this disclosure, to project a past inclusive of other
valued work. And who my group is, who I am, will not be known prior
to fiction's disclosure. This means not merely that there can be many
plausible claimants to fiction's present but also that these diverse presents will not coexist peacefully, threatening to divide both me and my
group against ourselves. Access to any present can jeopardize access to
others, can render them past or obsolete, and my group's discovery of
value beyond the present, that is, beyond what fiction is for us now, will
have the power to render us obsolete, to unmask us as "us." It is just such
radical stakes that represent literary success today. Fiction becomes present
by establishing an origin not in the past but in what is happening now.

   **11. The present of fiction must be located beyond modernism
and postmodernism, not before them.** In the twenty-first century, fiction's
present will not be established by repeating the formal innovations of
modernism and postmodernism independently of the historical conditions that gave them significance. Of course, what those conditions
were remains controversial. If there is anything less convincing than
postmodernism's self-promotional claim to have overcome modernism,
it is the self-promotional claim, repeated continuously by various figures
and movements over the last three decades, to have overcome
postmodernism. To discover the significance of postmodernity is to
rediscover the significance of modernism, discoveries that make possible the recognition of modernism's and postmodernism's limits, and
only afterward can the historical conditions necessary to their
significance be known. However, it seems uncontroversial that certain
literary gestures once polemically associated with modernism and
postmodernism have little impact on readers today, at least in their
most familiar embodiments, and the present consequences of this change
call for investigation. Does our present nonresponsiveness to formal
innovation, at least as an end in itself, mean that fiction's present can
now be established by directly representing contemporary events and
forces, perhaps in their global and local manifestations? Although the

value of much past fiction seems recognizable in some such terms, other forms of literary and artistic practice—essays, autobiographies, commentaries, and treatises, not to mention documentary film and video journalism—have at least as strong a claim as novels to represent our contemporary world. Is our present interest in previously marginalized voices, each with its unique inflection and perspective, an interest in the novel per se, or is it at bottom a turn toward autobiography? Is there any historically unprecedented task today that falls specifically to fiction? Such questions cannot be answered apart from the continuing investigation, by writers and critics, of fiction's form. That is, to know the historical conditions necessary to fiction's present significance is to discover, in our globally and locally contested present, what being a work of fiction means. This task falls to insiders. To be present, to produce its value here and now, fiction must know itself.

12. Fiction's present is the acknowledgment of fiction's past. Only with the establishment of fiction's present can the political, moral, and philosophical value of twentieth-century aesthetic innovation be recognized. In other words, producing the present requires radicalizing the past, locating our freedom's roots. This is how a revolution takes hold. If fiction is not to retreat from its history of problems and achievements then it must further, not merely repeat, the modernist and postmodernist exploration of the conditions of literature's existence, and within the context of global change and conflict this furthering means laying bare the consequences of these conditions for individuals and groups situated variously around the world. The twentieth-century investigation of language—an investigation encompassing textuality, writing, voice, interpretation, authority, temporality, subjectivity, and representation—does not necessitate the forms of fictional practice and achievement celebrated in the twenties and thirties or sixties and seventies, but it cannot meaningfully coexist with an uncritical acceptance of mainstream literary fiction today. The present and dominant appear synonymous only to the dominant. If our current valuing of diverse voices and perspectives is to produce a present, then it must show itself to be the present meaning of postmodernism's account of voice and modernism's account of point of view. In this way, our freedom from their history is achieved. Although prior to inhabiting a present no one knows what will produce one, the testimony of psychoanalysis is that repressing the past leads only to compulsion. For the twenty-first century to liberate a new episode in the history of fiction, writers and critics will need to locate points of contact between the formal conditions of reading and writing and the demands of a multicultural, globally organized, technologically complex, and economically constrained world. To demand that fiction accommodate itself to this history without acknowledging the historical specificity of fiction itself is to erase it. The present cannot be the past's denial. It is the absence of any *need* for denial. From such openness, the future is born.

Chapter 1

Fiction's Present

Brief Notes

Samuel R. Delany

The question of the present inflection of fiction is Janus-faced, looking aside to the novel's radically changed political, economic, technological circumstances and back to its history of achievement and problems.

—from the *symplokē* call for papers on "Fiction's Present"

The "call for papers" begins with an interesting comment, there. For me, it brings to mind that when Bakhtin noted that, by the beginning of the twentieth century, all artistic genres had been novelized, he was at a historical point that was beginning a process that allows us to say today that, by the beginning of the twenty-*first* century, all artistic genres have been "film-ized." That process takes us through more than half a century of novelized films that finally did as much as any social phenomenon to remove the novel proper from a certain preeminence in the job of social representation. One remembers the scene in Tim Robbins's historical drama *The Cradle Will Rock* (2000), in which, after New York art students have rioted over the destruction of Diego Rivera's Rockefeller Center mural, Nelson Rockefeller and William Randolph Hearst, who up until now have supported this representational, highly social art, do a coldhearted about-face and decide from now on to support only abstract art with no overt social messages, to avoid this kind of disruptive political response. The ironic point is not whether any such conspiratorial conversation ever actually took place at such a

11

financial pinnacle, but rather the scene's revelation of a social truth—
a moment in what Jameson might call the "political unconscious"—that
explains why, indeed, in an art field supported by those with more
money rather than those with less, natural selection is finally going to
favor the abstract. It happens for the same reason that, if epic singers
are going to be supported by ninth-century BCE kings and princes,
you're going to end up with the *Iliad* and the *Odyssey* rather than *Ger-
minal* and *Giants in the Earth*. The same turning away from the larger
social portraiture of the interrelations of the classes is evident in Julie
Taymor's totally gorgeous film, from two years later, that focuses on
Rivera's wife, painter Frida Kahlo (*Frida* 2002). Today, of course, a
critical discourse is in place that rushes to read the two films as pejo-
rative mutual critiques. In the light of Taymor's film, Robbins's looks
like an emotionally button-pushing, finally rather preachy socialist tract.
In the light of Robbins's film, Taymor's reduces to a kind of tragic-
glamorous fairy tale presented as objective reality, but that rigorously
cuts out the larger social context making the other film signify: different buttons pushed.

But, one wonders, why can't the two films be read as supporting
one another—expanding on one another, enriching one another? Finally, what would prevent a new, hypertextualized novel, say, from
embracing both approaches? But it would require a creative discourse
that paid much more attention to rhetorical texture than the novel
usually does, in either case, to plot—and in which rhetorical texture
would be seen as a site for the generation of meaning in itself rather
than as merely a supplementary intensifier.

Novels that aspire to broad-scale social representation are rarer
and rarer—even as commercial fiction relies more and more heavily on
plot, and even as it trains its readers to ignore style.

From *Pere Goriot* to *Invisible Man*, from Dickens to Flaubert, one
thing the novel has done is explain—dramatically—how areas of society
interact and affect each other, in terms of what this interaction inflicts
on individuals and their strivings and desires within their own social
spheres, or as they move from sphere to sphere. Paradoxically, both
Marx and Freud, who start out by enriching the range of explanations
of how our strivings and desires function, both in the family and the
state, may have finally managed to swamp the novel, because we now
know that what explains these things is, finally, too complicated to
"dramatize" in other than a truly simplistic fashion.

Finally, the novel (with the short story leading the way) becomes
a kind of extended "haiku" run to seed, where from time to time the
artist asserts, yes, there is an explanation somewhere behind it all, but

it is much too complex and, finally, boring to go into at any length while presenting the glimmer and flicker of the here and now, the shadows of memory and association in the forever lost.

Over eighty-two years, *Ulysses'* shift from eccentric experiment to the central text of the contemporary novelistic tradition indexes the rise of the novel as extended haiku, or in the case of *Ulysses* itself, eighteen extended haiku, each presented with some interesting techni-cal filigree to keep one interested in an implied but never-stated explo-ration—behind the fabulous verbal surface—of what Gertrude Stein several times called "the daily island life."

The opening decades of the twentieth century are marked by a kind of forking into two rivers: Stein starts us off along one, which leads up through Perec and a lot of today's playful writers, and Joyce leads the other, which carries us, frankly, to I'm-not-sure-what. It is a river that, by today, includes lots of ambitious, unreadable novels that really *do* try to explain things, as Joyce's work itself, once past *Dubliners* and *Portrait,* locates itself in the "unreadable" precincts first mapped out by Pater's *Marius the Epicurean: His Sensations and Ideas,* which also ceded Virginia Woolf the vacant lot on which to erect *The Waves* and the novels that followed.

> Can the novel establish itself in the present of global capital-
> ism without abandoning its formal distinctiveness?[1]

Bakhtin's point is that the novel is already established. As a dis-course, it is quite firmly in place, which is why we go on writing them. But we may need to trace out other subcurrents through its history in order to reawaken our formal interests.

Such a subcurrent that presently fascinates me is the one that takes in Baron Corvo's *Hadrian the VII* (1905), Chesterton's *The Man Who Was Thursday* (1908), Hughes's *A High Wind in Jamaica* (1929), Barnes's *Nightwood* (1936), Lowry's *Under the Volcano* (1947), Nabokov's *Pale Fire* (1960), and Russ's *We, Who Are About to . . .* (1978), as well as other novels in which great effort has gone into making the prose crystalline, vivid, *and* readable (without stylistic pandering), in order to allow a more or less lucid narrative structure to speak of things that most fiction, whether innovative or not, usually leaves unsaid.

The novel's existence as a discourse (like the poem's) is the ex-istence of a discourse that allows its texts to make sense (i.e., fundamen-tally it is a critical discourse). But when, indeed, we compare the critical discourse of fiction to the critical discourse of the poem, the discourse of the poem right now seems willing to welcome within its discursive boundaries a lot more material that *does not* "make sense"—with the result that, by and large, right now the poem seems more vigorous, healthier than the novel, at least to me.

Unreadable novels can revitalize the style of the novel.

But readable novels are what revitalize its structure.

Perhaps in this statement, both "readable" and "unreadable" need to be in scare quotes. Certainly, they are wildly inexact terms for what I mean—since most novels that are written to be readable I cannot read, while a few "unreadable" novels for me make the most interesting reading.

Does fiction continuing the tradition of modernist innovation have any reality for emergent political groups and cultures?[2]

The place where poetry trips up is in trying to prove that, yes, all of that "experimentation" is politically significant, if not actively subversive.

I think, for both the novel and the poem, the answer to this question should be a blunt "no." We will get farther if we accept that "no" than if we try, however subtly, however dogmatically, to convince more and more people that it does.

There is an expanded version of that "no," of course. It is this: The relatively small group of people that can, when it wants to, trace out the subversive allegories in all that stylistic difference just is not large enough or, frankly, powerful enough to make a difference, because it is dealing with a critical construct rather than the reading experience of (most of) the texts with which it deals. Indeed, this is precisely the point where the apolitical aspect of art, which critics from de Man to Bloom are always stressing, comes home, and should be welcomed there.

I think of myself as the model consumer—if not an ideal one— for innovative art. I am a self-styled Marxist, which is relevant only in that I think I am quite politically sensitive. I like innovative fiction and poetry as genres. I buy them in bookstores. I enjoy sitting back and reading them.

I still enjoy the narrative. I enjoy the ways that the rhetoric constitutes and disrupts that narrative. And when the rhetoric enhances the narrative, the insights, the intellectual content, and the structural richness of that narrative, as it does in the fiction of Guy Davenport, William Gass, Robert Glück, Charlotte Bacon, or R. M. Berry, as a reader I am at my happiest. At that point, frankly, I stop perceiving the fiction as traditional or innovative and simply think of it as very good writing.

But unless I enter into a particular type of dialogue with the textual rhetoric per se—a dialogue that something in the text has invited me to enter—as a rule I do not usually read the rhetoric itself as political. I read it as some sort of formal constitutive/commentary on or of the narrative, i.e., primarily as aesthetic.

I *do* think new art teaches us to read new discourses—and a changing society is always presenting new discourses to its citizens in order to help them negotiate the world. But I firmly believe that that is a task art only accomplishes at the level of groups or artworks. One work by itself never relates to politics in that way.

NOTES

1. Quotation from the *symplokē* call for papers on "Fiction's Present."
2. Ibid.

REFERENCES

The Cradle Will Rock. 2000. Dir. Tim Robbins. Burbank, CA: Touchstone Home Video.

Frida. 2002. Dir. Julie Taymor. Burbank, CA: Miramax Home Entertainment.

Chapter 2

Innovative Fiction and the Poetics of Power

Gertrude Stein and Christine Brooke-Rose "Do" Language

CHRISTINA MILLETTI

I like anything that a word can do. And words do do all they do and
then they can do what they never do do.

—Gertrude Stein, *Everybody's Autobiography*

STRAP-ON PROLOGUE

In 2003, *Critical Inquiry* (perhaps the most renowned journal in
academia) announced an unprecedented editorial symposium—what
editor and scholar, W. J. T. Mitchell described as "a kind of interdisci-
plinary summit conference of the human sciences"—on the state of
"big theory" (Mitchell 2004, 326). For an academic event, the tone of
the conference was decidedly political: "What can criticism and theory
do to counteract the forces of militarism, unilateralism, and the perpetual state of emergency that is now the explicit policy of the U.S.
government?" Mitchell asked. "What good is intellectual work in the
face of the deeply anti-intellectual ethos of American public life . . . ?"
(327). Yet it is to Mitchell's grim supposition about the role of the
literary—whether it will be possible "in the coming century . . . to determine the fate of literature and to secure some space for the aesthetic
in the face of the overwhelming forces of mass culture and commercial

17

entertainment"—to which I cautiously turn this examination of "fiction's present" here.[1]

On the face of it, Mitchell's questions may not appear to have much to do with a forum on the current state of narrative, with the craft and strategies of writing fiction. Yet his apparent object, I would argue, is nothing less than the fate of the written, of *language*—and, more specifically, a space for "difficulty" within the realm of the literary if one attributes to the condition of "difficulty" (as I intend to here) a loose assemblage of aesthetic characteristics bearing witness to a tradition of linguistic complexity, even excess. Let me therefore pose the following questions in the same spirit: What form of critical "engagement" does writing fiction offer writers and readers in the present moment when the conditions of doublespeak, redundancy, and propaganda saturate the media? What kind of impact can the praxes and strategies of fictional language be said to incur on the field of power? *Why is the imaginative terrain that fiction presents materially relevant today at all?*

This last question might at first seem alarmist or simply over-stated. Does not fiction, after all, continue to sell strongly in most bookstores? Moreover, was not Dan Brown (author of *The DaVinci Code*) recently assigned a "celebrity power ranking" of "12" by *Forbes Magazine*, that is, to set a context just below Tom Cruise ("10") and Brad Pitt ("11") but above David Letterman ("14) and Michael Jordan ("16")?[2] Yet Rachel Donadio's article in the August 7, 2005, edition of the *New York Times Book Review*—tellingly called "Truth Is Stronger than Fic-tion"—notes the precipitous rise in nonfiction sales since September 11, 2001, at the expense of the fiction market across the board. "We're in a dark cultural moment," *Esquire* editor Adrienne Miller reflects. "Fewer and fewer people seem to believe fiction is still essential for our emotional and intellectual survival." Indeed, the catalog of changes in cache literary publications is ominous: in 2003, *GQ* stopped publishing fiction; in June 2005, *The Atlantic Monthly* announced it would continue to publish fiction only in its summer issue; and even *The Paris Review* has indicated that it intends to feature more nonfiction in its pages. While editorial policy shifts are a matter of course, the significant question about this one centers on why it is occurring during what *Paris Review* editor Philip Gourevitch calls this "newsy time." Donadio's answer—to return to our opening motif—suggests that the culprit is "politics."

> As a rule, novelists shouldn't become editorialists, but it's safe to say no novels have yet engaged with the post-Sept. 11 era in any meaningful way. . . . To date, no work of fiction has perfectly captured our historical moment the way cer-tain novels captured the Gilded Age, or the Weimar Repub-

lic, or the cold war. . . . Nonfiction can keep up with the
instant messenger culture; fiction takes its own sweet time.
(Donadio 2005, 27)

Clearly, in Donadio's limited view, the concern of "politics" within the
realm of fiction refers to that strain of reality-based narratives whose
conventions, as Susan Suleiman reflects, "correspond to what most of
us . . . think of, in our less theoretical moments, as the 'natural order of
the world" (Suleiman 1990, 35). Such fictions, for Donadio, function to
make order of chaos—they are fundamentally "instructive," offer their
readers life lessons (she cites, for instance, Ian McEwan's novel *Saturday*, set just before the 2003 invasion of Iraq)—and she implies that it
is indeed order which, given the global rise of terrorism, readers now
crave. Her model, however, begs the question of agency. Whose "order"
is it? By means of what social, cultural, and political influences is such
an order achieved? How is fictional language shaped and arranged to
create that sense of order?

In this regard, the relation Mitchell asked his conference participants to consider—the connection between politics, language, and culture—is a productive means through which we might organize these
multiple threads of fiction's present and explore how—and to what—
they add up. Whereas Donadio puts the emphasis on narratives *about*
politics, for instance, Mitchell instead suggests that it is to language itself
that we must turn our investigation to better suss out the thorny relation
between politics and literature in the current moment. He would likely
prefer us to ask the following questions: In what way is "politics" revealed
in our *use* of language? How does power orchestrate language and therefore meaning—our interpretation of events? Toward what ends might
the less immediate situation of literature be useful in thinking through
how power shapes the immediacy of our daily lives?

Before addressing these questions through the work of Gertrude
Stein and Christine Brooke-Rose, however, I ought to fess up and admit
that I began this chapter by setting up something of a straw man. After
all, how surprising is it really that the tried patterns of realist narrative
have given up ground recently to nonfiction? One imagines that the
kinds of readers to whom Donadio refers would naturally be less likely
to turn to invented worlds and situations in search of a life "guide"
during difficult times, when "how-to" books pepper the shelves in ever
greater numbers and with far more direct advice.

Yet far from being troubled by this shift in readership, let me on
the contrary propose that such an atmosphere in fact presents an
opportunity *for* fiction—for a subtler, overlooked kind of narrative that
arises in the shape of "anti-stories," "new" novels," and "criti-fictions"

20 Fiction's Present

(among others). With their far more astute approach to aporias and impasses in interpretation, such "innovative," "arealist," and even "experimental" fictions accomplish the wholly different work of exploring how language *operates*—how narratives work to successfully convey meaning—often by showcasing or resisting those operations themselves. Such fictions do not just tell stories; rather, they investigate how stories are made—offering the reader a means for both understanding and, as I will argue, *resisting* the ways power shapes the narratives we read, inasmuch as the ones we live.

Novelist Kathy Acker distinguishes between the two forms by singling out realist fiction as an apparatus of control. As she argues, realist narratives do more than just teach. They in fact function to manipulate readers' perceptions. Innovative fictions, in contrast, present a playful disorder that invites readers to consider how their perceptions are formed. Though experimental fictions have been critiqued for being insular or abstract, she reminds us that all narrative is political—inflected with the concerns of power.

> If I'm going to tell what the real is by mirroring it, by telling you a story that expresses reality, I'm attempting to tell you how things are. By letting you see through my own eyes, I give you my viewpoints, moral and political. In other words, realism is simply a control method. Realism doesn't want to negotiate, open into, even know, chaos or the body or death, because those who practice realism want to limit their reader's perceptions, want to limit perceptions to a centric—which is to say society is always a phallocentric—reality. . . . In other words, behind every literary or cultural issue lies the political, the realm of political power. And whenever we talk about narration, narrative structure, we're talking about political power. There are no ivory towers. The desire to play, to make literary structures that play into and in unknown or unknowable realms, those of chance and death and the lack of language, is the desire to live in a world that is open and dangerous, that is limitless. To play, then, both in structure and content, is to desire to live in wonder. (Acker 2004, 17–18)

Put another way, narrative is never "merely" a form of entertainment or escapism. Consider, for example, the paradoxical—and troubling—role of the feminine in Dan Brown's now infamous detective thriller to which I referred earlier. Though he has achieved great renown by his recovery and promotion of the goddess figure hidden within the traditional Christ story, Brown's heroine-cryptographer, Sophie Neveu, herself sadly would be unable to decode a riddle even if she were given the key.

Whereas realist narratives, in other words, fail to question the systems they describe—and instead merely work to reinforce them— innovative fictions are in contrast deeply aware of their political investment. Though they offer few direct lessons, they discreetly inform us about the power of language, and the means by which power can be manipulated—and resisted—*through* its own operative structures. As Judith Butler notes, by deploying new and unfamiliar modes of language—by obstructing readers' expectations—"non-ordinary" meaning functions to "precisely contest what has become sedimented in and as the ordinary" (Butler 1997, 145). Breaks with accustomed usage present openings, highlight meaning's inexact foreclosure—the condition under which language can be troped and transformed so that mutations can take place. In such moments, the laws of language are made visible; the "ordinary" uses that normally conceal its operation are set aside, exposing how meaning is made.

It is likely apparent by now that a founding tenet of this argument will be controversial in certain circles: I am, after all, proposing that writing fiction is an intellectual, theoretical, and political praxis—that the act of (so-called) "imaginative" writing is nothing less than a radical engagement with the immediacy of the (so-called) "real" world. I also am suggesting that fictional language can be a space of resistance—a means of challenging political forces that defy penetration—and the narrative form, in particular, presents opportunities to critically examine the delivery of power in language and, therefore, the prospect of counteracting it through a self-reflexive engagement of the operations of language themselves. What follows then is an attempt to examine how such engagements occur in the work of both Gertrude Stein and Christine Brooke-Rose, and how their fictional *re-presentations* are useful to understand the political *present* now.

> And then I shall walk in with my
> hypotheses, like let sex equal why . . .
>
> —Christine Brooke-Rose, *Amalgamemnon*

HOW DOING *DOES*

Throughout her body of work, Judith Butler considers the relationship of subjects to discourse: how it is, in other words, that we *do* language.

In *Excitable Speech* (1997) in particular, she inverts the teleological proposition of *whether* or *not* a subject produces particular kinds of language acts, and she instead asks in what ways we become intelligible *through* language. For her, language is not a tool that merely allows meaning to happen. Rather, the relation between language and its users represents a complex "matrix of intelligibility" that makes us readable to one another. Language, in other words, represents a framework that constitutes both the "doing" *and* the "doer" alike: the subject always exists *in a condition of relation* to language that implicates the person using it, as much the addressee. Butler's premise—"we do things *with* language . . . produce effects *with* language, and . . . do things *to* language" because *"language is the thing that we do"*—therefore offers a framework for considering how language promotes as well as prevents access to power, how shifts in power occur at all (8, emphasis added).

Throughout Gertrude Stein's body of work, there is evidence of her deep appreciation for this relation. In "Portraits and Repetition" (1935), for example, she describes the difference between mere "repetition" (a well-known trait of her work) and what she calls "insistence." Corralling anecdotal evidence from crime, nature, history and, more locally, her own family, she explains the difference between the terms.

> It is very like a frog hopping. He cannot ever hop exactly the same distance or the same way of hopping at every hop. A bird's singing is perhaps the nearest thing to repetition but if you listen they too vary their insistence. That is the human expression saying the same thing and in insisting and we all insist varying the emphasizing. (Stein 1967, 99)

For Stein, in other words, repetition—the phenomena of "A equals A"—occurs only as "description," as a static, if elegant, body of writing that simply documents, and whose familiarity is comforting because it upholds and reinforces linguistic patterns to which we are accustomed. Yet such "soothing novels," she writes, cannot express the intensity of being alive that she prefers to capture in her own work.

> . . . . I can read any number of soothing novels; in fact, nothing else soothes me. I found it not a thing that it was interesting to do. . . . We in this period have not lived in remembering, we have lived in moving being necessarily so intense that existing is indeed something, is indeed that thing that we are doing. . . . The newspapers are full of what anybody does and anybody knows what anybody does but the

thing that is important is the intensity of anybody's existence. (Stein 1967, 108)

In contrast, Stein aspires to make writing "lively"[3]—and whatever is
lively, Stein argues, is neither set nor fixed: it moves, changes. By insisting on selected words, she generates their gradual transformation with
respect to their placement within a sentence: she creates epistemological shifts in meaning.

Consider the first line of her so-called "detective" novel, *Blood on
the Dining Room Floor* (1982): "They had a country house," she writes. "A
house in the country is not the same as a country house. This was a
country house" (11). While one may have had in mind a summer home
at Stein's first mention of "country house," she goes on to clarify the
reference, not by adding further description to it but by moving the
word "country house" relative to the other words in subsequent sentences. A "country house," Stein tells us, is *not* a summer home: as a
result, the reader gathers that her "*country* house" is "simple" as opposed to "refined"; it is not just *in* the country but countri*fied*. The
word "country" in the first sentence, in short, does not mean the same
thing as the word "country" in the second sentence, nor the third
sentence. As Marjorie Perloff (1981) notes, Stein wants us to ask not
just what "A" *means* but *under what circumstances* "A equals B or modifies
C or is in apposition to D" (76).

It might be said, then, that Stein's project is one of *differánce*: she
is fully aware and manipulates the gap between the signifier and the
signified. Constraining herself to a reduced vocabulary, her project
paradoxically exploits the often limitless possibilities of linguistic meaning by arousing a network of interpretation that permits multiple read-
ings to juxtapose, cohere, and collaborate at the same time. One might
take a lesson from her project and consider, in this regard, the current
Bush administration's peculiar (in)sensitivity to language in its coinage
of phrases such as "embedded journalists" or (the Afghanistan mission)
"Enduring Freedom." Both phrases are meant to impart strength: "embedded journalists" do not just accompany troops, they in fact become
indelible members of the units they cover. Similarly, "Enduring Freedom" seems to advocate the loftiest ideals of liberation. Yet both slo-
gans inscribe within themselves an opposing, and even a sinister,
intention. A keen reader must necessarily ask: Who exactly is an "embedded" journalist *in* bed with? What kind of news can such a lover be
expected to report? *Whom*, meanwhile, is enduring *whose* need for freedom? How difficult is such a freedom to bear? How long is the pain
expected to last—and by whom?

Like Stein, Christine Brooke-Rose's fictions arise from a similar concern for *differánce*, though they take an opposing extreme. Whereas Stein employs an "insistent" language of meaningful repetitions, Brooke-Rose advances a poetic which, as she writes in her novel *Amalgamemnon* (1994), "*recycles* words and weeds" to create a revealing, polyfilamental language. Showcasing an uncanny knack for recombinant word formations, Brooke-Rose merges languages and dialects, discourses of the past and the present, often deploying puns to poignant effect. The result is an "utterly other discourse" that comes to a head in *Amalgamemnon* by virtue of an amalgamated tongue (much as the novel's title suggests) that is uniquely her own:

> Never let anyone see you foresee them, keep quiet Cassandra, forecaster of your own pollux, keep your castrations in perpetual cassation for nothing will ever be exactly as you shall one day see it in retrospect, otherwise you would grow big with expectation and sexplode, the expected generation the expectoration or vice versa perhaps. Qui vivra verra, che sera sera, you shall see what you shall see and may the beast man wane. (Brooke-Rose 1994, 30)

Much as she does here, Brooke-Rose melds heterogeneous discourses into the confined space of a phrase or a sentence so that, as she remarks about her novel *Between*, "a sentence can continue correctly, but by the end of it we are elsewhere in time or space" (32). In fact, it might be said that Brooke-Rose redesigns meaning itself, recycles language to showcase its internal multiplicity by melding words and phrases—generating terms that can be said to have always already existed, such as "viceversatile," "sexcommunication," and "sexcess," among others, or putting phrases through a series of meaningful tropes.[4] For instance, the aforementioned phrase "may the beast man wane," which is already one transformation from "may the best man win," eventually also becomes in recurrent uses "may the boast man whine" and later "may the boss man whine" (30, 52, 57). For Brooke-Rose, as Judy Little remarks, language represents "constantly simulatable new word[s]," and it is the creation of such "non-ordinary" meanings from the ordinary that can be said to situate her project: the making of language a realizable site not just of resistance but of transformation as well (125).

This is perhaps made nowhere more evident than in a key phrase that Brooke-Rose deploys throughout *Amalgamemnon*—"And we'll all go on *as if*"—a trope on the (in)famous final words of *The Unnameable*, "I can't go on, I'll go on" (Brooke-Rose 1994, 7, emphasis added; Beckett

1958, 414). Grammatically speaking, "as if" signals the use of the subjunctive mood, and as a construction it provokes a comparative unit that Brooke-Rose does not go on to provide like a "dangling impossibility" (8). "We'll all go as if," in other words, always implies a subsequent phrase. In *Amalgamemnon*, we might all go on *as if* we were oracles, priests, supertechnicians, teachers, pig farmers, terrorists, tribes, aunts, nephews, stars, soldiers, and so on—these being just a sample of the many personas that occur throughout the novel.[5] In short, the subjunctive is a very particular choice used to suggest that what is said is "hypothetical" or "contrary to fact." Going on *as if*, in other words, implies going on *discursively*—a move into the conditional sphere that highlights its own constraint by and within language in which the "physical signifier is made more physical" as Brooke-Rose remarks (Friedman and Fuchs 1995, 32). Going on "as if," moreover, acknowledges the improbability of going *forward*—of progress or complete change—as discourses of power (as Foucault reminds us) are always waylaid by their past constructions. "Recycling" words is therefore an alternative model for critiquing systems of power, resisting the limitations of the systems in which we live.

As Luce Irigaray (1985) notes, after all, the issue is not to change the system so much as to resist its customary operation by "jamming the theoretical machinery itself . . . suspending its pretension to the production of a truth and of a meaning that are excessively univocal" (78). In other words, since alternative systems of power cannot be enacted in the face of an ever more opaque political discourse—as Bush "revealingly" noted in 2004, for instance, "We stand for things"[6]—the only plausible response is to prevent a continued pretension to consensus. Donadio, in short, has one thing right: fiction can in fact be an "instructive" medium. It teaches us the force of language—and how a language of power can be used to control. If, as Kathy Acker writes in *Don Quixote* (1986), "an alteration of language rather than of material usually changes material conditions," then Brooke-Rose's fictions are designed to alter language—to teach us to recycle language ourselves—so that we can act out and change material conditions as well (27).

INNOVATIVE FICTION ≠ INNOVATIVE FICTION

Naturally, not all fictions—even innovative fictions—work with the same particularity or intensity toward these ends. The "innovative" covers a vast array of fictions and authors—from narratives by Virginia Woolf, Kathy Acker, Ann Quin, and Angela Carter to those by Alain Robbe-Grillet,

Thomas Bernhard, Georges Perec, and Thomas Pynchon, to name several distinctive writers (among many others) whose projects, on the face of it, might initially seem to have little in common. As a term, however, "innovative" offers several compelling advantages. From the Latin root *innovare*, "to make new, renew, or alter," the term *innovative fiction* implies a break, a twist, a trope—a reconsideration of narrative language that can take up diverse shapes and styles: fictions, in other words, that engage the re-*presentational* question of language and the ways it shapes our perceptions. David Kellogg offers this distinction: "Innovation . . . is always a question of 'more or less.' [It] is always understood *in relation to a shifting center*" (101, emphases added). One can therefore imagine an "innovative" fiction that appears bound to various "traditional" poetics but that then breaks from them—takes specific risks—in order to question the limits of such forms.

The usefulness of the term *innovation*, I hope, is therefore apparent: it enables a means to describe writing *in relation*: the innovative does not take a stand *against* but instead showcases a *working through* of the very positions they represent. Its aim is to make readers reinvestigate how they perceive the world around them, what relations and assumptions they draw about their role as subjects in language: the way language functions to engage, describe, and distort our understanding of each other and the world. It aims *not* to be unfamiliar necessarily but to present a perspective that may not in fact *be* familiar. What is innovative, in other words, might be said to be in the midst of an ongoing transformation. What is innovative today may not be innovative tomorrow. And it is on today's fiction, with particular relation to the fiction of yesterday, which may help us begin to think about the tomorrow of fiction *now*.

NOTES

1. See http://www.uchicago.edu/research/jnl-crit-inq/features/specialsymposium.html.
2. See http://www.forbes.com/lists/2005/53/T5P9.html.
3. Stein remarks in "Portraits" that the act of telling a story—even the same story over and over—is not static "if there is anything alive in the telling." If a story uses "lively words," then it will shift, transform, reveal, and conceal itself, just as living things do (1967, 99).
4. See Brooke-Rose (1994, 23, 14, 18).
5. The subjunctive mood represents a verb tense that is used very little in English but with which Brooke-Rose would be altogether familiar, both as a polylinguist (she was born in Switzerland, raised in Belgium and England, and now lives in France), and a writer and scholar whose work reveals a concern for

grammar. In *Between*, for instance, she forgoes the use of the verb "to be." *Amalgamemnon*, meanwhile, is written only in, as she writes, "non-realizing tenses" (that is, in the future and conditional tense). Her most recent novel, *Next*, meanwhile, forgoes the use of the verb "to have."

    6. August 5, 2004, Davenport, Iowa.

REFERENCES

Acker, Kathy. 1986. *Don Quixote*. New York: Grove Press.

———. 2004. The killers. In *Biting the error: Writers explore narrative*, ed. Mary Burger, 17–18. Toronto: Coach House Books.

Beckett, Samuel. 1958. *Three novels: Molloy, Malone Dies, The Unnameable*. New York: Grove Press.

Brooke-Rose, Christine. 1994. *Amalgamemnon*. Normal, IL: Dalkey Archive.

———. 1998. *Next*. Manchester: Carcanet Press Ltd.

———. 2007. *The Christine Brooke-Rose omnibus: Four novels: Out, Such, Between, Thru*. Manchester: Carcanet Press Ltd.

Butler, Judith. 1997. *Excitable speech: A politics of the performative*. New York: Routledge.

Donadio, Rachel. 2005. Truth is stronger than fiction. *New York Times Book Review*, August 7, 27.

Friedman, Ellen G. and Miriam Fuchs. 1995. A conversation with Christine Brooke-Rose. In *Utterly other discourse: The texts of Christine Brooke-Rose*. 29–37. Normal, IL: Dalkey Archive Press.

Irigaray, Luce. 1985. The power of discourse. In *This sex which is not one*, trans. Catherine Porter, 68–80. Ithaca, NY: Cornell University Press.

Kellogg, David. 2000–2001. The self in the poetic field. *Fence* 3.2 (Winter): 97–108.

Mitchell, W. J. T. 2004. Medium theory: Preface to the 2003 Critical Inquiry Symposium. *Critical Inquiry* 30 (2):324-35.

Perloff, Marjorie. 1981. *The poetics of indeterminacy*. Princeton, NJ: Princeton University Press.

Stein, Gertrude. 1937. *Everybody's autobiography*. New York: Random House.

———. 1967. Portraits and repetition. In *Gertrude Stein: Writing and lectures 1911–1945*, ed. Patricia Meyerowitz. 98–122. London: Peter Owen.

———. 1982. *Blood on the dining room floor*. Berkeley, CA: Creative Arts Book Company.

Suleiman, Susan. 1990. *Subversive intent: Gender, politics, and the avant-garde*. Cambridge, MA: Harvard University Press.

Chapter 3

To Have Done with Postmodernism

A Plea (or Provocation) for Globalization Studies

TIMOTHY S. MURPHY

To begin, a caveat: this is not really an objective argument for the abandonment of postmodernism as the privileged interpretive framework for analysis of the present, so much as it is a plea for another perspective to begin systematically contesting the stranglehold that postmodernism has too long exerted over the study of contemporary culture: the perspective of globalization studies, which I take to be a historical step beyond the radical linguistic indeterminacy of postmodernism rather than a retreat from that indeterminacy. Or perhaps it is merely a provocation, a blunt instrument intended to get a long-overdue argument started. In any case, let me explain.[1]

The proliferation of conferences, broadcasts, books, and articles dedicated to the issue of globalization suggests by its range—which runs from business administration to the humanities and in some cases even to the physical sciences—that something more is at stake in this notion than mere op-ed punditry or intellectual fashion. As many critics have noted, globalization does not signify a fundamentally new phenomenon, at least not when its elements of commerce, mobility, and social hybridization are considered separately, but clearly there is something new in the orders of magnitude that these elements have now attained and in the speed at which they now interact. I would like to propose that we treat globalization not as a totally new thing but as a threshold across which the growth and acceleration of long-existing trends has only recently pushed us. At this threshold, the quantitative changes produce a qualitative shift, which is what I think we mean to emphasize when we talk about globalization as a pressing issue. The goal of all the aforementioned conferences and so on, then, is to determine

29

what this qualitative shift entails within distinct fields of knowledge and inquiry and in the relations among these fields.

I would further like to suggest that the problematic of globalization, whatever new complications and contradictions it carries along with it, has one tremendous merit from a literary and cultural point of view: it heralds the radical reorientation, and perhaps even the end, of the tortuous debates over postmodernism that have dominated literary and cultural studies for the past twenty-five years. Now there are many contending, indeed mutually exclusive, definitions of postmodernism currently in circulation—this is to my mind one of the biggest problems with it, the exasperating indistinctness that allows it to be all things to all people—but for my purposes here it will refer to the decomposition of the overall cultural project of modernism, which was the reconstitution of a more or less rational, creative, and tolerant society from out of the shattered fragments of the ancient traditions of national, ethnic, gender, and power conflict that no longer seemed viable in the accelerated world of the twentieth century.[2] Henry Adams's continually recommended and ultimately useless education can stand as a literary emblem for this project.[3] Sympathetic cultural historians have justifiably called modernism "Promethean" in the range of its critique and the energy of its invention, but from the postmodern point of view, modernism simply sought to replace the supposedly "natural" conflicts between inherited traditions with a self-consciously artificial consensus that was equally destructive and false.

Jean-François Lyotard, the most prominent left-wing proponent (as opposed to critic) of postmodernism as the self-criticism of modernism, argued that modernism's reliance on what he called "grand narratives of progress"—both idealist, like the Hegelian eschatology of redeemed spirit, and materialist, like the Marxist redemption of social existence through political revolution—to overcome the contradictions of inherited tradition was itself a continuation of that same tradition, and hence it was guilty of the same ultimately totalitarian sin of imposing a destructive consensus and uniformity on an irreducibly multiple and diverse world (or, rather, on the language games that constitute the social world).[4] For Lyotard, the postmodern is marked by a widespread "incredulity" toward these grand narratives—they seem unbelievable and irrelevant to most of us. We know that time continues to pass, but despite this the world does not seem to be getting any better, any more civilized, any closer to a goal, whatever that might be. The world is perhaps getting more technically efficient, however—recall that Lyotard's model of postmodernism was originally conceived in the context of a study of advanced technology and its social legitimation—so the only residually utopian future we can still imagine revolves around the constant stream of new technologies, each of which promises to meet a need that the technology itself creates. According to Lyotard, the criterion of technical efficiency or "performativity" provides the only broadly applicable framework for grasping historical change, and it is indifferent to questions of direction, qualitative value, or goal. Of course, a few Marxists and Hegelians (not to mention Christians, Jews, Muslims, and others) still cling to grand narratives, but for Lyotardian postmodernists those people are somehow stuck in an outmoded, modernist, or even premodernist worldview that refuses to acknowledge what is really happening. The upshot of this is that collective action (which is what grand narratives underwrote) is no longer possible, and only atomized, individualistic forms of contestation remain, mainly struggles over access to information and media.

Interestingly enough, Lyotard's left-wing version of postmodernism found a strong echo on the right, in the overtly Hegelian thinking of Francis Fukuyama (1992), who argued after the collapse of the Soviet Union that history in the grand sense, by which he meant history as the chronicle of gigantic world-convulsing conflicts between mass ideologies and ways of life, had come to an end in the universal triumph of free-market capitalism and the gradual spread of representative democracy around the world. Time would of course go on, he claimed, and people with different agendas would still disagree and struggle, but only at local or individual levels governed by the invisible hand of the market and the long arm of the liberal state's police forces. This perspective too is a kind of postmodernism, though it generally refuses the label: Fukuyama agrees with Lyotard that history, having lost its grandeur, and the future to which it claims to lead, having lost its promise, are not what they used to be, and he further suggests that the only thing we can do in response to this situation is define the irreducible diversity of our cultural backgrounds and situations according to their relative values on the global market. The fact that such profound similarities in practical outcome can arise from such radically different philosophical and political points of departure demonstrates how little real difference exists across the postmodernist spectrum.[5] Some critics see convergences of this kind as evidence of postmodernism's underlying contradictions, which would then imply that some kind of dialectical resolution to those contradictions could preserve the model's critical productivity. My view is that this assessment is mistaken, for two reasons. First, the convergence of viewpoints can be explained just as easily by appeal to the indistinctness, or even incoherence, of postmodernism as a category as it can by such dialectical sleight of hand, and second, if there are in fact contradictions underlying postmodernism, then they have repeatedly proven to be irresolvable in its terms and require a radical change of perspective to make them productive.

The great merit of globalization, then, is to have revealed the profound limitations of these diametrically opposed versions of postmodern disengagement and dehistoricization (and, I would claim, the many versions in between). The huge, indeed world historical, conflicts to which globalization has given rise—of which the current situation is a particularly acute but otherwise not unusual example—compel all of us, not just the Hegelians, the Marxists, and the professional historians, to attend once again to the large contours of historical struggle and change, to rehistoricize the resolutely anti-historical conceptual field bequeathed to us by postmodernism, and to make another effort to find common cause amid the profusion of atomized economic subjects and cultural particularisms. These conflicts demand not that we live according to a single prewritten "grand narrative" but rather that we take an active part in the construction of whatever narratives, of whatever magnitude, we will have to live through in the coming years. In this effort of construction, the most important precedent to be found is the work of Fredric Jameson. He has long argued that postmodernism is the cultural logic that corresponds to, but at the same time masks, the process of evening out the uneven development of global capitalism, an unevenness that was once the subject of the well-known "three worlds" theory, among others.[6] I would argue that this evening-out process is precisely what the word "globalization" is intended to name: in crossing the threshold of globalization, we are constrained to acknowledge that there are no longer three distinct (economic/political/cultural/"existential") worlds because the second world, international socialism, has effectively collapsed and fragmented, while the first and third worlds now interpenetrate one another almost completely. High-rent, high-rise financial districts dot what was once the "nonaligned" "third world," where the affluent speak English in order to do business, and the metropolises of the Western industrial "first world" are honeycombed with areas of intense poverty, linguistic polymorphism, and cultural separatism that result from forced economic migration. This interpenetration does not mean that economic development and hence real power are now evenly distributed among all groups or regions and therefore that inequality no longer exists—far from it. It simply means that the world market no longer has an apparently clear-cut outside or alternative, that resistance to the market no longer has a dominant model to imitate or an ideological line to follow, and so everywhere we look we find that capitalism has replaced not only the developmental mechanisms of the socialist world but also virtually all of the precapitalist productive practices that had survived modernism. This is the situation that Marx called "real subsumption" or the "specific mode of capitalist production" (1976, 1023), in which capitalist relations of production penetrate all levels and regions, leaving no geographic, economic, or cultural area untransformed.[7]

Although the "three worlds" model has fallen into deserved disrepute, no comparable overall model emerged to replace it during the reign of postmodernism. Indeed, the fundamental postmodern principle of linguistic indeterminacy and slippage, Lyotard's insistence on the incommensurability of language games and its variants, stigmatizes any such "totalizing" effort as "totalitarian" and effectively rules it out. At this point Jameson's well-known appropriation of Kevin Lynch's concept of cognitive mapping becomes relevant (Jameson 1991, 51–54). Like Althusser's famous definition of ideology or the Situationists' notion of psychogeography, cognitive mapping is a subject's "Imaginary relationship" to her "Real conditions of existence," and thus a critical project of constructing a "situational representation on the part of the individual subject" of "that vaster and properly unrepresentable totality which is the ensemble of society's structures as a whole" (51). This "situational representation of totality" is precisely what postmodernism, in almost all of its forms, has not only failed to provide but ruled out a priori (Jameson 1991, 330), and it is what Jameson calls for in the conclusion to his book: cognitive mapping of the "new spatiality implicit in the postmodern" (418). This, I would claim, is what the various models of globalization offer, and as such they provide the (plural) basis for a new proliferation of globalization studies, studies in the cultural consequences and possibilities that follow from the evening out of global capitalism's functional processes.

This evening out of capitalism or interpenetration of worlds has important consequences for literature and the arts in general. Most obviously, the notion of distinct national cultural heritages is becoming increasingly untenable as populations with different backgrounds come into prolonged contact, intermarry, and exchange cultural values, beliefs, and practices. We are approaching a belated and an unexpected fulfillment of Goethe's prophecy of *Weltliteratur*, which Marx and Engels echo in the *Communist Manifesto*:

> The intellectual creations of individual nations become common property. National one-sidedness and narrow-mindedness become more and more impossible, and from the numerous national and local literatures, there arises a world literature. (Marx and Engels 1962, 38)

We can see this synthesis beginning to coalesce already in the Anglo-European cross-fertilization of high modernism itself, in Eliot's and Joyce's casual polylingualism, but during the postmodern period a much broader synthesis takes place in the case of magic realism, for example, a diffuse literary movement that numbers among its contributors major writers from the United States (Toni Morrison), Latin America (Gabriel García Márquez, Isabel Allende), Mediterranean Europe (Italo Calvino), the Arab world (Naguib Mahfouz), and Asia (Salman Rushdie). In the masterpieces of magic realism as in high modernism, however, local specifics of cultural heritage generally remain central and dominate the global elements of inclusive style. For example, in Calvino's *Invisible Cities* (1974), perhaps his finest achievement, it is the Venetian explorer Marco Polo, cartographer of the forking paths of immanent discovery, who evokes the allegorical cities for Tartar emperor Kublai Khan, who is the cities' transcendent ruler but as such knows little or nothing of their diversity. Toni Morrison's version of magic realism, most powerfully deployed in *Beloved* (1987), is even more precisely delimited by its national situation: the historical legacy of American slavery and the literary legacy of Faulkner's and Hurston's Southern modernism. In these examples, the local is granted priority over the global, even in those relatively rare cases in which the mutual co-implication of local and global is explicitly recognized (as in Rushdie's case). In short, while magic realism is one tremendously important form of what we might call "international postmodernism," it does not constitute a literature of globalization.

In my view, the decisive elements of a more genuinely global kind of literature can be seen in the cyberpunk movement, which at its best—in the work of William Gibson and Haruki Murakami, among others—mixes diverse cultural frames of reference without privileging any one of them as a center and demonstrates how fully the local and the global interpenetrate and mutually define each other. Gibson's "Sprawl" trilogy,[8] for example, posits advanced information technology, "cyberspace" (a term Gibson himself coined), as the arena of continuous, nonhierarchical interchange between cultures widely separated in physical space and historical tradition: high-density Japanese urbanism meets Caribbean Santeria meets European titular aristocracy meets the high modernism of Joseph Cornell's boxes. In these books cyberspace itself exemplifies and enacts the co-implication of the local and the global, since through it one can get from anywhere to anywhere with virtually no privileged intermediary steps. Murakami's work, for example his novel *The Hard-Boiled Wonderland and the End of the World* (1991), is not strictly cyberpunk to the extent that it is not simply a manifestation of the newest generic orthodoxy in the field of science fiction, but it shares with Gibson's work an assumption of the almost immediate translatability of local cultural traditions and forms on a global scale—which includes, of course, their mistranslation. Literary works like these may be said to be "denationalizing" in their frames of reference, which does not make them fully denationalized or decontextualized but rather requires them to be situated at a global level in order for their full context to become intelligible. Similar forms of decentered or equal-opportunity hybridization can be found in the global cinema of Bollywood (an important locus in Rushdie's *Satanic Verses* [1988]) and Hong Kong, and in the many forms of so-called "world music" that spring from the proliferating contact zones between formerly distinct musical traditions.

These new artistic and literary genres constitute positive syntheses of diverse cultural materials, but each of them arises out of a conflict that may or may not be clearly legible in the content or form of the artwork itself. This has always been true, of course: the notion that art relies on conflict goes back at least as far as Aristotle's *Poetics* and some of the mythological texts of Asia and the Americas. For many centuries the conflicts that generate art have been organized around several variable, but nonetheless traditional, axes mentioned earlier: ethnicity, gender, class, and nation. These axes are obviously still with us, but in crossing the threshold of globalization they have been displaced, overdetermined, and complicated in unprecedented ways. To investigate these complications, I would like to propose three descriptive and analytical categories that run skew to those well-established axes of conflict and thus offer us insights into the unexpected possibilities of creativity that the new millennium has in store.

I propose these categories as tools for mapping lines of cultural alliance and struggle in the world of globalization, tools that are intended to replace the outmoded categories of "three worlds" theory and other modern or postmodern models of difference and hybridity that were once forms of resistance to capital but have now been absorbed within it.[9] The fact that there are three is the first point I would like to stress, because it seems to me that many of the popular and even specialized discourses on the subject of globalization assume a fundamentally binary division of parties and perspectives. For example, analysts who equate globalization with the impending triumph of so-called "American" economic and cultural forms like the free market and republican democracy over one-party planned economies on the one hand and precapitalist aristocracies of caste or sect on the other appear to fall naturally into two camps: those who favor such globalization, like its primary beneficiaries, the multinational corporations along with their stockholders and representatives, and those who implacably oppose such globalization, like the protectionist, separatist, and nativist groups that can be found in significant numbers in almost every nation today. Thus, in both the mass media and scholarly publications, we often see an apparently monolithic opposition between corporate globalization and protectionist anti-globalization, conceived as mirror-image world-historical forces in contention for the future of humanity.

While dualisms of this sort make possible very simple and power-ful rhetorical oppositions between the affluent and the impoverished or between the progressive and the reactionary, depending on whose politics are being dramatized, they make very misleading analytical tools because they reduce every critical intervention to a crude referendum on the status quo. We are called upon to be either for corporate glo-balization as it now stands or against it. That is why I have found the inclusion of the third term, "counter-globalization," to be necessary in order to complicate the oversimplified, us-versus-them logic of the common journalistic dualism. I take the term from what I have found to be the most sophisticated, penetrating, and useful model of the contemporary world system, Michael Hardt's and Antonio Negri's *Empire* (115), where it serves to name the project of what we might provisionally call an alternative globalization, that is, a form of world social and economic organization that would preserve, extend, and intensify the flow of information, production and human subjects that underpins the corporate form of globalization but at the same time activates circuits of radical democracy that have been trivialized and instrumentalized when they have not been actively foreclosed by that form of globalization.[10] Counter-globalization or counter-Empire is another word for a populist "globalization from below," which con-fronts corporate "globalization from above" on different terrain and with different aims than nativist or protectionist anti-globalization.

As Jameson reminds us, globalization is at root an economic cat-egory, one that describes the institutional framework of the present era of multinational or transnational capitalism, but as a result of the accel-erated development that this era has witnessed, a qualitative threshold has been crossed, and now everything is tending to become economic. Thus the economic ceases to be a narrowly defined category: the estab-lishment of global market mechanisms for fine art, pollution credits, insurance risk, adoptive children, affect, and other contemporary (ma-terial and/or immaterial) objects of exchange demonstrates this clearly. This expansion of the economic sphere is in fact one of the elements of globalization to which anti-globalization movements object most strongly.[11] The same point also can be made from the opposite direction: Italian economist Christian Marazzi has argued that the most recent mutation of capitalism constitutes a veritable "linguistic turn" in the global economy and economists' study thereof, corresponding to philosophy's linguistic turn (following Wittgenstein, Heidegger, and Derrida), as the new global marketplace increasingly comes to rely on communications media and information technology that constitute not merely the infrastructure of production and exchange but privileged objects of consumption as well.[12]

In response to the situation that these models define, a theory and practice of counter-globalization cannot just raise an abstract, formalist argument about the logic of the excluded third. It must propose a form of resistance that is not simply opposed to globalization, and thus is not an avatar of anti-globalization but instead differs from globalization and anti-globalization alike. It cannot quite be a compromise between the two, a tempering or balancing of their respective excesses, either, though in a certain sense it does take shape in the conceptual and cultural spaces between them. It is, I would argue, fundamentally other in one crucially important way: counter-globalization is the condition of genuinely new cultural expression, expression that self-consciously situates itself in the present historical conjuncture and addresses itself to the future that is bearing down on us, and as a result I believe that counter-globalization is a necessary condition for radical democracy in the new millennium. Counter-globalization should be our horizon of expectation for the literature of globalization as well.

To understand what this means, it will be useful to consider the forms of cultural expression that accompany the initial dualism of globalization and anti-globalization. Globalization depends upon the increasingly frictionless and direct flow of commodities and capital from locale to locale around the globe, and this flow numbers among its key exchanges the circulation of cultural products in the broad sense: films, books, artworks, crafts, and so on. These forms, whatever their points of local origin and whatever the specifics of their local meanings might be, are all transformed through this process of exchange into commodities, and they are in fact produced with that exchange in mind. Commodity status is not added onto them as an afterthought, as they are being shipped out of their sites of manufacture, but incorporated into them from the very beginning. By virtue of their quantity and the patterns of their movement, they acknowledge that they exist to be purchased and consumed, even when they preserve the material forms of a cultural heritage that predates commodity relations. In this sense, the cultural expression of globalization is the culture industry, very

much in the sense that Max Horkheimer and Theodor Adorno defined
it in 1944 (1972, 120–67). This overdetermining commodity form imposes a reductive unity of meaning on cultural expressions: what the
products of the culture industry express above all is exchange value or
money, and therefore from the point of view of the market a culture
and its expressions only have value if they make money.

Anti-globalization, which generally seeks to "preserve," or more
accurately reestablish, the insularity of local social, religious, and economic cultures against the inroads of the global market and its exclusive commitment to exchange value, expresses itself through the
reactivation of traditional aesthetic and artifact forms as emblems of an
unsullied, precapitalist or noncapitalist local, national, or transnational
culture. This was already the case during the era of decolonization, as
Chidi Amuta and others have noted, when many of the newly independent nations of Africa and Asia promoted one or another particular
cluster of indigenous expressions to the level of generalized national
identity as a way of reasserting a cultural autonomy that had been
suppressed during the colonial period. The painfully contradictory
results of this kind of forced generalization, especially in the cases of
African nation-states that, as a consequence of colonialism, yoke together large numbers of tribal groups with distinct languages, heritages, and aesthetic forms, are well known (Amuta 1989, 62–64). In
some cases this "postcolonial" promotion takes shapes that are hard to
distinguish from the culture industry of globalization itself: the mass
manufacture for export of indigenous arts and crafts, for example.
However, it also takes more unique forms whose commodification may
not be so immediately obvious. For example, many indigenous communities around the world preserve their cultural heritages by encouraging cultural tourism, which encourages traditional artists, artisans, and
performers to display those heritages in context to visitors from foreign
cultures. However, even here commodification emerges as the defining
difference between premarket cultural practices and their postmarket
avatars. Although "authenticity" is the commodity for sale, inauthenticity
is the only thing that can actually be bought. In rituals and other cultural performances, the market pressure to provide access to the expressive events results on the one hand in the publicizing of forms that
were formerly restricted in access or the secularization of acts that were
formerly sacred, and, on the other hand, it results in the regular repetition of formerly time-specific activities like seasonal festivals. As Leslie
Marmon Silko reminds us, it would be a serious mistake to think that
such ceremonies have not always been changing throughout their his-

tory, but it also would be a mistake to attribute the kind of abrupt changes we are discussing here to an autonomous cultural development (1978, 126). The upshot of this is that even anti-global cultural expressions often are forced to retool, fossilize, and commodify themselves according to the demands of the culture industry in order to survive on the terrain of corporate globalization.[13]

Both terms of the globalization/anti-globalization dualism thus lead to cultural and aesthetic redundancy or uniformity, and at the same time they impose sociopolitical conformity and hierarchical control on extraordinarily diverse populations. This is obvious in the anti-globalization tactics of theocratic fundamentalism, authoritarian nationalism, and ethnic cleansing, but it also is clearly visible in the practices of corporate globalization, which has long proclaimed itself the most influential emissary of democracy. The terms that global capital has tended to dictate to debtor nations as the conditions of its investment erode those nations' democratic institutions by imposing broad public service reductions, often against the will of the people, in order to create more favorable tax and regulative environments for increasingly mobile corporations and investors.[14] Clearly the nation-state, democratic or otherwise, has ceased to be the controlling level of organization in the global economy. Indeed, recent events suggest that this "post-Fordist" economic model that has become the norm in "underdeveloped" and debtor nations is now being imported into the economies of creditor nations such as the United States in order to roll back the progressive tax and regulative accomplishments of the past century of labor, feminist, civil rights, and environmental activism.[15] In order to afford our "war on terrorism" and the subsidiary wars it entails while cutting taxes to stimulate the hobbled economy, we will be asked to cut spending on all other elements of the public budget, including noncommercial scientific research (the very thing that has made possible the current information infrastructure of the global market), education, and the arts, no matter how badly a majority of us may want to pursue or provide them. Then, if we make our communities more attractive to investment by further reducing taxes and weakening safety, health, and environmental standards, we may get jobs that will someday, in an undefined future, generate enough noncorporate public revenue to permit us once again to fund basic scientific research, education, and the arts. It is a surprisingly simple gambit that will complete the process of corporate globalization by bringing it full circle back to its birthplace in the former "first world," and it remains to be seen if this gambit will actually work in the face of rising resistance.

At this point, I would like to turn to the cultural possibilities opened up by my third term, counter-globalization. These possibilities are beginning to take shape *between* the rigid oppositions of globalization and anti-globalization, just as a substantial number, perhaps a majority, of the most significant cultural achievements of the past thirty years, those masterpieces that have most often been called "postmodern" or "postcolonial," took shape between the first and second or first and third worlds of that older model. Here we can think not only of aforementioned magic realism but also the "historiographic metafiction" of Thomas Pynchon or the reflexive genre-bending of Joanna Russ.[16] Counter-globalization is a discontinuous and dissensual set of movements that contests both terms of the globalization dualism, and in so doing it must make use of themes that are not reducible to that dualism and aesthetic forms that are not already compromised by it. This makes the cultural expressions of counter-globalization somewhat difficult to recognize and categorize, from the points of view of pro- and anti-globalization alike, and I note this as a way of acknowledging that my remarks on the subject are necessarily schematic, conjectural, and incomplete.

Nevertheless, some patterns that indicate the shape and direction of the culture of counter-globalization are clearly beginning to emerge, and not only in the guise of cyberpunk fiction. For instance, the most interesting protestors of Seattle and Genoa (such as the Tute Bianche, Ya Basta!, and the Free Software Foundation), those who are not members of trade unions or other conventional representative organizations, seem to group themselves around and communicate through elements of the new media—most often participatory forms like hypermedia, noncommercial hacking, digital art, and zine publication. If their public statements can be taken as a reliable indication of their means and ends, then these groups aspire to a state of collective creativity, production, and consumption abetted by instantaneous communication and continuous information exchange—a utopia of radically redistributed material and intellectual abundance that some critics have tried to model via Marx's notion of "General Intellect."[17] Most groups like these have yet to present fixed cultural products to the world, artifacts that can be analyzed and assessed in relation to the masterpieces of previous movements, but that is only because the forms for those artifacts have not yet stabilized; the same was true of the endless improvised choruses of New Orleans jazz before the invention of the LP record. Perhaps the recent commissioning of short stories specifically designed for online "instant messaging" systems marks one possible beginning of such stabilization, though I am skeptical of that genre's long- (or even medium-) term viability.

However, the demands these movements make for radical democracy, by which I mean democracy beyond the scope of the nation-state and its new taskmaster the global market, present a challenge that cannot be answered without calling into question both the fundamental assumptions of anti-global isolationism and cultural "preservation" on the one hand and the most basic operations of globalization in its corporate form on the other. Global commerce has begun to outstrip democracy as earlier it outstripped cultural tradition, but the cultures of counter-globalization appear to recognize that the response to the former dilemma must be more complex, sensitive, flexible, and forward-looking than the response to the latter has been—as complex, sensitive, flexible, and forward-looking as the new human collectivity that is becoming conscious of itself through the networks of distributed cognition and immaterial teamwork. No longer conceivable as an exclusive ethnic or national *Volk* or people, this collectivity must embody the differential inclusiveness of what Hardt and Negri call the multitude.[18]

To conclude, one final, less technophilic, but perhaps more readily graspable example: the Zapatistas, who speak, write, and resist as indigenous peoples exploited by a colonial nation-state, Mexico, that is in search of its own privileged place in the global economy. But they did not demand the world's attention on New Years' Day 1994 in order either to demand their share of globalization's profit or to essentialize and nationalize their cultural heritage as a defense against globalization. Like the other collective participants in the culture of counter-globalization, they have interrupted the small talk of the global status quo, the everyday language game of performativity in the untrammeled pursuit of the same old goals, in order to raise the big question of other goals and the means they might require. This is the question of history—not the history that subsumes us within vast processes or grand narratives that depend upon a fictive transcendent subject but the history we construct as we go. As Subcomandante Marcos puts it in perhaps his best-known parable of the struggle, "The Southeast in Two Winds,"

> The storm is here. . . . Now the wind from above rules, but the wind from below is coming. The prophecy is here. When the storm calms, when rain and fire again leave the country in peace, the world will no longer be the world but something better.[19]

And perhaps the globe will no longer be postmodern but something better.

NOTES

1. This chapter first took shape as a talk given to a nonspecialist audience at one of the conferences on globalization to which I refer in the second paragraph, and I have chosen to retain some of the casualness of that situation in this slightly more specialized version.

2. The breadth of this project can be suggested, if not really measured, by the philosophical distance between one of its most prominent early ideologues, the "artificial" high-church Anglican, T. S. Eliot (see his late essays, especially "The Idea of a Christian Society," reprinted in his *Christianity and Culture* [1960]), and its most prominent current defender, Jürgen Habermas, the "reformed" Frankfurt School Marxist.

3. See Adams (1999), as well as Cottom (2003).

4. This is the argument of his book *The Postmodern Condition* (1984), whose original date of publication, 1979, marks the beginning of postmodernism's critical ascendancy.

5. More such examples are readily available, such as the liberal John Rawls's prefiguration of postmodernism in his anti-transcendent *Theory of Justice* (1971), the "proceduralism" of which closely resembles Lyotard's account of the performativity criterion. See Hardt and Negri, *Labor of Dionysus: A Critique of the State-Form* (1994), chapter 6.

6. See Jameson (1991, 307–310, 404–405). Negri has advanced a very similar claim in his brief essay "Postmodern" (1989, 200–207).

7. See Marx, *Capital*, vol. 1 (1976, 1023–25, 1034–38).

8. See Gibson's *Neuromancer* (1984), *Count Zero* (1986), and *Mona Lisa Overdrive* (1988).

9. On this absorption into and unconscious complicity with capital, see Hardt and Negri (2000, 137–46, 150–56). Briefly, the reliance of the so-called "politics of difference" (such as many versions of postcolonial critique) on assumptions regarding the strict binarism of hierarchical power structures (racism, sexism, etc.) makes that politics vulnerable to co-optation by capitalist models of "diversity management" and the like that eschew simple binarism in favor of subtly differentiated niche marketing that treats ethnic and gender diversity as a range of new business opportunities and not simply as an Other to be radically excluded.

10. A word on my preference for this book (and its recently published sequel, *Multitude: War and Democracy in the Age of Empire* [2004]) over other insightful models of globalization (such as Giovanni Arrighi's *The Long Twentieth Century* [1994]): while Hardt and Negri can certainly be criticized for a number of overstatements, understatements, and even errors in their interpretation of the emergence of Empire out of the ashes of traditional imperialism, they have the great merit of focusing most of their analysis on the features that make the present state of things genuinely new in relation to the structures of the past. Virtually all the other models of globalization I have examined focus primarily on the continuities with or repetitions of the past (the structure of

the "systemic cycle of accumulation" in Arrighi, for example), and thus they offer comparatively little in the way of new opportunities for intervention, whether scholarly/critical or activist.

11. For example, tertiarization (the shift from a primary or manufacturing economy to a tertiary or service-based economy, with the concomitant lowering and precariousness of wages) and the global sex industry (both tourism and media) are common targets of critique and resistance from protectionist anti-globalization forces as well as counter-globalization groups.

12. This is the argument of Marazzi's book *Il posto dei calzini: La svolta linguistica dell'economia e i suoi effetti sulla politica* (1994).

13. In this regard, the intervention of the U.S. federal government in the legal definition and guarantee of authenticity of Native American handicrafts (to say nothing of the legal definition of tribal membership through blood quantum) would be an instructive case study.

14. See Soros (2002) and Stiglitz (2002).

15. "Post-Fordism" refers to the systematic abandonment by nation-states of "Fordist" welfare structures (such as national health care and pension systems and other elements of the publicly funded "social wage") that once moderated the impact on workers of traditional "liberal" (that is, laissez-faire) capitalism.

16. Historiographic metafiction is Linda Hutcheon's term for the key strand of postmodernist fiction that she claims interrogates and criticizes the fundamental assumptions of historical knowledge; see her *Poetics of Postmodernism: History, Theory, Fiction* (1988). Regarding Russ, see her novel *The Female Man* (1975) and her critical polemic *How to Suppress Women's Writing* (1983).

17. See Marx (1973, 706). See in particular Virno's contributions to *Radical Thought in Italy: A Potential Politics* (1996).

18. See *Empire* (2000, 60–74, 209–18, 357–63), as well as *Multitude* (2004), passim.

19. See *Zapatistas! Documents of the New Mexican Revolution* (1994, 46). See also Rabasa (1997, 399–431).

REFERENCES

Adams, Henry. 1999 [1918]. *The education.* Oxford: Oxford University Press.

Amuta, Chidi. 1989. *The theory of African literature: Implications for practical criticism.* Atlantic Highlands, NJ: Zed Books.

Arrighi, Giovanni. 1994. *The long twentieth century.* New York: Verso.

Calvino, Italo. 1974. *Invisible cities.* Translated by William Weaver. New York: HBJ.

Cottom, Daniel. 2003. *Why education is useless.* Philadelphia: University of Pennsylvania Press.

Eliot, T. S. 1960. The idea of a Christian society. In *Christianity and culture*, 3–77. New York: Harcourt Brace.

Fukuyama, Francis. 1992. *The end of history and the last man*. New York: Free Press.

Gibson, William. 1984. *Neuromancer*. New York: Ace.

———. 1986. *Count zero*. New York: Ace.

———. 1988. *Mona Lisa overdrive*. New York: Bantam.

Hardt, Michael, and Antonio Negri. 1994. *Labor of Dionysus: A critique of the state-form*. Minneapolis: University of Minnesota Press.

———. 2000. *Empire*. Cambridge, MA: Harvard University Press.

———. 2004. *Multitude: War and democracy in the age of empire*. New York: Penguin Press.

Horkheimer, Max, and Theodor Adorno. 1972. *Dialectic of enlightenment*. New York: Continuum.

Hutcheon, Linda. 1988. *Poetics of postmodernism: History, theory, fiction*. New York: Routledge.

Jameson, Fredric. 1991. *Postmodernism, or, the cultural logic of late capitalism*. Durham, NC: Duke University Press.

Lyotard, Jean-François. 1984 [1979]. *The postmodern condition*. Translated by Geoff Bennington and Brian Masumi. Minneapolis: University of Minnesota Press.

Marazzi, Christian. 1994. *Il posto dei calzini: La svolta linguistica dell'economia e i suoi effetti sulla politica*. Bellinzona, Switzerland: Casagrande.

Marx, Karl. 1973. *Grundrisse*. Translated by Martin Nicolaus. New York: Penguin.

———. 1976. *Capital*. Translated by Ben Fowkes, vol. 1. New York: Vintage.

Marx, Karl, and Frederick Engels. 1962. *Selected works*, vol. 1. Moscow: Foreign Languages Publishing.

Morrison, Toni. 1987. *Beloved*. New York: Knopf.

Murakami, Haruki. 1991. *The hard-boiled wonderland and the end of the world* (*Sekai no owari to hard-boiled wonderland*). Translated by Alfred Birnbaum. London: Hamish Hamilton.

Negri, Antonio. 1989. Postmodern. In *The politics of subversion: A manifesto for the 21st century*, ed. 200–207. Cambridge, MA: Polity Press.

Rabasa, José. 1997. "Of Zapatismo: Reflections on the folkloric and the impossible in a subaltern insurrection." In *The politics of culture in the shadow of capital*, ed. Lisa Lowe and David Lloyd, 399–431. Durham, NC: Duke University Press.

Rawls, John. 1971. *Theory of justice.* Cambridge, MA: Harvard University Press.

Rushdie, Salman. 1988. *The satanic verses.* Dover, DE: The Consortium.

Russ, Joanna. 1975. *The female man.* Boston: Beacon Press.

———. 1983. *How to suppress women's writing.* Austin: University of Texas Press.

Silko, Leslie Marmon. 1978. *Ceremony.* New York: Penguin.

Soros, George. 2002. *Soros on globalization.* New York: Public Affairs.

Stiglitz, Joseph. 2002. *Globalization and its discontents.* New York: W.W. Norton.

Virno, Paolo, and Michael Hardt, eds. 1996. *Radical thought in Italy: A potential politics.* Minneapolis: University of Minnesota Press.

Zapatistas! Documents of the new Mexican revolution. 1994. Brooklyn, NY: Autonomedia.

Chapter 4

Fiction's Present without Basis

LESLIE SCALAPINO

In the evening, the day the U.S. invasion of Iraq began, I went to a reading series held at a private home. The host was in jail, arrested during a huge anti-war demonstration that blocked buildings and streets of San Francisco. Fourteen hundred arrested, twelve hundred arrested the next day (the extent of the demonstrations never reported nationally). The audience (all writers) at the reading, and the readers, discussed the fact that language has been destroyed. It is only propaganda and lies. Saying that we are liberating them, 'we' mow down their people. (Jalal Toufic, in *Forthcoming* (2000), comments that in Lebanon, "Even guerrilla operations by Lebanese against military targets in the part of Lebanon illegally occupied by Israel are termed terrorist!"[1]) The writers speaking used words to the effect: 'they (those saying they're liberating) have destroyed language, we must destroy language (in order to make it)'.

I think language that is poetry or fiction is the only language that *can* destroy language in that sense (to remake it).

That may not be an answer to the question posed (for a consideration of 'fiction's present'): "Does fiction continuing the tradition of modernist innovation have any reality for emergent political groups and cultures?"[2] Destroying language (to remake it) may be alongside that question.

"Can the novel establish itself in the present of global capitalism without abandoning its formal distinctness?" My sense is: it is its formal distinctness if it 'transforms' the time it is in—'transforms' in the sense of to be only *its* language, syntax, and structure in *that* time. It can change the *space* of the given—the space given as that language there, which rearranges changing the conception (*present tense*) of the outside given.

47

That is, fiction's present is the act of changing the language *then*. The present *is* (phenomenally) a form of fiction, in being created ahead of us unknown. The present is not engaged in this sense, however, in MLA Style Manual language. Critical, explanatory language (intentionally regularized) is removed from the present *as* its space (is not the present of that language)—meaning, the intent of critical language is not that of being: the act of changing the present as real-time space (as language, itself a form of real-time space, which can change space outside not mimicking it—conceptual as also a *physical* change). Critical language is to be within shared terms, what has become that already. My argument is that the language of poetry and fiction can be a new space by being (in the text) *as* given, there.

Yet the language of theory (such as Deleuze's and Guattari's *A Thousand Plateaus: Capitalism and Schizophrenia* [2000]) is also written 'physical' space, that work a kind of summary that reconstructs modern terrain according to a description that we then recognize as present information (though "Treatise on Nomadology—The War Machine" is a conjecture on "Thought, the State, and Nomadology," which is not about actual nomads, in Mongolia, for example, it is created theory/future)—but the writing of that vision of reality (which one can accept in the same way one accepts news, if news were that, anyway the way one accepts observation, as the language of supposed rational/'straightforward' exposition) does not change its space except to enhance it. It leaves that space in place, intentionally prolonging it, adding to it rather than altering it as the shape of the language in which it is delineated, in a duration as to constitute a history of the present. Dropping a distinction between fiction and poetry as types of language is indicative of the current change also reflected in writers dropping the distinction between art of language and discursive language. Yet there are still distinctions. The language of fiction and poetry can change the created setting vertically/horizontally at once by that setting being differently the space that is syntax, rather than that setting being solely intellectually created (its very presentation depending on appearing as objective fact, therefore without *apparently* attempting its own transmogrification *there*).

An example of intellectual construct's resistance to its meaning occurring *as* the medium of its language, which for example in poetry would be its syntax shape and sound (yet as its language constituting change of its own terrain—I am now altering my construct to indicate that its resistance to such written change can be part of its own energy) along the lines of Deleuze and Guattari, is the work of Jalal Toufic (who is highly conversant with their theory and influenced by them). Jalal Toufic's writing can be regarded as a new fiction eschewing characters, plot, and emotive impetus or resonance in a form of duration that is radical. Toufic's (2000) *Forthcoming*, using a 'syntax of discourse,' begins with a discourse on refusal as the language, rejection of embodying action, emotion, and character. I'm viewing Toufic's *Forthcoming* as a work of fiction by its being intentionally a counterfeit that demonstrates withdrawing the possibility of there being fiction: in that, in relation to event as (what he terms "surpassing disaster," such as in contemporary Iraq, Bosnia, Lebanon, and Rwanda, as in earlier but still present Hiroshima) observation or reportage, seeing at all, has been withdrawn, both intentionally, and from possibility at all (given the nature of comprehending these events). Yet in his view, 'fiction' can comprehend by being counterfeit, only if it demonstrates itself as that.

Toufic's project begins at the point in time of conventional fiction already having been displaced. *Forthcoming* is a form of 'fiction' that is only its theory, as film and literary theory indebted to Deleuze, Nietzsche, Shakespeare, and others—to create a glass (text's space), one that is not reflecting (as would a mirror): the two sides of the glass in which one sees oneself/surpassing disaster/history, not by comparison or similarity/analogy—but via the glass being itself only a dichotomy, by an alternate space or element being created next to (outside of) the dichotomy. The image of the glass is proposed toward the beginning of *Forthcoming* in Toufic's rewrite of a scene from *Hamlet* in relation to his conception of "surpassing disaster" (as in Lebanon and Iraq); the function of his theoretical glass is to enable the shattering of any image (false in any case) by a mismatching of the gazes looking into it: "In this adaptation, Hamlet has been stamped by the mismatch of the gazes during his encounter with the ghost" (2000, 32). The difference of their seeing (still demonstrating, however, the ghost's, Hamlet's, and the queen Gertrude's private 'interiors,' not yet entire substitution) is necessary to the shattering of the image: "This is merely the inmost part that can be reached by a glass, one therefore that still pertains to the logic of reflections and mirroring and thus does not reach the realm and level of substitu/tions, where specula are undone" (ibid.).

Toufic's rewrite of the scene from *Hamlet* is composed of notations on taping for substitution of itself/the tape, on interviews with the director and with the playwright (*not* Shakespeare but the substitute who rewrites, thus presumably Toufic unnamed). The rewrite of *Hamlet* also is woven no-analogies ("where one can mistake as identical different things, and as different identical things"), such as Toufic's interjection that is a statement of the concept ('meaning') of a film's action as apparently a kind of "dumb show" now of *Hamlet* (but *Hamlet* as the structure of something else), though the actions are different

(2000, 30). Speaking of Hamlet's queen, he produces by no-analogy a separate 'no-action': "In Coppola's *Bram Stoker's Dracula: Love Never Dies*, Dracula's wife kills herself in fidelity to her husband on being misinformed that he was slaughtered in battle" (ibid.). The text is a proposing by addition of 'extensions,' demonstrations that are not analogous though they seem to be.

His argument (a form that is usually analogies, his being this series of additions that are 'not-analogous') as it unfolds is construct to see outside of itself. *As* intellectual construct, his 'analogies as no-analogy/as if 'only' prolonged analogy' are not rationally constructed or divined. His intellectual constructs intentionally restrict (are "radical closure") emotional/as dumb-show dramatic expression; as in his statement, given his own context of "surpassing disaster," that he cannot laugh because he would not be able to stop, therefore must have only a serious framework (a construct that this reader remembered/thus misremembering, as intentional suppression of emotion).

The 'destruction' of action as a basis of writing, *to be fiction*, is necessary in order for Toufic to construct *Forthcoming* as two sides at once of a glass in which one sees a different view than one is capable of seeing—just as Gertrude in Toufic's *Hamlet* begins, by Toufic's description in the play within the play, to see her own action in marrying her husband's brother/the husband's murderer, an action that by its nature is psychologically impossible for her (because it is her own action) to see. Toufic's alternate space is rendered by withdrawing the possibility of seeing otherwise (otherwise than that given, or *not* given in that it is unseen by her except through Toufic).

Toufic, a filmmaker as well as writer, is an Arab from Beirut, where he presently resides, though he has lived and taught in the United States. He makes context of "surpassing disaster" the only space—the alternate ('to be able to surpass disaster') being simultaneous. Both meanings of his term are the glass, the writing bringing all onto one spatial plain with which he begins his text, "Every Name in History Is I," his dissolution of character to be his space only:

> To fight the anonymity with which the war enemy is killed
> even by precision bombing, the soldier has to receive, from
> their state of being already dead, the calls of the unknown
> persons who will soon be murdered by him. Such a call is
> possible in the non-linear time of undeath. The Jacob Maker
> of David Blair's *Wax, or the Discovery of Television among the
> Bees* (1992) has to receive the call of the two Iraqi tank
> soldiers at whom he is shortly going to fire a missile during

the Gulf War, and to whom he is invisible (whether because he is flying a Stealth fighter or because the radars of their unit have been blinded). In the state of undeath from which the call is sent, and in the state of death before dying in which it is received, one at times feels: *every name in history is I. Every name in history is I* is one way to fight the reduction to anonymity and generality. (Toufic 2000, 17)

The singular spatial plain is thus proposed on the first page of the text, a construct fulfilled there and later as not-entirely disparate blind shards of thought in displacement in which characters, dramatic plot, and (any) action is stricken to render the text a state of undeath. Toufic is a character in the text only as someone else, thus dead:

As long as I, as dead, have not totally disintegrated into disparate blind shard of thoughts and affects functioning mostly according to *displacement* and pure association of sounds, figures, etc., I will try, through the most incredible contortions—which are not felt as such since they are allowed by the non-linear time and the non-exclusive disjunction reigning in the realm of death or death-before-death—to arrive at a semblance of justice, discovering that I, who will shortly kill, was a victim of the dead, was killed by them: it is because I, as Zoltan Abbassid, was murdered by them in 1919 that I, Jacob Maker, will take revenge on them ("being dead, vengeance is my life") in 1991 by firing a missile at their tank . . . I, as Zoltan Abbassid, was killed in 1919 by the (Iraqi) dead taking the form of (Mesopotamian) bees (some fly their B-52 warplanes and drop bombs on an enemy whose radars have been rendered inoperative, killing a large number of people without feeling the least ethical qualms. . . . Vengeance, the indefinite *par excellence*, here becomes a circle, therefore contained; with the consequence that guilt is as it were done away with, since we are dealing with a series of reactions with no initial action. (Toufic 2000, 17–18)

In *Forthcoming*, the author appearing as the character of someone else spoken of in the third person in an event—no direct action—is thus in a perspective of fiction, even when the events are autobiographical occurring in real-time. These inserts of the author as a 'spoken' third-person character (as if not himself to himself, and as if possibly someone else rather than the author, to the reader) are given "radical closure" (cease abruptly, as such are linked to a 'comparison'/analogy that again punctures both sides of the glass, the glass of fiction/real-time). The abrupt entry or departure/"radical closure" of the character (the author as 'only' a character) is to withdraw, while at once making, the assertion of actual *other* people or himself—but these on a nonexistent plain (except as his text)—in order to have as text space an exchange between two that is a "momentary perfect concordance through a thought that belonged to neither" (Toufic 2000, 37).

Toufic thus substitutes character and action with film concepts and their plots. Or his characters (where they are not himself) are dead as figures of analogy, such as Lazarus, that only demonstrate Toufic's 'logic' only conceptions that define the meaning of events ahead of or 'behind' (create nonlinear space) the event itself then, to close as precluding its having its own action: "Past a surpassing disaster, the memorial and memory have to pass through the ordeal of the impression of counterfeit since the events and knowledge they are accessing are being resurrected" (64).

Toufic uses the Buddhist term the "gateless gate" (meaning 'no eyes, no ears, no nose'—no frame, theory, or senses): "that is exactly how I too feel," referring to a "momentary perfect concordance through a thought that belonged to neither" (37). His removing of action/motion (holding the glass of the text up to motion) is a form of feeling to prevent all motions ceasing, in those in the undeath realm (those suffering a surpassing disaster). The text is 'the subject/as the time/which is motion/still' of photographs, the following paragraph being one such photograph or more than one:

> the threatening conditions under which the photographer was taking them; the aversion of his or her look on encountering the gutted, decomposing corpses; the proximity of the dead—come to prevent the world's desertion of those suffering a surpassing disaster from turning into a radical closure—against those freezing, not as corpses (*rigor mortis* is still a variety of motion) but as creatures of the undeath realm, all motions, including the restless immobility of the living, appear blurry; the entranced states in which the encounter with the dead often occurs.
>
> —Those from the aftermath of the "civil" war were due mainly to the withdrawal of what was being photographed.
>
> Like so many others, he had become used to viewing things at the speed of war. (Toufic 2000, 11)

The author as 'a character only' (stillness) is thus a participant, is only motion in the undeath realm.

Removing action as the basis of text, the removal a means of *rendering* real-time, Toufic substitutes intellectual construct (an abstract of the event as a philosophical or theoretical concept, not the event's action or purport) preceding the event itself—either historical event in real-time, or actions of an event as intentional illusion-making in fiction. His language reverses chronology by defining 'ahead of' the event's own occurrence. "Nostalgia precedes the past, makes its occurrence" (85). So the past had no other occurrence than separation (from it). He is creating a separation of thinking and being by a continual "radical closure" that he links (duplicating Nietzsche) to (only) *willing* an event's eternal recurrence (having control over 'occurrence at all').

Interjecting myself as author (my no-analogy, appropriate to his own gesture): Toufic's construct, as was Nietzsche's, is a cycle of power that recreates as itself—'not being controlled by event, *willing* it' is one having a predatory relation to outside, a relation that also separates one from 'being' in/that is action (except as 'acting upon,' though Toufic's intent is not to duplicate vengeance). His language is still a description of freedom without being its performance: "Freedom from nostalgia implies either remaining detached even while the event is happening, letting it *self-liberate*, or else, on the contrary, willing its eternal recurrence. And these two states that let go of the event—a letting go clear in the absence of nostalgia—are kindred. The willful are simultaneously those most apt to create real change" (79–80).

My insertion of no-analogies: In my fiction, *Defoe* (2002, 1994), the screen/figure through whose eyes/flesh-as-text the context appears and is linked is named "The Other." The Other sometimes reflects conflicts and performs actions in episodes the author actually was performing. The Other (unlike the author, however) was in love with James Dean, who is killed and is turned into a deer. He is only the image that is that 'real' person (man who is an actor in *Rebel without a Cause*, named James Dean)—yet the writing in *Defoe* is a spatial and image rendition of sensation of flesh (such as in sexual sensation with him, physical hallucination outside of oneself). Similarly, there are action scenes of running, of being hurled above motorcycles and hoods of cars in sheets of traffic—which are one (the reader) being in a motion of action (as sight, produced in reading) the conceptual way one's spinal cord makes (outside) actual motions (that occur inside) rendered by one's brain, and actual even if one cannot move outside (I had a cervical disk injury and wrote much of the second half of *Defoe* lying on my back 'supplanting motion

with conceptual motion the same'). My conceptual action was by being the opposite similar to Toufic's action/withdrawn (though we had not read each other).

Perhaps Toufic's theory of the undead implies that the spine's conceptual (actual, felt) motion is 'as if the same' as cultural intellectual construct (in the glass: as if the same as the space in *A Thousand Plateaus: Capitalism and Schizophrenia*; or is 'God's' conception, therefore also determinism as within 'outside' will)—that being in the physical sensation of movement is also nostalgia: the spinal cord's creation of conceptual motion outside in front of one (when one could not move) felt by one, which is an actual movement, is the same as an intellectual construct of memory while parted from that which one remembers. Thus, any action is fiction. I also held the latter view (as Toufic might, I am conjecturing). I was writing in relation to a space outside language, which can be duplicated as language, though the space may be outside even (language's) postulation there. My intent was: 'as' 'physical' action free ('experience' as text only) that is without imposition; is not either as 'will' (which would only be further imposition, supposedly of one's own, on oneself)—nor limited in the particular event/context (of the action), that is, not only dramatizing a character. Toufic, while recognizing performative language, which enacts events as being closest to will, chooses willing eternal recurrence, which is by definition only repetition (2000, 79). His intent is to perform the space of our being the realm of the undead *because* it is the present.

Sensation itself is in part socially derived, constructed. A characteristic of being now in the imperial present: one is conceptually divided from one's own sensation (from tactile even), isolated from one's physical motion in real-time (as also *from real-time*, as it's occurring). The separation effected by conceptual division itself is in conversational and conventional language the imposition of explaining all instants as outside (of writing, of one). 'Meaning' (social only, it is a translation, a summary) is outside of itself. Toufic comments on the acceptance of cyberspace as "real" space, that this concordance is an indication of the space being transformed by our will. The mode of addition of statements of dislocation in Deleuze's and Guattari's *A Thousand Plateaus: Capitalism and Schizophrenia* is a method of increasing the gap between the text and the reader, prolonging the gap as discourse that is without summarized or emotional resolution.

Speaking to the subject of 'fiction's present' entails answering, 'What *should* one write?' (future) as being fiction's present, the corollary being: '*Why* is one writing that?' (the latter question is still present-time).

For example (my sense of conjecturing a language, which may be different from that implied by the people speaking on the occasion mentioned earlier, the day of the U.S. invasion of Iraq), parallel language by crushing syntax: crushed as syntax of the language, spatially— as it had been the *same language* as lies—that reverses, is 'only' simple, does not duplicate double think (a syntax that drops out double think by incorporating *that is* motion as pre-text, pre-formation).

To destroy or crush the language by expanded paragraphs: During the Gulf War, I wrote the fiction titled *Defoe* in sections of which there were sheet-like paragraphs (or consecutive, non-stop, one-line phrases) that included everything above and below a conceptual 'text-horizon line' (as text, therefore not *visible*) as if with the *actual* sun and moon together on a line at once (as a paragraph). A paragraph would be 'across,' and above and below, a conceptual line *of the paragraph's* (produced by the paragraph) as if in the midst of it (but also imposed: by my having seen the sun and the moon on the same horizon line descending and ascending beside the ocean once—in real-time)—which by including other (night) was to destroy the language of that paragraph. The space of the paragraph (that is) expanded outside of language. The conceptual 'rim' or horizon line, as line of concentration, was also imposed: as mind phenomena by the writing of these passages occurring alongside the fact of (in the context of the build up to and the bombing of Iraq in the '90s—and other events, such as someone I knew having a bone marrow transplant for leukemia on the day of the first bombing, their later dying) my trying to sit (sitting meditation); the paragraphs were the written form of this practice (a procedure sometimes outside language as spatial and sensation, or being language space that is conflating rational and emotional) as sitting's mind phenomena action held up as a mind formation to that real-time present in an extended framework that is the first 132 pages of *Defoe*. 'Rim' is one's *direct constructing* of the image-illusion. Change action outside with one's mind changing, an action that is even seen at its instant as total illusion.

In the syntax of phrases (in *Defoe*), perception is created by its struggle created in the outside:

> They who are the few viewed as respectable are caught in conventionality for him which is not in waking life. It is not in it or in dreams.
>
> They are restricting one to conventionality not in their dreams, or later. And yet one struggles in their narrowed rim. (Scalapino 2002, 25)

The physical seeing as an action of the reader is 'located' in the center of a phrase that's a motion, empty in the sense of their not creating the sight, that as movement is there without its own beginning or its end:

> Sheep trotting with a crazy eye on the beige-rust cliff passes me. Its senseless globular eye is floating in the mist.
>   Black robes blowing walk ahead on the beige-rust grass.
>   On the rim.
>   A robed no eye-hole muscular movement not from it.
> (Scalapino 2002, 22)

Thus the intent is that the 'outside' is viewed—as not *actually* arising from oneself. People are viewed in actions as in real-time present, not in seeing that's an ideal of them but an instant of multiple seeing (physically in the syntax that's constructing a 'rim'), a phrase containing at once various states of the same action in time. The same instance seen entirely, as say fighting, and also not fighting, is seen at once:

> One says she's defending against attacking coming from them,
> really coming from her to them . . . we're just tubes.
>   tubes with pumps alongside the cars—coming from one's sleep and after dawn
>   who're in silence
>   not fighting (Scalapino 2002, 11)

As part of reversing or taking apart the entire construction, there is no conversation between people in *Defoe*: conversational language is convention only—one would have to speak as what is inside and outside at once, be outside convention. Beside outside, which is not allowed here (in our conversational customs). At the time of writing that novel, my sense of a sentence as action or emotion was: its writing/ *now*/present has to be earlier (before Daniel Defoe 'ordered,' made an order of, the sense of character as 'being reported'—that the character of a person is represented, as in a talk show). (At the airport in Reno this week, there was a gaggle of girls lying on the floor waiting, who, going around the circle, lounging but their mood tense, 'forced' each other to voice how many casinos, and which ones, their parents owned, after first 'forcing' the circle one by one to describe how each did their wash, how often they washed their bedding.)

I remarked joyfully in the text of that earlier book *Defoe* that now I had become a hack—by the paragraphs only being action scenes (therefore not reproducing character, invoked as reading even). These scenes are 'physical' actions as text only. Outside-motions *actually* not *being* language, these outside-motions are seen by the reader, anyway, as if arising only as text (as if running or hurling is being produced by *one's* language there only, not as sight either, only reading). The end of *Defoe* has simple phrases, which are not complete sentences, but are the mid-action of mid-seeing; 'physical' action in my particular crushed language there being, to perception, both faster and slower at once than it would have been if differentiated by ordering it as linear (linear is: described/explained from the outside). (Inside a phrase that is a part of a motion, the reader cannot differentiate whether motion as that syntax is fast or slow, whether the syntax is rage or meditation or thinking; as text, it is these at once—which changes the reader's attention in the text's content.)

Why intend to have even physical action be (as if) *only* produced by text/syntax (occurring as the act of reading), since physical movement and conceptual movement/impressions/seeing/reading are by their natures different?

Defoe, a fiction that is 'within' its language, was not to be a virtual reality but actual (in contrast to Jalal Toufic's text *Forthcoming*, which is neither actual nor virtual, is intentionally removed from either of those by not being 'within its language'). In *Defoe*: see even one's actual physical movements in one's real-time as illusion in the instant of constructing these motions (seen as dual—that is, as motions also being illusion, as the setting is—because they are mental, reading).

To reiterate for clarity: Sights of objects and people 'outside' come out of emptiness (they are text's sights only) but 'come' as the physical seeing of the reader's in their seeing (reading) syntax that is a phrase as a 'rim' of one being inside-out: *as one's seeing only*. A 'rim' is comparison (of two levels of concentration) narrowed to be beside each other seen there held, as such constructing itself (text), being one's mind there only (the observer seeing itself: as not being 'there'). The action of 'seeing *not* being there' has to occur (in a phrase) in order to be seen: "Which is completely manipulated. It's not seeing the observer (who's looking at itself) or it. One can do this, not seeing myself or it— it must occur in oneself" (Scalapino 2002, 8).

The syntax is thus a deconstruction method akin to the Tibetan exercise of the observer being observed (by himself or herself) as meditation practice discovering there is no object observed/as no observer. In *Defoe*, the observer (reader) looks at her or himself there (in the sentence or paragraph) so that seeing becomes: there is not that which is observed because the observer has been 'dispelled as the object seen' (no observer).

There was this red disc, a soft empty disc of a cloud
hanging over the desert with cobalt or indigo lake in it where
I was. The huge rose soft disc and another small red disc
reflected the rays of the setting sun which were not red in
the rest of the sky since there was nothing there.
        The huge rose disc hung there without moving. Just in
silence not coming out of the person.
        Their having any and one agree with them—and one
struggling with that or one is not there, isn't there.
                wasn't there before, to push out the huge empty rose disc
                disc floating on the desert, with the cattle that come to
the edge of the blue water and the white desert—not com-
ing from it. (Scalapino 2002, 11)

'Rim' then is practice of deconstructing as a conceptual line in
space which one 'reads' before one: on which the inside of the inside
(perception, physical seeing) and the outside of the outside (events,
sights) occur, both as if at once on that conceptual line in space (created
by a phrase or paragraph)—real-time being the *reflections* as if visual yet
of the paragraph (text only—as if the paragraph as itself space were
empty and only reflects the outside world; and this is all there is of self).
        As an action, this construction of illusions (that I am calling a
'rim') has to occur as a long duration, sometimes long paragraphs and
also length of text to constitute the sense of real-time.
        Any narrative goes *before* and behind real-time, constructs a sense
of outside real-time by providing setting as framework defining a motion even, as only in relation to setting and effect—future. The 'future'
can occur in the syntax being altered (disrupted from linear progress)
to predict outside of its own first postulation. (Toufic's text also pre-
dicts outside its postulation by its discourse being the *subject* that is of
refusing to change that postulation continually. Toufic's 'fiction' has
not been replaced by language of theory, he has replaced 'language of
theory'—as present formal genre.)
        Toufic conjectures that if he were to allow himself to laugh at all
he would not be able to stop, would be torn apart by it: therefore the
refusal to admit any emotive language or expression into the waves of
detail (centuries of history of the rise and deposing of Islamic sects in
close reading that's no-analogy, for example) hurled as if against the
reader (as if in opposition, in the reader's face, as the sheer duration
as intervention on the part of the author of these passages akin to
holding a breath, which has the effect of splitting open the text 'as'
without allowance of emotion). Toufic's text is, I think, a brilliant ex-

position of at least two levels of language occurring at once by a level being missing or absent, but as if erupting only by being left out. 'Intuitive' space, or any changing of the space given, is everywhere suppressed throughout to an intentionally 'intolerable' extent by a language constructed as solely intellectual in a way that is exterior to the subject or a self, the exclusion changing that space as suffering (which is *not* there, however).

In *Forthcoming* (meaning 'not there yet'), an anti-fiction-self-portrait as fiction, the *experience* of suffering is a double. Chapters are doubles of each other and of the subject. For example, the chapter "Radical Closure Artist with Bandaged Sense Organ" is an analogy to Van Gogh cutting off his ear and delivering it to a prostitute, after which he was hospitalized. The chapter becomes an installation (perhaps only there as the chapter, not an installation shown elsewhere?), thus an analogy to Toufic himself, a filter of the senses by listing what would be shown: reproductions of Van Gogh's *Self-Portrait with Bandaged Ear and Pipe* and *The Reaper*, texts of letters to Van Gogh's brother Theo, Magritte's *This Is Not a Pipe*, reproduction on canvas of *Shoes*, *Wheatfield with Crows* as seen in Kurosawa's film *Dreams*, and a showing on monitor of Toufic's own video *Credits Included: A Video in Red and Green*, described in the text as shot inside the Fanar Mental Hospital in South Lebanon. His text gives no other description of his own video; I have seen this video, however. The inmates speak their 'mental illness' as an alternate reality (shock) that is the same as being in/their actual reality, their society as being total war. Their and Toufic's authorship are "radically similar" here to Van Gogh cutting off his ear; Toufic's alternative title to the chapter given as "Ear to Ear," referencing David Lynch's film *Blue Velvet*: "They discovered that under certain conditions the ear is no longer an organ that allows one to locate more or less approximately the source of a worldly sound, but is where the unworldly sound 'is'" (2000, 108).

The text of the chapter "Radical Closure Artist with Bandaged Sense Organ" is thus a filter of the senses, which itself functions as irruptions; in cinematic matte, which his text is *not*: "the impression that the dancer before them is not fully in the space where he or she ostensibly is; and, not diluted with and thus not filtered by the eyes themselves, by-pass them, functioning as irruptions" (2000, 106).

Toufic's writing is irruption as "temporal atomicity," which he describes in the chapter "Middle Eastern Films *Before Thy Gaze Returns to Thee*—in Less than 1/24 of a Second" as the predominant Islamic conception of time (as opposed to film camera and lens from Renaissance Western monocular perspective). Islamic time is expressed as irruptions: "People are unaware of these perpetual acts of appearance, disappearance, it is both that the appearances, disappearances then appearance occur before 'thy gaze returns to thee' and that the form appears following the disappearance of an earlier one is radically similar to it" (Toufic 2000, 116). In Islamic time, the flicker of perpetual disappearance itself produces a disappearance. Creatures are not subsistent in themselves, but return to that which alone has subsistence, God: "If one is enjoined not to forget God for an instant one reverts to Him, thus remembering Him" (121). Toufic delineates a "repetitive invocation," echo arising in the form of the recurrent resolution back of the non-subsisting entity to Reality" (121).

Real-time history and (also that as) self-portrait is analogous to the arabesque creating in reality myriad ones "each radically similar to the other without being identical to it" (125). The double as a reproduction is many self-portraits (as if 'of outside'):

> The arabesque, especially the one where the figures are juxtaposed rather than interlaced, is doubly my mirror: the multiplication of its basic figure gives me a spatial rendition of my temporal multiplication, the abstraction of its unit figure reminds me of my own abstraction, my being without a nature and proper characteristics. The effect of lightness produced by the arabesque is double: at the level of the architectural object, through covering the solidity of bricks or stones with shimmering glaze tiles that etherealize them; at the level of the subject, who, on seeing the recurrence of the figure, is divested of the weight of time and even of his own nature and characteristics. (125)

Toufic creates etherealizing terms such as "radical closure artist" and "radically similar" to make an arabesque that is the Islamic conception of seeing in relation to the Western current Renaissance perspective that is being applied 'everywhere' in real-time.

"Radically Similar." (As I mentioned, at the time I wrote *Defoe* Toufic and I had not read each other.) My text *Defoe* is current Western Renaissance ocular seeing. The reading of its syntax *has* to be as the syntax the reader seeing that seeing (which is one's), that which is 'our' constructing of events, actions, and seeing or even one making motions within events (future). That is, the syntax is a spatial place that does not reinstate one's prior self: by the syntax being a double of 'outside one' and 'inside one' at once (experience of which both exists and also 'does not exist outside the text,' *then*, is experience as reading).

Power, force, authority. Toufic's formal enactment as text of "temporal atomicity" is couched in the authority of "the predominant Islamic conception of time," that is, couched in the dominant conception, in its setting, of his own vast culture, which is ancient and modern at once. His text is 'radical' in that it enacts, it is, Islamic seeing in the irruptions that are (plural) the structure of seeing, as entirely different from the Western seeing manifested also in real-time now as force that is overwhelming and conquering Islamic nations. His multiples of absences (the absence of experiencing even) mirror authority of accumulated social experience in text-only conceptual in relation to real-time force.

In *Defoe*, thinking, physical sensation apprehended spatially, emotional rupture, and seeing are only 'inside' the reader experiencing seeing and moving *as* the Other: a woman who is always without social power, thus in common interpretation most likely presumed to be an aberration, or a rebel, from her society; yet neither of these, she is a double who also has no existence. The text without conceptual authority from any source has to alter the given seeing (of her culture) by not reproducing any power as illusion of a character in interior speaking and thought or in the 'outside-as-the-text'—in that one's comprising the same seeing as power and the same seeing at all as her own culture, which is dominant, merely reproduces it in the text. One must change real-time experiencing *there*.

The intent in *Defoe* was: enforced social perspective is surpassed, by motion (as the text) occurring before formation even. (The text's motion is before the text, in order not to have formation, rather than definition being before the text/event, as in Toufic.) The separation of sight and reading is outside and inside one, just as the spinal cord produces one's motion felt out ahead of one when one cannot move. One is not one's own motion, nor is one one's sight. Produced there as reading. Being outside is not produced anywhere, and this is 'occurring' as direct constructing of the image-illusion. (Writing: Outside not-produced is active, is one's attention as a [a 'rim' is:] ' *'rim'/direct constructing of the image-illusion at once in the text'.*) A joyful state.

The meditation scheme of *Defoe* is spatial, in that phenomenal horizon and dawn or dusk being *also* words—language and phenomena as doubles, as if language-space is *also* without-language. Thought of an essay is different, can articulate the 'space of word-wordless.' Thought there, that is, in the essay, is outside, is a gesture reciprocal to experiencing.

At the same time, the breakdown of mind itself (that is, mind is inculcated layers of assumptions, which then are the *way the mind works*, as dichotomy then, socially contrived) is only possible in the art of language—in that the language of discourse (of theory) has already made hierarchical dichotomy, *is* that (judges 'intellect,' insofar as it is removed, to be superior to 'experience'—without 'language of discourse' incorporating awareness that the way the mind works, and as only that specific language being used, is only experiencing). Toufic in *Forthcoming* makes a structure that enables perception outside of his language of discourse by an (discourse's) absent double.

I intended *Defoe* to be hack writing in the sense of breaking down its being as a literary object that is rarified, not 'literary' but a receptive state of attention. But in a graduate seminar of a PhD program in the Comparative Lit Department at UC Berkeley, where I visited in 1995 to discuss *Defoe*, two of the students remarked with hostility that this text could not be read by the public, that it was too difficult. I replied that format genre of novel, intended to be commercial, will not disrupt social-political misrepresentation (what the format itself *is*), unless it's a disruption of its own format (isn't format then).

On the evening of the day of the U.S. invasion of Iraq, the women and men discussing language being destroyed were young. They were hopeful. None considered how many people would read the language they were forming, only how their sense of language should be and why. They conveyed an exciting sense of the phrase 'destroy language,' their sense quite different from my language, though I had even thought that same phrase (even thought it earlier that day).

What's happening now (this war as a change in the future world, reinstituting imperialism as an acknowledged, accepted goal) gives a sense that they are (saying we are liberating them, as 'we' mow down their people) destroying language at all (in America, but not elsewhere), so that language is only useless, figure out how—as 'we' crush language, any—it being useless is simple not mimicking alongside *is not* their 'U.S. world'—as language without authority basis.

I recently received a request to respond, as a writer, to Beckett's work (how he does or does not influence writers now). A page of text accompanied the request that was a quote from Larkin dismissing Beckett and modernism.[3]

REPLY TO LARKIN ON BECKETT

In Part 1 of *Molloy*, which begins the trilogy *Molloy, Malone Dies, The Unnameable*,[4] all events, actions, memories, occur as memory spoken as present-time by one addressing a "you" as if there were someone else listening—yet the one speaking is almost always old (even while in

sexual actions), enfeebled with minimum memory, occurring in a text
of two paragraphs, one a page and a half and the other eighty-two and
a half pages. Actions are the same as movements, brought onto the
same level as each other in the one long paragraph as is time, duration
in the paragraph, distinguished, for example, by the moon said to be
moving relative to the room in which the speaker is (Beckett 1991, 39);
or by past as present events (puncturing real-time), such as his being
waylaid by a woman who kept him for observation while the speaker (as
if in present but implying a future without these particular events) lies
on the ground in her garden or barely eats, actions that are occurring
in the movement of inertia which is that of nature (his own *as* the
universe's, or the universe's as his), being a "pre-established harmony"
(62) that is actually the author's constructed "mythological present"
(26), his speaking-in-present-tense. His predilection to be within inertia, however, is his nature, not the nature of someone else who might
choose activity within the nature's movements. Yet the speaker's reason
occurs at all as: the phenomena of the literal forest as color. That is, the
senses are phenomena outside, apparent and occurring at all (color
and movement outside) only as the one long paragraph, which cannot
be color and is movement as its own language. Movement (distinction
and action of events) is *by* comparison as relative, such as himself to the
forest to seeing to color:

> The forest was all about me and the boughs, twining to-
> gether at a prodigious height, compared to mine, sheltered
> me from the light and the elements . . . I stumbled, but the
> darkness was not impenetrable. For there reigned a kind of
> blue gloom, more than sufficient for my visual needs. I was
> astonished this gloom was not green, rather than blue, but
> I saw it blue and perhaps it was. The red of the sun, min-
> gling with the green of the leaves, gave a blue result, that is
> how I reasoned. (Beckett 1991, 83)

Molloy voids or empties out actions as plot as the vehicle of apprehension or impetus of fiction.

Beckett in his prose (fiction) changed the relation of the speaker
in the text, either writer or reader-as-if-writer, from being a 'voice' to
being only the act of speaking. His text is then also speaking, which is
in relation to the act of hearing. "That I am not stone deaf is shown by
the sounds that reach me" (295).

The distinction he made is that speaking, as pre-text-before-text-
(in his prose works, hearing is in silent reading), is not 'voice' as

expression of a personality (expression of its supposed psychology), as if "one" as entity existed, which presupposes the entity as separated from the outside.

In the plays, the speaker is in real-time space, but like the prose is also only speaking and hearing, not dramatizing events—the speaking (of chatter in the plays) is as if directed or in reference to silence, regardless of the number of characters. The plays crack open conversational (out-loud) speaking—to puncture the barrier that is speaking, as such.

Beckett was recognizing we do not get into real-time, ever. So his pre-text (before text)—using *The Unnameable* as an example—is *not* one of the senses, or *not* another of the senses, one after another stripped as being mere pretext that's a barrier. "There is no night so deep, so I have heard tell, that it may not be pierced in the end, with the help of no other light than that of the blackened sky, or of the earth itself" (300).

Hearing (in Beckett's prose) is only 'from' ventriloquism (speaking that is also silent text). Hearing is not arising there in a virtual picturing of oneself (the reader) as if moving in Beckett's landscape animated as mind, which is then spoken as gone—it is in relation to literal hearing of a sound only that's the text's sound—not virtual, actual.

Speaking in a silent text (silently reading prose) is groundless (not existing, a silent note in non-occurrence). Beckett's eliminating any ground *is* the action (of making no action/as no basis of: imagination/speaking/seeing). By puncturing the fictional illusion, Beckett is making a 'reverse text' that is itself illusion of 'being' and real-time space:

For example, the text asserted as being only color (grey, then black, then no color) is also pretext in imagination—color is not in the possibility of text. Thus the separating of the *act* of seeing from text there, one's undergoing the experience of making/seeing (this elimination), is a palpable space.

The characteristics of my writing and that of others in the present coincide with elements of Beckett's examination, because his was basic. My sense is that present writing can begin from the point he reached and continue from there. Not reproduce conceptions he already abandoned, already demonstrated groundless.

NOTES

1. See Toufic (2000, 75).
2. Quotation from the *symplokē* call for papers on "Fiction's Present."

3. Gary Adelman asked writers to comment on their valuing of Beckett's fiction. He sent with his letter a comment by Larkin on Beckett.

4. See Beckett (1991).

REFERENCES

Beckett, Samuel. 1991. *Molloy, Malone Dies, The Unnameable: Three novels by Samuel Beckett.* New York: Grove Widenfeld.

Deleuze, Gilles, and Felix Guattari. 2000. *A thousand plateaus: Capitalism and schizophrenia.* Minneapolis and London: University of Minnesota Press.

Scalapino, Leslie. 2002 [1994]. *Defoe.* Los Angeles: Green Integer.

Toufic, Jalal. 2000. *Forthcoming.* Berkeley, CA: Atelos.

Chapter 5

Convinced by Fiction, Convinced by History

Three Novels

Joseph McElroy

Rereading J. M. Coetzee's *The Master of Petersburg* (1994) because I do not quite trust my memory and its inventions, I find myself on the track of what I mean when I say that history in fiction must convince me, finding in a Haymarket rooming house, a police station, children in the street, or a "madness . . . running through the artery of his right arm down to the fingertips and the pen," many Dostoevskys here settled in a familiar one who "on the heels of remorse" has a "voluptuous urge to confess." Only somewhat like the Dostoevsky in another book I have recently read for the first glorious time, Leonid Tsypkin's *Summer in Baden-Baden* (1987), indeed with such a difference that I wonder if I do have a key to this particular convincingness I would like to pin down, that I seek and find in both books, as indeed I write in the shadow of my *bête noir* of making things more complicated, a dream from which I have just woken at daybreak on a Sunday.

It must convince me. But convince me of what—this novel that visits and invents another time we already know about? Though nowadays the past is often not so much slipping out of memory as for most American citizens never having much been there in the first place. So readers are glad of a good read and our shared past and a tale that builds, like *Cold Mountain*. Facts set moving with made-up talk and behaviors either of persons nowhere to be actually found in the chronicles establishing the era and events the novel recalls, or of persons who actually existed—for me I confess an uncomfortable liability, too easy to do—like the famous in Don DeLillo's *Underworld* Polo

67

Grounds—and with an effect on the authority of the narrative I must question, remembering at random Thomas Bernhard's imaginary Glen Gould in *The Loser*.

I recall pleading an imaginative centrality of science in conversation with John Barth thirty years ago, who retorted, "What about history!" Indeed. Yet the particular kind of fiction I have in mind here is quietly to one side of Barth's transporting work of parody, *The Sot Weed Factor*, or Thomas Pynchon's poignant, sometime drolly anachronistic contemplation, *Mason and Dixon*. Perhaps it is our era (a history we cannot help being *in*) that says history is whatever we say it is—a fiction without limit—but for the willing reader too (and all to the good that we still read). I have to say the Rosenbergs' Times Square execution never got to me in Robert Coover's *The Public Burning*, with all the epidemic truth at large through a colossal explosion of political psycho-fantasy. Historical figures in a made-up setting, it is probably not history in fiction Coover is writing so much as satire, which granted becomes part of the "history" of American writing. Quicksand beckons me trying to find a corner of imagination for a novel whose ground is a history intersection, its mind not brio of invention but, on the one hand, contained inside a factual spirit while, on the other, acknowledging how it got there. To be convinced by the turn of both these aspects upon each other.

This kind recommends itself in three books I've recently, almost by accident, read or reread for quite other reasons—only now to lump together as if an authority more august than what our brains do casually all the time had deemed these a threefold demonstration of the limits and chances for imagination in the novel's more modest slant into or embrace of history: the two Dostoevsky books, and yet another writer's book out of my apparently random reading and arbitrary choosing, Ford Madox Ford's 1905 novel about Katherine Howard, *The Fifth Queen*, and, through her, most curiously about Henry VIII.

Coetzee and Tsypkin hand us Dostoevsky in transit, driven, weighed down, combative, manipulative, pious, sleazy, unstable, guilty, at risk, a living experiment, a character ingeniously persistent, perhaps plausibly a genius, palpably a man, needing women (but for what?). Summoned back to Russia from Germany on the occasion of his stepson's suspicious suicide, and traveling necessarily incognito, Coetzee's Dostoevsky unfolds unexpected step by step Pavel's life, stepping into that life and the cloaked circumstances of his death. Thus to unfold the seeker in his grief and self-interest who "[refuses] to accept limits to what he is permitted to know," Coetzee, sometimes as heavy-handedly as his arbitrary ventures into his protagonist's mind waking and asleep, parallels with this partly invented life moments from the novelist's fiction.

The perilous climax affords Coetzee what may have been in part a pretext for writing the book: a chance to stage a completely convincing debate and showdown between the notorious and masterful anarchist S. G. Nechaev (1847–82) and our former revolutionary now (as Coetzee's puts it in an essay) a "great Christian philosopher" who, having "lived through the debates of his day with the intensity of an intelligentsia held down under censorship, . . . [had] [a] capacity to push . . . to its limits [the] . . . analysis of . . . self [and] soul . . . greater than in a purely secular thinker like Freud." Coetzee's sober, thrifty prose cannot quite touch the Russian sensibility only point to it. This helps him, however, seem to document the clandestine, but not implausible, errand of 1869 together with a number of other fabrications.

Coetzee might even be said to compound the use of "history" invented in the substantial gap of our knowledge of Dostoevsky's time in Germany. For it is *The Possessed* that his Dostoevsky sits down to write when he returns to Dresden, that is, out of the overwhelming experience in Petersburg which, like Pavel's rescued diary, is made up by Coetzee, but which we are asked to accept in detail as the material inspiration for Dostoevsky's actual novel. Adroit, of course, and yet to be reckoned with, as I grope further to grasp what it is that might convince me in this kind of novel. The verifiable historical situation, let us say, into which imagination folds or plants a potential like the human potential the actual situation itself possessed. Maybe this means no more than intelligent, dynamic characters—"of more than ordinary worth and interest," in James's phrase more blunt than we give him credit for. But no, I mean an original exchange between impersonal forces, even in Nietzsche's sense, brought to bear upon a chaotic mystery of choices personally constituting at its most interesting everyday life *itself* as experimental.

You are in mourning for yourself, Anna Sergeyeva diagnoses Coetzee's Dostoevsky returned from Russia. Leave it to her to say it all when given the chance, though the young wife, Anna, of Tsypkin's *Summer in Baden-Baden,* between dictating sessions and the perpetual carryings-on of her impossible husband, must understand him in another atmosphere entirely. Tsypkin's novel, itself a docu-miracle rescued out of the late Stalin period, turns even more complexly upon what is and is not made up. Indeed, what is imagined only partly out of Anna's actual published memoir by the narrative presence Tsypkin's astonishing style and devotion to his subject and the novels conjures from inside and outside with his own first person and the slippery immersion of it in a third-person history of fourteen years of the Dostoevskys abroad, a postmodern reciprocity of multiple loci.

Baden-Baden, though, for the gambling; for the endless humilia-
tions, pawnings, money worries; for the boarding house world, the social
nuances and snobberies, Dostoevsky's envy of other writers—the Who's
best debate, his anti-Semitism puzzled over by the narrator, himself not
alone among Jews who have loved Dostoevsky's work; the sometimes
absurd helter-skelter comedy of eccentric habits in museums and restaurants and on the street, somehow so much more intimate than
Coetzee's grim limiting of what even his contradictory and dynamic
Dostoevsky can choose to be. Is it how I would like to write (or do
write), this rapid mass (mass transiting) of brimming impressions never
quite off track or out of focus?—merging with the person-in-progress
and his often violent work like the answer to every pedestrian literary
biography I ever read. Even to, like Nabokov in many of his passages
about the imagination finding its exact, luminous shadow somewhere
between the large and the small, frank hints of how Dostoevsky looking
at a painting absorbs an image for future use—"the first crystal to form
in a supersaturated solution—and the remainder, perhaps still hidden
by a thick mist, would have to come by itself" (which reminds me that
this deprived and very part-time novelist Tsypkin, his health and so
much else at stake, untimely dead, who never saw a word of his published nor expected to, was a full-time medical researcher). The imagination and even science of knowing somehow build a whole person
who finds himself.

The abiding gamble of the life, the temperament—to persist in
your own being or gift embracing the impulse you are seized by—
brings elements organically together as if you committed your power to
forces beyond your control in order that they might take you where you
can go. The history is social, the names we know (Goncharov, Turgenev,
et al.) venally passing in the many turns, accelerations, and locomo-
tions of the prose, the opinions, the breath and precarious life unde-
niably of this master hardly giving a thought to the death ahead soon
to be enacted with the extended agony and authority for which Tsypkin
finds room in all his resources, no less a lightness, not least this accurate tourist's later visit to a deserted Petersburg museum, once (or still)
the house where Dostoevsky died typically, we learn, at that moment
full of people.

Three books, I said, three writer's books. Where writing is rendering to the reader what is the reader's, and is thinking, and thought not
only life's slave (Hotspur) or a waiting sickness (Hamlet), but in its
evolution what History ultimately *means* (R. G. Collingwood), that is,
History is the history of thought. But wait. I said "three"? How is *The
Fifth Queen* a writer's book?

Only listen to King Henry the rhetorician readying in his head a speech with which on his return home to greet his clever, beautiful Kat. Proud of his style, like an American novelist, and of her for her mind, her unmatched classical learning (but beware her Plutarch), her written or spoken words—" 'I have had better converse with thee,' " says he, " 'than with man or child this several years. Thinkest thou I will let thee go?' " (Ford 1963, 230). Indeed, *yes*, she does—foresees it early on, and will say so, this passionate Roman Catholic woman who would gladly retreat to a convent and who may lose her way in the treacheries around her but knows herself not slenderly like the king; for, court wit and love aside, in this minefield of spies and ecclesiastical politics—from a relenting royal letter written but not yet sent to the pope, to Privy Seal's little Tom Delay book of political debts, to messages that may turn treasonable—words seem everywhere a dark liability as well as a pleasure, and Henry's illegitimate daughter Mary angrily closeted writing her commentary on Plautus will witheringly call "every woman's part" what we see everywhere yet ultimately at a crux of history see the new queen, in a final speech to her husband, refuse: that is, "to gloss over crimes of their men folk." For Katherine is "too proud to fight the world with the world's weapons," to use her power to save her skin with words written and spoken. She makes her choice, again with words in a long and matchless speech that is to force Henry to act out the meaning of his slippery, feckless, temporizing, and unstable positions and do away with her.

The riveting story I leave to the reader, the structure of scenes and play of comedy against the hard, breathtaking intricacy of the drama. Ford's language is convincingly early-sixteenth-century Edwardian, as unfussed with as rich. The production a virtual theater everywhere in the depiction of rooms, hallways, exits, entrances, roles; a mention of *Menechmi* but pivotally an Italian interlude written by the contemporary classical scholar-teacher, Nicholas Udall, an important and sleazy player in the machinations of the romance and the author of the first English comedy; Shakespeare echoing often in Mousetrap and turns of phrase and plot from *Hamlet, Macbeth, Othello, Julius Caesar,* more. All the prose so fully sensed, thought, true, acute as a "banner . . . all red and white against a blue sky," where "in a gust it cracked like a huge whip" that the shifting portrait of the king might seem only one more coup to relish. Set twenty-five years before the birth of Shakespeare, Ford's novel seems to have made good a Shakespeare (or Shakespeare-and-Fletcher) late-period failure with its own Henry VIII, his stagey, charming, vain failure and presence in conjunction with his steadfast queen as fully exposed as perhaps only the later form could manage in the modernist hand of Ford's own invisible presence nonetheless opening to the winds of interpretation, as Jameson says, among other things that history is "what hurts."

Distant I do not deny from that undoubted and sometimes clumsy comi-tragic dramatist Dostoevsky, but in its tensions making congruent a literary means (and culture) with a painful, unavoidable history. As everything at stake in Tsypkin holds us inside an elapsing time that presses passion, intelligence, risk, and the experiment of our lives upon us. For the surely overstressed etymology of "peril" in "experimental"— by now a virtually meaningless literary term—may at least remind us, as Coetzee and Tsypkin and Ford do, of what is truly in the balance. Yes, one might write about a writer, if our lives are seen as an infinitely divided narrative of choices haunting us to make the most interesting ones, in which case a writer ideally might be close to that action, living it, recording it, making it up out of what we know.

REFERENCES

Coetzee, J. M. 1994. *The master of Petersburg.* New York: Viking.

Ford, Ford Madox. 1963 [1905]. *The fifth queen.* New York: Vanguard Press.

Tsypkin, Leonid. 1987. *Summer at Baden-Baden.* London: Quartet.

Chapter 6

American World-Fiction
in the Longue Durée

JOSEPH TABBI

PAPER EMPIRES, EMPIRICAL FICTIONS

Critics are not forecasters, but their formal investigations, if these are keyed to the present, occasionally put them ahead of poets and novelists when it comes to articulating the next stage in a literary development. Thus it was Toqueville, a social critic and historian, who anticipated Melville when he argued that the coming of age in American literature would be something "fantastic, incorrect, overburdened, vehement and bold" (Toqueville 1840, II, 62, cited in Delbanco 2005, 117). It was Emerson, a minor poet but a major critical writer, who in his own time (circa 1844) anticipated Whitman when he lamented, "We do not, with sufficient plainness, or sufficient profoundness, address ourselves to life, nor dare we chaunt our own times and social circumstances" (Emerson 2006, 1651).

In periods of economic chaos, political transformation, and generic flux, critical writing (freed of the necessity to present recognizable characters, plots, conventional settings, and lifeways) can itself produce a profile for a society's renewed self-imagining. The editor of a 2005 cluster of essays in the *electronic book review* (Pease 2005), writing about the literary reception of *Empire* (2000) and *Multitude* (2004), refers to Michael Hardt and Antonio Negri as plausible successors to Thomas Pynchon and Don DeLillo. A prominent theorist speaks of Hardt's and Negri's "transformation of political science into political science fiction" and treats *Empire* no differently than the fiction of Kathy Acker, Brett Easton Ellis, or Richard Powers: all are involved in a project that would replace representation itself—aesthetic and political representation—with

73

fictions of bodily, perceptual presence (Michaels 2004, 173). This apparent turn away from avowed fictions toward what has become today a capacious and widely circulating mode of conceptual writing was echoed by another *ebr* contributor, the one-time fiction writer and current art historian William S. Wilson, who called *Empire* Hardt's and Negri's "world-poem" (see Wilson 2005).

Wilson also notes that despite the numerous and varied responses to *Empire*, nobody seems bothered by the fact that the authors scarcely glance in their writing toward works of contemporary fiction or the arts, and when Hardt and Negri do write about characters in fiction—Melville's Bartelby, or Musil's Count Leinsdorf—we could be discussing actual living personages, instances of a particular social group or political identity (the poor whose world-changing power is in the refusal of work; the aristocracy whose extensive, administered imperialism contrasts with an intensive, networked Empire in a state of continual emergence). In this critical world-fiction, we find no imagination of "character" as an embodiment of the hopes, desires, and observed behaviors of a particular author at a particular moment in time. Nor will we find, in *Empire*, a political program, or, in *Multitude*, much in the way of practical development toward the self-formation and self-realization of a networked society. Poets can be prophetic without being politically responsible. So if Hardt and Negri failed to anticipate a momentary regression in Washington toward colonial and unilateral nationalist policies, then their work will not stand or fall on that basis. Despite their currency, Hardt and Negri are not participating directly in the official political or literary culture, and this separation puts them in the company of philosophers, literary theorists, novelists, and prophets—which is to say, all those who "assemble qualitative shifts into a narrative mapping of a global system much as their postmodern predecessors, such as DeLillo, William Gaddis, and Thomas Pynchon, once did" (Pease 2005).

Hardt and Negri work much as world-novelists and -poets have always worked: broadly, prophetically, and often apocalyptically—and that can help explain why their work is received more favorably, generally, in literary-critical communities than in established political and social disciplines.[1] The authors' living situation, Hardt in an academic setting known for conceptual innovation, and Negri until recently in prison, helps create the separation from a common culture that is (according to theorists of apocalyptic discourse) a precondition to the imagination of a "complete reconstruction of the body politic" (Taithe and Thornton 1997, 11, cited in Foster 2006). Typical of their refusal of common discourse is the recasting of familiar terms—not "imperialism" but "Empire," not "individualism" but the cultivation of "singularities," not even common culture itself or "the commons" but rather "the common." All this linguistic innovation (focused not on a signified object but rather on a material transformation of language itself) points to a reconstruction that is global conceptually, not just geographically.

If theorists, then, are renewing the language and setting terms for the material transformation of society, is there still a place for fiction writers at the vanguard of the present?

THE PRESENT SITUATION OF THE LITERARY

For all its expansiveness, contemporary theory remains restricted to the realm of linguistic and literary innovation. At a remove from state power, criticism continues the "cultural' and "linguistic turn" in literary discourse, although now with a renewed focus on the material substrate of signification in literature and perception in the arts. The increased prestige of culture and linguistic formations within literature departments developed for good reason: the poststructuralist discovery of an irreducible difference between word and thing, consciousness and communication, offers one way of understanding the emergence of the world-system itself in the creation of professions capable of communicating internally (through a specialized language) and avoiding communication externally (with other professions, protected by their own professional languages and protocols, and with a mass audience that, to the extent it is "mass," is left unprotected from the environment of sheer information and commodity exchange). No longer tied to the capacities of individual consciousnesses or even groups, the world-system instead grounded itself in networks of communication and monetary exchange that were capable, over time, of developing on their own, requiring only legislation and a measure of military protection from the state. These systems, though not immediate in their exchange of money and information, are so fast as to *appear* immediate and beyond the "control" of linguistic and cultural communications. In this sense, the world-system infrastructure can be said to have entered the realm of "nature"—the perceptual—while literary production remains in the measurable, historical present of written communication.

As technology creates ever faster, increasingly automatic communications below the level of consciousness, language and the material of signification itself have become an object of study in text-centered disciplines that are increasingly delimited under the rubric of "Cultural" or "Area Studies" whose common interest is "the self-referential capacity of

language and signification" (Chow 2006, 11).[2] If the current disposition
of knowledge into specific areas is perceived, increasingly, more as an
obstacle than an aid to those who wish to alter the course of the world-
system, then the first line of action (for those desiring change) is not
to enter directly into world politics or media ecologies, still less would
writers be advised to "stubbornly resist" a culture conceived as "monolithic" (Reeve 2006, 3).[3] Rather than continue to throw words at a
system that has successfully closed itself to communication, what is
needed is for authors to reconceive their own position within current
knowledge structures—and this reconceptualization is as necessary for
those in "Creative Writing" as it is for those confined to departments of
"Islamic Studies," "Cultural Studies," or any of the hyphenated "American" studies that have emerged in the past few decades.

It has been suggested more than once, and not only by academic
critics, that the "present condition" of fiction writers has to do with
"their institutionalization within universities," right there next to the
theorists, Teachers of English to Speakers of Other Languages (TESOL),
Technical Writing, and Freshman Composition teachers (White 1998,
116). Novelist, cultural critic, and independent press publisher Curtis
White understood, even as members of the Associated Writing Program
held a panel expressly to denounce the threat of literary "theory" to
creativity, that the real danger to the cultivation of literary writing in
universities was more from the other two camps, Comp and Tech Writing. White very soon recognized the danger that English departments
"would become service departments, functioning in the name of commerce" (White 1998, 117–18). In such a situation, "innovation" in literature is, in itself, no more risky or subversive than the concurrent
drive to reinvent the market and extend commerce to all aspects of
experience: both literary innovation and capital accumulation have in
common, as their only defining feature, the fact that they are now
conceived as being endless—that is, without boundaries and hence
without the possibility to alter or set directions for the systems that
license innovation and mostly encourage (rather than repress) enjoy-
ment on the principle that desire, too, is endless and so a boon to
further accumulation. It is entirely understandable, under such circumstances, that the leading innovators in both theory and fiction writing
display a not-so-hidden desire for Empire (capitalized after Hardt and
Negri, and too frequently reified), although imperialism is now to be
described in the open-ended, networked fashion that fiction has traditionally employed for its own experimental and expressive purposes.
Obversely, the minoritarian desire for an alternative to Empire, when

it finds expression, often takes apocalyptic form, because no other end to the current system is imaginable.

FICTION'S (AND FICTIONS) PRESENT

"Postmodern fiction," writes White, "is not necessarily merely an expression of the postmodern condition. Postmodern fiction is also a strategic response to the condition" (White 1998, 114). This formulation, when I first encountered it in the mid-1990s seemed fair enough as a defense of fiction by John Barth and, among my closer contemporaries, Kathy Acker and Mark Leyner. The authors White references in his essay were still in circulation, if not exactly popular; the cultural "condition" was still unfamiliar enough, and the readership for literary writing still sizable enough, that a response in detail, in fiction, was called for. By exaggerating and exacerbating its worst features, writers—so we supposed—could help other writers (and an audience newly connected through the Internet to new, more focused marketing strategies) recognize the underlying system within the veneer of constant change. Ideology critique would allow us to see the market's abuses for what they are, and we would be moved, presumably, to want to overcome the present moment of late capital. When change does not come, however, and markets and reception media are enthusiastically embraced, not spurned, the literary disturbance eventually stops being needed or even noticeable, and the alternative to Empire becomes less and less distinct:

> And then I thought that, one day, maybe, there'd be a human society in a world which is beautiful, a society which wasn't just disgust. (Acker 1988, 227)

White characterizes Acker's strategy this way: "Is our culture dead? Then I'll be deader than death. Is our culture ugly? Then I'll be uglier than ugly. Her destination, paradoxically, is new life and beauty" (White 1998, 115). But an end is not a destination, and Acker's assertion of beauty in the closing lines of *Empire* sounds more like an afterthought than anticipation. Her book is an "Elegy" not just for the "World of the Fathers" (the title of its first section) but for the world as such, as a subject of imagination and representation. Having succeeded in coming to terms with "theory," at least as a generator of new language, Acker and others of her literary generation created a sensibility in an audience who would prove to be as comfortable with writing on the body as with writing in books, and as happy reading *Empire* as *Empire of the Senseless.*

One argument of this chapter is that the line of fiction represented by Acker and faithful to the resistive strategy outlined by White has not so much played itself out as positioned itself in a postapocalyptic neverland, where all these writers can do is anxiously await the end of the system that once gave it its edge, during a period of worldwide market expansion and consolidation through the 1980s and 1990s. As an alternative to this radical line and the enabling "postmodern condition," I would pose world-systems theory and the longue durée in particular, with its vision of a society that originates in particular circumstances, develops in time, and seems to be undergoing a prolonged, though one hopes not an endless, crisis. The aesthetic consequence of this shift in perspective is a recognition of other, less vocal modes of resistance, not Acker so much as Lynne Tillman, not DeLillo or Pynchon so much as Harry Mathews or Joseph McElroy—writers who, while different from one another as they are from their better-known contemporaries, are similar in their practice of a kind of constrained classicism, in which every sentence marks, in every turn of every phrase, an awareness of the limits on what can be communicated through institutions, academic, commercial, televisual, governmental, biological, and so forth. And where writers exercise expressive freedoms, these too tend to be imagined within further formal constraints, often arbitrary and wholly unnecessary, but of the writer's own making.

To write under constraint is to recognize that choices, though determined, can also have surprising outcomes. Economic systems, for example, have Kondriatief cycles and bifurcations, when small decisions at various dispersed locations turn out to have system-changing effects. Even pure mathematical systems (by Goedel's theorem) are unable to eliminate, from within, the possibility of contradiction. The situation within social and literary systems is of course not so clear-cut or measurable, but one can say that an author, by willingly engaging constraints outside herself—that is, outside one's own merely expressive freedoms—might then produce changes in language and consciousness that would not otherwise be discoverable. However fertile the imagination of "senseless" languages and fluid forms in writers such as Acker and Hardt and Negri, these languages and forms (when they are picked up and repeated) are quickly solidified and turned into commodities by the much more powerful, always better organized corporate culture that such expression is purportedly meant to resist or redirect.

Tillman's (2006) latest work, *American Genius: A Comedy,* offers a middle way between radical materialism (a reduction of "meaning" to mere "sense") and transcendence (the search for a position "outside" of culture). Her work represents neither an identification of the author's personal "Genius" with Empire nor a claim for an exclusively literary, wholly textual position outside of institutional power. The Genius that she sings is still "American" and wholly naturalistic, though Tillman's America is not (like Dreiser's "American Tragedy") bound by the imagination of the developing nation-state. Tillman's novel in fact thematizes the problem of boundaries at the level of the human body, not the nation, not "society." The constraints of embodiment are given through a sustained discourse on skin and textiles—the natural and human-made boundaries between self and environment, which let in only what the human body is able to process (or, when it fails to do so, erupts in psoriatic lesions, a melanoma, "Higoumenakis's sign" of the resurgence of syphilis, and so forth [Tillman 2006, 31]). The skin is a boundary, and all boundaries (marked as such) are of necessity part of the system, not the environment. All boundaries, like postmodern fictions, are thus reflexive by nature, without reference to an "outside." Any reaction to a toxic environment will be, then, if not deadly, successful, only if re-sistances are already present within the self and the various languages it has internalized. This ineluctably reflexive "American Genius," how-ever epical, tragic, or apocalyptic in its range, is first of all "comic," because it cannot escape its own constraining skin.

Tillman, Acker's contemporary, offers an alternative sensibility, no less materialistic, no less aware of Empire's colonizing of conscious-ness. But what distinguishes Tillman and Acker—and it is what I want to argue can distinguish world-fiction and a merely innovative or reflective narrative—is the pace at which the information is presented and the simultaneous channeling of perceptions, communications, and different levels of interpretation. In almost any passage in Acker, we might observe one of the distinctions I have been describing between perception and communication ("the I who desired and the eye who perceived"), but instead of engaging that difference as a source of narrative invention, in Acker the difference is flatly stated. What we get is not a conflict conducive to change but rather a mere "multiplicity" of voices and perspectives that one finds, for example, in this passage from *Empire of the Senseless*:

> I thought all I could know about was human separation; all
> I couldn't know, naturally, was death. Moreover, since the I
> who desired and the eye who perceived had nothing to do
> with each other and at the same time existed in the same
> body—mine: I was not possible. I, in fact, was more than

diseased. But Schreber had given me hope of a possible
solution. A hope of a possible solution. A hope of eradicat-
ing disease. Schreber had the enzyme which could change
all my blood. (Acker 1988, 33)

Tillman similarly acknowledges the incongruity of perception and consciousness, but instead of a flat statement of "human separation" (and
a consistent reduction of Schreber's schizophrenia from psychoanalytic
to chemical terms), we have in Tillman a consistent deployment of this
constitutive difference, so that what is perceived, though it develops
below consciousness and remains outside imaginative apprehension, is
made to emerge, over time, in relation to different aspects of her
narrator's first-person consciousness (as it considers other consciousnesses, like her mother's):

> Everything is a problem in some way, I can't think of any-
> thing that's not a problem from the past for the future, and
> I often worry, frowning to myself, unaware that I'm frown-
> ing, my lips turning down involuntarily, which I've been told
> to stop doing since I was a child, because it creates the
> impression that
>   I'm sullen and also etches fine lines around the mouth,
> but I can't. My father worried about the future, which pre-
> sumably he could imagine, but I can't, just as I can't imag-
> ine lines like tributaries running from the river of my mouth
> the way they do from my mother's, who was angry, who'd
> abandoned her girlish hopes of marrying a violinist named
> Sidney, and who often speaks of him now that my father is
> dead, wondering where Sidney is, and also wondering where
> my father is, if he is outside, waiting for her in the car that
> he loved. She might have seen the future in us, if we'd
> been someone else's children. By the time I knew my
> brother, he was thirteen and I was two, so he and my par-
> ents were the future that lived with and preceded me, it lay
> before me and also excluded me, so I didn't consider it,
> not when I was a small child, since it was already in their
> lives. (Tillman 2006, 7)

The writing of experience on the body, another common theme in
Acker and Tillman, gestures toward a signifying reality beyond or beneath either writer's ability to "imagine": but where Acker's response is
to set down the body writing, as a blood-in-your-face material reality

indifferent to meaning or interpretation, Tillman includes that unimaginable signification effortlessly among family thoughts, as they come to her, or not. Information in Tillman arrives in real time, but the reality is always that of cognition, not material signification alone, and the time of the narrating is set to match the pace of memory and projection. This is not the time of endlessly deferred signification licensing boundless innovation and interminable social critique but a hitherto never experienced time brought forward through a change in consciousness. One should not assume that such literary reflexivity merely sets a powerless subjectivity (a "raised consciousness") against a recalcitrant power that is indifferent to consciousness. We will hear more about the potentially world-changing nature of a sudden alteration in consciousness when we turn to Melville, an originator of the cognitive line I am trying to identify in this chapter. Here, in Tillman, we see the life-changing possibilities in the juxtaposition of an aging Mother, going senile, a child, for whom the future has no reality, and a woman (the narrative consciousness) whose capacities allow her to move in and out of these different consciousnesses and different temporalities. In childhood, there is no need for imagining a future, since that exists already in the lives of adults, a world apart. In world-fiction, the future is brought to present consciousness, even as unnoticed perception takes form, not immediately, but through verbal repetitions, following multiple sightings. Nobody denies the existence of a bodily presence more immediate than writing and imagination. And nobody pretends to bring this immediacy directly to the page. Nonetheless, it is possible, over numerous iterations, for the lines on the page to evoke the impossible-to-see lines on a face as they cease to be another's and become one's own.

HISTORY AS FICTION, FICTION AS HISTORY

I recognize that apocalypse, which has always been future-historical, always ever an event "to come," may not be the first genre that comes to mind as a description of present fictions and (this volume's titular) "Fiction's Present." Derrida's typically negative call, that there should be "No Apocalypse, Not Now," has been the established postmodern position—a somewhat nervous, collective, mutually unassured Deconstruction. Departments of literary and cultural studies have remained under the sway of this model for quite a long time now, and even the explicitly political branches of theory tend to cast their activism, in terms consistent with deconstruction, as a call for textual and cultural, rather than material, transformation.

To some extent, Deconstruction's trademark self-consciousness is comprehensible as the peculiar cultural form taken by an awareness that we humans, for the first time in world history, can now end it through military or ecological interventions—a situation that makes "the end" something immanent, within the collective power of multitudes, not transcendent, under the control of monarchs or states: that we ourselves, collectively as a living, breathing, consuming, and excreting presence, might bring about our own end can also intimidate the pursuit of systemic, structural change.

I opened this chapter with a discussion of Hardt and Negri because their radical materialism poses, among other attempts to meet the current world-system with an equally current, systematic criticism, an apparent alternative to the postmodern consensus based on negativity and cultural critique. As Wilson remarks in his essay, materialism is without negations, and it is inherently optimistic, since material nature is beyond the deductions of abstract logic, and technologically induced innovation cannot be domesticated by language (not even a language whose "plainness," contrary to most disciplinary criticism, can be directed unflinchingly on "our own times and social circumstance" [Emerson 2006, cited earlier]). This material orientation then is more than a set of intellectual concerns: materialism is also the reason one finds few regrets and few recriminations in the work of world-systems theorists, because "any destructions, and even horrors, can be made to serve here and now" (Wilson, private correspondence; see also Harootunian 2004).

A materialist criticism also is purportedly without illusions, since these depend on thought rising above material objects and forces, negating them, or relying on some (imaginary) reassignment of reasoning powers to aesthetic representations culturally and political representatives of the state. The refusal of negations, in Hardt's and Negri's thoroughgoing political materialism, is a refusal of transcendence and also a refusal of social and governmental hierarchies. The distrust of illusions in such writing situates materialism in much the same position as apocalyptic fiction of the current period—those works of imagination that attempt to communicate without the illusion of settled "characters," without recognizable settings, and without plots that proceed linearly through a person's youthful immersion in multiple possibilities; toward maturity as this person makes (or neglects to make) significant choices, reducing possibility to probability; and unfolding toward a happy or tragic conclusion (in death, marriage, or the achievement of some alternative social identity). Diverging from this linear model, contemporary world-fiction tends rather to proliferate possibilities in a networked fashion consistent with today's political, material, and informational networks. These too have beginnings; they have lives during which they have developed and terminal transitions (though not necessarily consistent with the pace of such developments over an individual human lifetime). It is not yet clear, however, if fiction as such can exist without illusions, or if narrative can proceed on multiple tracks in nonhuman time and still be compelling.[4]

The perpetuation of a world-system, which its leading analysts put at around 500 years, can take some of the urgency out of utopian and apocalyptic narratives; the comparatively brief ascendancy of an anti-systemic, Soviet social state deflects Hardt's and Negri's assertion of their commitments, as "communists," away from any programmatic politics. But if, as many commentators believe, the world system has entered a period of deep transformation (or increasing chaos), and if that transformation is materially driven, not conceptually or rhetorically urged forward, then that leaves us still with past expressions, including the religious language of apocalypse and the political language of social revolution. Alternative languages need to emerge, and the consistent recasting of familiar language, making the terms of discussion one's own, is a development in this direction. But there is no guarantee that literary forms and languages will develop or, if they do, that they will develop in synch with material transformations that are themselves mostly nonverbal and unrepresentable. After all, the market economy had been in existence already for close to three of its five centuries, before a proper world-literature emerged, notably in the incipient Russian and American Empires, giving form to Empire's assumptions and eventuating in a properly "modernist" development centered in Europe.

What eventuated in Russia and America, though, has been something different from the European logic of imperialism and the literature of colonialism. It is not accidental that the first accomplished world-fictions, by Tolstoy and Melville, only fitfully comport with the genre of a "novel." The counterposing of history and fiction that uniquely characterizes these two authors is tellingly rejected by Alfred Doeblin, the author of a competing world-fiction, who insisted that "the historical novel is, in the first place, a novel; in the second place, it isn't history" (cited in Caserio 2004, 107). Neither Tolstoy nor Melville, Pynchon or Gaddis, or Vollmann or Norman Mailer could disengage their work so clearly from "history"; Tillman, as Madame Realism in her journalism of the 1980s and 1990s, speaks in the same cadences as the narrator of *Motion Sickness* and *American Genius*; Mathews, the Oulipian author, uses rational constraints to the same purpose as Mathews, the

purported spy, in *My Life in CIA*. The same social and political transformations that disturb a bounded, national development (in the former
Russian and American world-systems) also affect generic boundaries
and individual expression in the arts.

Y2K, SEPTEMBER 11, 2001, AND OTHER SHAPES OF THE SIGNIFIER

The durability of classic and canonical fictions and the persistence of
generic distinctions through all projects of revision and deconstruction
in the past two or three decades may be no less surprising than the
persistence of the worldwide capitalist economy itself. Brian McHale
and Randall Stevenson (2007), in their conclusion to the *Edinborough
Companion to Twentieth-Century Literatures in English*, capture the odd
mixture of anticipation and routinization, cultural diversity and commercial homogenization, apocalyptic terror and enui that accompanies
any "sense of an ending" in the period of the longue durée. These
editors arrive at their formulation, tellingly, in an effort to conclude
their own collective project of mapping literary history through detailed investigations, by several scholars, of literary achievement from
particular locations at particular dates.

Inspired by the French Annales project (itself inspired by the
historian Ferdinand Braudel, who coined the phrase "longue durée"),
the *Edinborough Companion* eschews linear history with a series of "thick
histories" set in particular locations on particular dates—Joyce's Dublin
1904, Wolfe's visit to the London Impressionist Exhibition, "on or about
December 1910," when "human nature changed," the anus mirabilis of
modernist poetry, 1922 (which saw the publication of *The Waste Land*,
"Sunday Morning," "Hugh Selwin Mauberley," and "Spring and All");
Berlin 1989, Johanesburg February 11, 1990, the placelessness of the
Web in the palindromic year 1991, and so forth.

The volume's American and British coeditors conclude by
reflecting on the cultural discourse surrounding two world-class candidates for end points, Y2K and September 11, 2001, whose extensive
media presentation nicely defines the two moods of our quasi-apocalyptic
present. Even though the dates are wholly arbitrary in their numerical
materiality, a mass consciousness was able to condense around them
wholly as an outcome of global media culture, but the consequences
for each date are quite different and beyond the control of media
alone, of language, or material representation. The one, projected
catastrophe, the "millennium bug" that threatened to damage operat-

ing systems set up for calendars dated 19__, was prospective, scheduled, anticipated, endlessly reported, and ultimately "anti-climactic" (McHale and Stevenson 2007, 274). The other was retrospective, unanticipated, but recognizable in hindsight as a realization of "the many representations, in verbal fictions, but especially in films and on television, of the way the world ends" (ibid.). One distinctly minor literary response, the willingness to write within the constraints of numerical materiality, arguably emerges as an anti-narrative strain that participates fully in the enormously powerful, counter-narrative tendencies of contemporary media culture. Such narratives take a middle way, between pure materiality and subjective interpretation, and their authors do this by demonstrating the power of narratives to emerge precisely when the author, or a mediated culture, restricts control by responding to a numerical materiality outside of consciousness (in this instance, a Christian calendrical date known universally, if not acknowledged by all the world's religions and cultures).

Recognizing the relative stability of world-system formations, analysts (following Braudel) have posited the notion of a longue durée, that is, a long-lasting "structural time" that reflects "continuing (but not eternal) structural realities." Within the longue durée, one can mark events and a "cyclical time of ups and downs," including the emergence and disappearance of states, political systems, entire industries, and cultural movements. In fact, the concept of a world-system is meant to replace the national state as a unit of analysis, since "the defining feature of a world-economy is that it is not bounded by a unitary political structure" (Wallerstein 2004, 240). Nations of course persist in the world-system, and they can resist Empire with a vengeance—as the Baltic and Central Asian states emerged in 1991 to help break up the Soviet empire, and as in 2005 France and the Netherlands reemerged, in all the nationalist pride of their peoples, to resist further systemization by voting down an (admittedly diffuse) draft for a European constitution.[5] Resistance to the world-system also builds itself around identities—defensive communities, or, more properly, "interest groups," gathered in the name of God, ethnicity, and family—and these resisting forces have found powerful expression through uniform literary genres, which remain more numerous and more often read than current world-fictions. Nonetheless, as identities cannot be understood apart from the networks they resist, neither novels nor poems today can be understood apart from the material networks and institutional frameworks that bring them into existence.

Like the national literatures that preceded them, world-fictions will develop self-consciously and publicly, with their particular goals and their distinction from past national literatures clearly articulated. Like the world-systems, world-economies, and world-empires that world-fiction often (but not exclusively) takes as its subject, an emerging world-literature needs to erect barriers as much as it engages with current practices and forms. My hyphenation of "world-fiction" is meant to emphasize that I am not talking about fictions and narratives of the world, but rather about fictions and narratives that are worlds in themselves, semi-autonomous and self-constructing. It is not necessary for world-fiction to encompass, topically, the entire world or even for exemplars of the genre to be international in scope, although often they are, as a proto-world-fiction such as *Gravity's Rainbow* and *The Recognitions* has been, as William Vollmann's "Seven Dreams" series strives to become, and as collaborations (like the one between Steve Tomasula and Stephen Farrell) enact at an operational level, in the coproduction of image and text. What makes these works world-fictive, however, is not their global subject matter but their tendency rather to become global in their form and layered in their temporality.

Similarly, while such works surely engage new media, new material cultures, and newly collaborative networks, world-fiction does not need to be produced, necessarily, in another medium. My purpose is not to call for the production of new literary objects, but for literature in whatever medium to become more robustly integrated in networks of production and circulation. Further, if the book is indeed to continue as a progressive force in the current media ecology, authors may need to become more, not less, conservative at the material level (of pages, lines, signifiers, and bounded form), eschewing the temptation to allow images to distract from printed text (and the conceptual, continuous "thought track" that text uniquely generates). In an environment of enforced and endless change, authors need to employ all the defense mechanisms afforded by the traditional printed book, even as a nervous system needs to close itself off from an environment of noise and other, interfering systems. Only by closing itself at the level of material structure can the book remain open to innovation that must be, strictly, internal to the practice of the literary, not coextensive with the media environment that literature needs to reflect, and reflect on.

I will have more to say about the self-enclosed, solitary, "nervous" nature of American world-fiction in my concluding reading of Herman Melville, one of the exemplars of the late nineteenth-century "American Nervousness" analyzed "anecdotally" and in more psychoanalytical, less cognitive or systemic, terms by Tom Lutz. For the moment let me note, simply, that if productive networks in multiple media now define the present, then fiction needs to create in readers an experience of presence, bringing to consciousness the experience of living in "an integrated zone of activity and institutions that obey certain Systemic rules" (Wallerstein 2004, 17). Hardt and Negri make a parallel claim for the development of states in response to global networks—namely, it is not enough that governments should recognize networks that both support states (through lines of communication and financial exchange) and disturb them (through the use of these same networks for the development of terrorist cells). It is necessary, these authors argue, for states to *become* networks, and if a connection between literary objects and states seems far-fetched or metaphorical, then the conceptual technology underlying both developments turns out to be intriguingly homologous. As Walter Michaels (2004) has argued in *The Shape of the Signifier*, the turn in contemporary politics to a preferential discussion of "culture" and "identity" rather than class "politics" is consistent with the apparently more abstruse discussion of material signification in literary criticism, with its emphasis on the physical features of texts: both are understandable as a historical development involving a loss of hope in programs for achieving economic equality on the one hand and a common ground for argument and interpretation on the other, both of which, the ontological and the economic, were once thought capable of overcoming cultural, geographic, and biological differences by involving all peoples in argument, interpretation, and the articulation of intentions, activities that do not depend on subjectivity or subject position. Both the political Left and aesthetic progressives have learned to live with this development, Michaels argues, by developing a kind of conceptual defense mechanism, a common "technology" for "reconfiguring ideological difference (i.e., disagreement) as cultural, linguistic, or even geographical difference" (Michaels 2004, 15).

In Michaels's account, the Cultural Left emerges, through a vigorous engagement in previously unexplored areas of expression, as a sort of Research and Development wing for the Right, naming, and so making available, further expansion and new markets. In this regard, Michaels's critique of academic cultural politics is consistent with my critique of Acker and the line of contemporary fiction devoted to unconstrained and endless innovation: by reducing meaning to marks on a body, page, or screen, cultural and creative innovators lose their polemical edge. What is left out of Michaels's reading, however, is the structuring of consciousness in literary works, which is necessarily a combination of material presence and communicative utterance. What I am suggesting, by attending to the cognitive dimensions of what may be, admittedly, a minor strain in current literary production, is not a "middle way" between material identity and communication ("body/ontology"

and "meaning," in Michaels's terms) but an alternative "way" that recognizes the irreducible differences between perceptual and communicative processes and therefore makes their opposition meaningless.

If we move away for a moment from "ideological" technologies to
the way that actual, material technologies operate at the level of perception and cognition, then the outlines of an alternative material
culture might begin to emerge more clearly. One can accept that consciousness, like culture, is a "construction," but each is constructed
differently, and that *difference* is itself very real. The kinds of distinction
I am talking about go deeper than differences in interpretation; they
have less to do with "ideological" argument or even spatial organization
("cultural, linguistic, or . . . geographic difference" [Michaels 2004]),
and more to do with differences in processing time. Such differences
are historical, but it is a history whose political culture is constrained,
increasingly, by the development of new media with different claims on
human time and attention. Presence, a perceptual phenomenon, is of
course produced in time and "constructed" by the brain in collabora-
tion with external stimuli, but the cognitive construction is so much
quicker than constructions out of language, as to seem immediate by
comparison. The structuring power of literature, similarly, is much slower
than visual, sonic, and filmic media, so that the relation becomes not
one of opposition but of differing constructions, the production of an
alternative presence.

I will now turn to an example of a work of literature, arguably
one that inaugurates a new genre in world literature, that exploits
precisely this temporal difference in counterposing the perception of
present danger with a calm, imperturbable (but wholly false) consciousness of racial reality. The world-changing power of *Benito Cereno*,
far from developing a consensus through rational or polemical argument, occurs when the material world imposes itself in all its relative
immediacy, on a consciousness whose language had not, hitherto,
allowed for such disturbances.

As an author working in a period when print was for the first time
having to cohabit with photographic, telegraphic, and other nonverbal
media, Melville senses and adroitly engages the temporal in the modern city and its moving microcosm, the commercial whaling, factory, or
slave ship. Melville's narrative, remarkable as much for its pace as its
language (so different, almost chastened after the linguistic excess of
Moby Dick and *Pierre*), makes possible a hitherto unavailable expressive
register by exploiting the difference between the pace of printed discourse, unfolding with the slowness of events in a dream, and the speed
of events aboard a ship held hostage by rebellious slaves.

FROM MOMENT TO MOMENT, MIND TO MIND

The relative material stability of the printed book itself has been, from the mid-nineteenth century, a way to maintain the experience of presence. The book's somewhat longer duration than conversational or journalistic media recording similar events has been a way of giving shape (if not permanence) to the new society. The book's history (including its production in fixed editions, the development of international copyright, and the development in the United States of authorship itself as a distinct literary profession), is deeply involved in the postrevolutionary, democratic notion that political change was normal, not an anomaly. That there must be, as a consequence of a successfully built nation, a "renaissance" of native literary energies meant that material development (the achievement of "bread and covering," in Thomas Jefferson's words) would extend to the intellectual realm, allowing for more than the occasional "strong mind" that is capable only of "[emitting] a flash of light" (Jefferson's letter of 1845 to a British contemporary, cited in Delbanco 2005, 74). The paradox of a society built (for the first time in history) on endless capital accumulation, technological progress, and popularly controlled political change is that (to maintain stability) change needs to be perpetuated continuously and indefinitely. For much of the history of literature in the United States, the institution of a nation-wide literacy, the invention of authorship, and an independent book trade were all ways of creating cultural stability in the midst of material change, while the requirement of innovation ensured that literature did not lose touch with a culture that changes from moment to moment.

A self-consciously "modern" society, like a national literature, does not last forever but it can last a while, and one of the challenges to criticism is to explain how these different temporalities can coexist in structures that remain the same over time yet change from one moment to the next. At a time of crisis, when the world-system encounters problems it can no longer resolve, more than explanation is needed: the critic needs to participate, together with novelists and artists, in the creation of new conceptual forms, responsive to but distinct from the forms being produced in the overall media environment. Even more, writers need to participate in the creation of newly robust networks of literary production—although this will mean a different conception of what a writer is, namely, a participant in a common, collaborative concern that recognizes distinction in the act of literary creation but distrusts commercial celebrity and academic stardom. To be an author today means striving to be not a lone genius ("American" or otherwise) but rather one among a collection of singular but communicating talents. In this sense, the construction of a literary network is consistent with the preference, in materialist discourse, of horizontal and immanent constructions over vertical, hierarchical, and transcendent constructions: "The horizontal is associated with the immanent and the lateral, as with two authors working side by side passing ideas from brain to brain" (Wilson 2005).

The paradox of communication through material media is that a communicating system, such as a brain or an intellect, in the first place needs not to open itself but rather to protect itself from the media environment which to some extent forms it. In cognition, as in communication, boundaries need not be subverted, but they do need be distinguished and continually maintained against an indistinct environment, not least the environment of other systems and other consciousnesses: "People need to be protected from others, who may hurt them, as I need to be protected," writes Tillman in *American Genius*. Here is a narrator who "Listens to others more than most people, sometimes at my peril" (2006, 17). The systems model might resemble elitism in the requirement of clearly drawn boundaries and a willingness to recognize only those who achieve the distinction of an original "voice" or an established critical standpoint. A culture of distinction differs from elitism, however, in that no distinction ever raises the intellect above the environment in which it exists: rather, distinctions create further distinctions, in a process similar to the continuation of a conversation or the growth of a narrative.

The entire discipline of critical writing, with its emphasis on accurate citation and responsible (or at least, responsive) commentary, is a way of coordinating ideas that by definition cannot be communicated materially among perceiving minds: I read, in the initial journal appearance of *Fiction's Present*, a citation of Dorritt Cohn by Robert Caserio, on the need for fiction to distinguish and limit, rather than subversively cross, boundaries and celebrate the breakdown of borders. (Caserio is concerned specifically with the line that separates history and fiction in James, Cather, and Vollmann.) With this literary citation, I find the support not of a literary authority but rather of a collaborator working along lines consistent with my own project and distinguished, I hope, from the critical commonplace that (as Caserio puts it) "every passing moment" should solicit "comprehension of our submersion in an in-between element" (2004, 106). Once "subversiveness" becomes not a resistant but a dominant position, submersion in the "in-between" can begin to look not like freedom but rather like lukewarm commitment, and endless innovation becomes a way only to suspend engagement.

Emerson had always understood the need for criticism, no less than fiction or poetry, to be in and constitutive of the present. He argued that authors should be introspective not retrospective; that they should achieve insights not from the study of past works or emulation of European contemporaries "but by the intellect being where and what it sees, by sharing the path, or circuit of things through forms, and so making them translucid to others" (2006). The critic, working in concert with the imaginative writer, is not reflecting present concerns (the concerns of everyday media) so much as he or she is taking responsibility for producing the present. And this is true even when the critic is writing about past authors. A welcome trend in recent Melville criticism is the understanding that a major author's importance lies not in any expressed attitude (or complicitous silence) toward slavery, patriarchy, queerness, ecological destruction, or any of the politically charged issues of the time (or ours). Still less is the continuing topical "relevance" of these issues a reason to revisit the political decisions and evasions of past authors. Indeed, as is shown by the renewed recognition of *Benito Cereno*, what makes a work or an author worth going back to is the way that deeply held conceptions of relevance and impossibility, registered in present consciousness, can be entirely, dangerously mistaken. That Captain Delano, boarding the San Dominick, does not see the effects of a slave mutiny is less an indictment of one man's intelligence or conscious racism than a way of showing, in excruciating, foreboding detail, how "race" has been naturalized in the mind of a representative American so that, despite this character's relaxed and detailed investigation of every aspect of the ship's life, during his entire time aboard the San Dominick the truth never occurs to him—that the mutineers have arranged a masquerade in order to hide the fact that they are in fact running the ship and keeping the Spanish captain, Don Benito Cereno, in a condition of terrified suppression. Cereno, the captive captain whose serenity hides deep and persisting turbulence, remains held precariously in the present; Delano, the unsuspecting visitor, is for most of the narrative comfortably, perceptively, and wholly mistakenly in a state of critical suspension.

"NOT CAPTAIN DELANO, BUT DON BENITO"; NOT POE, BUT MELVILLE; NOT ACKER, BUT TILLMAN . . .

In closing, I want to consider *Benito Cereno* as an exemplary production of presence in fiction, and I will offer this work as a reference for subsequent productions appropriate to our own, somewhat altered,

circumstances. My analysis centers on the "in-between" (Caserio), undecidable, genially critical but deeply blinkered consciousness that gathers around the narrative's main focalizer, Captain Delano. In an
otherwise insightful and appropriately worldly biography, *Melville: His
Work and World,* Andrew Delbanco refers several times to Delano's stupidity, foolishness, or "doltish" behavior (2005, 157; then again on pages
235, 240, 141, 242). But the visiting captain's slowness to pick up on
hints that are everywhere has less to do with intelligence than with a
structuring of perceptions or, more precisely, the production of
blindnesses that do not simply limit understanding but rather constitute a person's ability to perceive from one moment to the next. Hence
the sensuous slave woman holding a child, in Delano's mind (as observed through Melville's roaming narrator), is a composite of certain
ideas regarding nobility in a state of nature: "naked nature, now; pure
tenderness and love, thought Captain Delano, well pleased":

> He was gratified with their manners; like most uncivilized
> women, they seemed at once tender of heart and tough of
> constitution; equally ready to die for their infants or fight
> for them. Unsophisticated as leopardesses; loving as doves.
> Ah! thought Captain Delano, these perhaps are some of the
> very women whom Mungo Park saw in Africa, and gave such
> a noble account of. (Melville 1987, 2011)

Rather than absorb the sexual, maternal immediacy of the woman
and child he observes, Delano characteristically retreats into literary
reflections that comfortably codify experience and keep him at a
safe distance.

The retreat into categorical understanding characterizes every turn
of the narrative. The black "assistant," Babo, holding the arm of his
master, in Delano's view has to be acting out of concern for the master's
well-being. A man or a woman, a master or a slave, only partly consciously selects from the environment of variously embodied information certain salient details for observation, and that "part" will be
revealingly different depending on the perceiver's gendered or racial
character. What is evident to one person, within the seemingly free flow
of words, actions, gestures, and glances, will not be evident to another
person—but these different meanings are less the result of conscious
interpretation or intelligence than they are the result of institutional
and cognitive constructions that have been set well in advance of any
empirical observation at any given time. That the visiting captain persists in his misapprehension testifies not only to the perpetuation in

him of racial stereotypes but also to the production of consciousness in the present—and it is no accident that Melville here, in his one fiction that explicitly and consistently focuses on race, creates (in advance of European modernism) an American version of stream-of-consciousness narrative. As one critic noted, Joyce's and Wolfe's contemporary, who contributed to the Melville revival, rationality in *Benito Cereno* retreats before "the unconscious mind, stealing silently between the eyes and pen . . . as it suggests, offers, presses and overwhelms the conscious mind, and makes it less an equal than a servant" (Freeman 1926, cited in Delbanco 2005, 148).

Constructions of a narrative present are powerful not primarily for what they include but for all they keep out of consciousness; at the same time, social constructions are equally powerful and also slow to admit change. The quietly building, dramatic tension within Melville's short novel of course depends on Delano's intellectual lassitude: "a person of a singularly undistrustful good nature, not liable, except on extraordinary and repeated excitement, and hardly then, to indulge in personal alarms, any way involving the imputation of malign evil in man" (Melville 1987, 1991). Rather than blame Delano directly, Melville's narrator appeals to the wisdom of the reader, who is enlisted to decide "whether, in view of what humanity is capable, such a trait implies, along with a benevolent heart, more than ordinary quickness and accuracy of intellectual perception" (Melville 1987, 1991). More than mere delicacy, the narrator's indirection regarding Delano directs the reader to the actual location of narrative "events" in the sustained correlation between two minds—namely, between registered perceptions in the mind of a character and their moral reflection in the mind of a reader.

The setup is, by necessity, slow, even excruciating, depending on how observant the reader is in fact, or whether the story is being read for the first time. However, when the realization of the true state of affairs does reach Delano, it comes suddenly, in the form of a shock: only after Delano has stepped off the San Dominick does Cereno manage to free himself long enough to leap over the rails and onto the departing craft. Cereno is followed by Babo, who is finally recognized by Delano as deceitful and murderous, but not until "the black" is observed "writhing" in search of a hidden dagger, which he intends to use not against Delano but rather against his "master," Cereno. The recognition, which in a single moment disrupts every fixed conceptual schema within Delano's mind, when it comes is given in a markedly awkward sentence, whose grammatical organization itself threatens, at every clause, to come apart or collapse into itself:

Not Captain Delano, but Don Benito, the black, in leaping
into the boat, had intended to stab. (Melville 1987, 2030)

Delbanco calls this, not unreasonably, one of "the most contorted
sentences in all of Melville's writing; gnarled, syntactically disordered,
a stretch of twisted prose in which subject, verb, and object seem to
want to merge with one another" (Delbanco 2005, 241).

What Melville captures in the sentence is not just the confusion
that arises in an episode of violence but the coming apart of distinctions that have hitherto upheld an entire worldview. Specifically, the
comforting assumption that the slave is "other," and safely contained in
this alterity, is disrupted at last—a development that I have been describing in cognitive terms but that is also recognizable in terms of
apocalyptic discourse theory. As Wendy Foster (2006) notes in her study
of contemporary novels of subversion, the apocalyptic mode distinguishes itself from conventional narrative by its reduction of space and
time to an inescapable, looming, and "pathological" presence. Foster
writes, "[t]here is no 'elsewhere' through which the narrative is mediated, no allusive past through which the pedagogy can be safely codified
and distanced; rather, what is foregrounded is the immanent present in
all of its pathological flatness. The 'elsewhere,' thus subtracted from
the apocalyptic scene, is replaced by the body itself, at once estranged
and perverse in its function as catastrophic remainder" (2006).

Acknowledging this apocalyptic context, Melville does not entirely
do without his own authorial attempt at codification and distancing.
The biographer, Delbanco, has described in some detail how Melville
makes use of medieval apocalyptic iconography in the figure of Delano
suppressing Babo's writhing, snakelike body, much as Christ is figured,
variously, with one foot on a snake, or holding down an infidel, Muslim
soldier. My concern, which is consistent with Foster's interest in present
fictions by Kathy Acker, Chuck Palahniuk, Brett Easton Ellis, and others,
is less with Melville's source than with the structuring of consciousness
through apocalyptic rhetoric. The slowness of Delano's coming-to-
consciousness, indeed the extended and sensually tantalizing way that
such realization is withheld, becomes itself one of the great embodiments of the longue durée in modern fiction. Significantly, the visiting
captain's private world-fiction is altered, not through any careful analysis or raising of consciousness but through violence. As Delbanco no-
tices, the retrospective reconstruction of all that went on before takes
the form of a sexual release. Understanding, when it does arrive, comes
to and through the whole body, with a potential not for political reform
but for reconfiguring all the fragile, semi-conscious logics that bind a

society together (with the races and peoples the society suppresses, somewhat as the civilized psyche represses spontaneous physicality).

Even a cognitive structure that seems as if it will last forever, as this narrative shows, can be shaken up violently and dramatically. As long, however, as the shake-up is experienced individually, in the mind of a single person, there is no guarantee that the disruption will eventuate in social and political change throughout the world-system. In the story, the murderous slave eventually is captured, the rebellion is contained, and the experiences of the persons involved get papered over by official history. (A similar denouement occurs in *Billy Budd*, where the eponymous hero, recognized even by his examiners as innocent, goes down in documentary history as an instigator of rebellion, and his accuser, the patently evil Claggart, goes down as a martyr.) The realizations momentarily achieved by Delano are not conveyed to the culture at large—not yet. (The story appeared in 1856, years before the outbreak of civil war.) Any translation of an individual cognitive understanding would have to wait, some several decades, for a corresponding institutional and structural change. The Civil War and, later still, the institution in the United States of civil rights in the 1950s, may have brought Delano's personal consciousness into wider social currency. Possibly there are not so many unconscious racists in positions of institutional power today in the United States. Even so, this transformation in consciousness does not mean that structural conditions of institutional racism have been addressed—not when discontent in the United States is contained by a penal system that since the institution of civil rights has expanded dramatically, and not as long as worldwide economic disparities indexed to race are widening, not narrowing.

The presentation of documentary history, in *Cereno* and *Billy Budd*, is not incidental to the production of presence in these fictions, and neither does the inclusion of documentary history, in all its authenticity of detail and deposition, in any sense blur the distinction between history and fiction. Fiction's role, contrasting with history, is to give palpable form to a potential for change in consciousness. That same potential, when it is realized in fiction, can be felt not through the constraints of legal language and textually supported institutions but rather, most palpably, as a production of presence in the prose itself. One of the merits of Delbanco's biography is that it is more about the "work" and the "world" that Melville inhabited than it is about the private life of an author. (This is partly the result of a relative lack of documentation—Melville never saved letters, and only a relatively brief stage in his professional career was recorded in the press, from his debut with *Typee* through the publication of *Pierre*, and Hawthorne, whose notebook entries give the clearest, most telling glimpses of the man, died a full forty years before Melville.) The present is lost as much to consciousness as to posterity, but what remains are the noted observations of an author's environment registered (in Delbanco's words) in "the pattern of images" Melville used to capture the emerging modern city, whose mark is left "in the nerves and sinews" of an author's prose (Delbanco 2005, 117).

Particularly distinctive is the deformation of the novel's own material presence in response to the city's textual environment:

> The city itself was a circulating collection of newspapers, leaflets, business cards, broadsides, tabloids, placards, signs affixed to carriages. (Delbanco 2005, 119)

These things were cited by Melville, and (because their medium also was print) they could be occasionally reproduced in the pages of *Moby Dick*. The work, however, was never in competition with the city environment of textual production, and it is likely that today any work of comparable quality that emerges from the links, chats, text messaging, banner ads, and interactive media will not be, simply, another innovation along these lines. If Melville could cite a mostly textual City of Words, print literature today cannot be expected to cite modes of signification that are of their essence, moving. But a literature contemporary with electronic environments will be capable, like Melville's work, of registering media effects:

> Moving clause by clause through Melville's New York prose is like strolling, or browsing, on a city street: each turn of phrase brings a fresh association; sometimes we are brought up short by a startling image requiring close inspection; sometimes a rush of images flickers by; but there is always the feeling of a quickened pulse, of some unpredictable excitement, in aftermath or anticipation. And if New York broke open Melville's style, it opened his mind as well to the cosmopolitan idea of a nation to which one belongs not by virtue of some blood lineage that leads back into the past, but by consent to the as-yet-unrealized ideal of a nation comprehending all peoples. (Delbanco 2005, 119)

"The cosmopolitan idea of a nation" fairly describes the cultural context for the production of presence in Melville, although the cosmopolitan tone, which reached cultural predominance in the literary modernism of Eliot and Pound, is less and less often heard in American writing. It is not clear whether a culture of globalization can be cosmopolitan, nor is it clear, today, whether or to what extent the currently realized idea of a nation will continue to shape the literary imagination. Personally, I cannot imagine the willful "nation building," in areas not historically given to nationalist feeling, playing much of a role in our understanding of global culture—especially when no attempt, none, is being made officially to establish an American cultural presence in those countries where the United States maintains a military presence.

Nor is it clear that the sensibility Delbanco rightly finds expressed in the patterns and pacing, the "nerves and sinews," of Melville's prose, the organization of chapters in *Moby Dick*, and even the appearance of the page itself, will take anything like these forms in a media environment where the letters and lines are in flux, not fixed by print. Fictions of the present need not be about the Internet or the emerging global city; from a literary perspective, what the Internet reveals is exactly how much operational language, textual matter, and environmental noise the book had been able, more or less successfully, to keep out of present consciousness. So if the endlessly inventive, wide-open, nervous style of *Moby Dick* settled into the more formal, more cautious, and more constrained prose of "Bartelby" and *Benito Cereno*, then that marks a recognition, on Melville's part, of language's medial limitations as much as it shows a personal evolution in a major literary style.

Benito Cereno, like Poe's "Purloined Letter," is a narrative whose object—racism—is in plain sight. Poe presents the blindnesses of rational inquiry and its attendant ironies in a front-brain way: he offers for observation two intellectuals discussing competing techniques of investigation, with a concern less for justice than for the sorting out of power relations between rationalist and intuitive worldviews. Poe's brief, ratiocinative narrative introduces to world-literature the genre of the detective novel. Melville presents the act of intellection raw—through a third-person, limited narration that hovers somewhere between a character's purposely limited focalization and a consciousness as large as the sea and the sky. In devising a cognitive profile of racism and its blindnesses, Melville also, almost incidentally, invents the modern psychological novel. The two approaches—Poe's discursive, and Melville's cognitive—represent alternative, not necessarily incompatible developments within the establishment of an American literary practice—practices that might map onto present alternatives by Acker and Tillman, as discussed earlier. If American fiction has operated at a level of innovation that could contribute to world literature new genres and the articulation of new identities, then that is partly because the world-system itself has until now encouraged endless innovation within a context of endless accumulation of capital. A similar attention to form will of course characterize any world-fiction today, but it is not at all clear that the perpetuation of an endless innovation, for its own sake, is now called for. A literature of formal constraint is at least as likely to characterize the present moment of literary history. Neither is it clear, how or whether the term *American,* will describe what is unique to an emerging world-system—although the presence or absence of writers of fiction, whatever their country of origin, will make a difference in how we imagine what comes next, when the end comes to a system that has lasted a long time.

NOTES

1. An indication of Hardt's and Negri's separation even from social theorists of the Left is that no reference to *Empire* or *Multitude* is to be found in any of the recent volumes on world-systems analysis written or edited by Immanuel Wallerstein, an author who is equally important to the understanding of world systems in this chapter. There is just one reference to *Empire* in Harry Harootunian's pamphlet, *The Empire's New Clothes,* arguing that Hardt's and Negri's postnationalism merely lets the United States off the hook, since according to Hardt and Negri no country, not even the United States, is now able to form the "center" of an imperialist project (Hardt and Negri 2000, 2, cited in Harootunian 2004, 18).

2. Chow places the development of "Area Studies" within the context of the expansion of the American university system after World War II, a continuation of the wartime mentality that wishes to organize knowledge against a perceived enemy. The technological context presented in this section is meant to complement, not contradict, Chow's analysis.

3. My citation comes from a leading column in the current issue of the *American Book Review* (September–October 2006), but I easily could have found similar citations from any issue of this journal during the past decade or so. The moralistic defense of pure literary "innovation" in the face of a hostile corporate culture can go on indefinitely, until resources run dry, which has in fact happened with this particular issue of *ABR.* As this is the only general-interest print journal that still regularly reviews titles published by independent presses, one is grateful for its relocation to the University of Houston-Victoria, but one also looks forward to a more nuanced targeting of the critique, with a bit more reflection on the place of the literary within these cultural systems worldwide.

4. My experience with network writing in electronic environments so far resembles novel reading less than earlier engagements with art-world and conceptual writing which, while capable of creating vast networks of participant-observers (a la Fluxus), have never generated the mass audience produced by novel reading and, later, film.

5. The post-Soviet nations have been, however, distinctly limited in their sovereignty, and my own observations while traveling in Latvia and Ukraine suggest a dependence of newly "independent" nations less on European sponsorship than on grey economies and the flight of populations (see "Riga under Western Eyes," http://www.electronicbookreview.com 08-20-2006).

REFERENCES

Acker, Kathy. 1980. *Empire of the senseless.* New York: Grove.

Caserio, Robert. 2004. James, Cather, Vollmann, and the distinction of fiction. *Symplokē* 12: 1–2: 106–129. Reprinted in this volume.

Chow, Rey. 2006. *The age of the world target: Self-referentiality in war, theory, and comparative work.* Durham, NC: Duke University Press.

Delbanco, Andrew. 2005. *Melville: His world and work.* New York: Knopf.

Emerson, Ralph Waldo. 2006 [1844/1847]. The poet. *The Heath anthology of American literature.* Boston: Houghton Mifflin.

Foster, Wendy. 2006. The apocalyptic body in contemporary literatures of transgression. Dissertation, University of British Columbia.

Freeman, John. 1926. *Herman Melville.* London and New York: Macmillan.

Harootunian, Harry. 2004. *The empire's new clothes.* Chicago: Prickly Paradigm,.

Hardt, Michael, and Antonio Negri. 2000. *Empire.* Cambridge, MA: Harvard University Press.

———. 2004. *Multitude.* New York: The Penguin Press.

Lutz, Tom. 1993. *American nervousness, 1903: An anecdotal history.* Ithaca, NY: Cornell University Press.

Mathews, Harry. 2005. *My life in CIA.* Normal, IL: Dalkey Archive Press.

McHale, Brian, and Randall Stevenson. 2007. *The Edinborough companion to twentieth-century literatures in English.* Edinborough: Edinborough University Press.

Melville, Herman. 1987 [1855–1856]. *Benito Cereno. The Harper American literature.* Volume 1, 1990–2043. New York: Harper & Row.

Michaels, Walter. 2004. *The shape of the signifier.* Princeton, NJ: Princeton University Press.

Pease, Aron 2005. Writing futures: Hardt and Negri's notation politics." http://www. electronicbookreview.com 12-18-2005.

Reeve, F. D. 2006. Croesus and crisis. *American Book Review* (September–October) 27:6:3, 15.

Taithe, Bertrand, and Tim Thornton. 1997. The language of history: Past and future in prophecy. In *Prophecy: The power of inspired language in history 1300–2000*, ed. Bertrand Taithe and Tim Thornton, 1–14. Gloucestershire: Sutton.

Tillman, Lynne. 2006. *American genius: A comedy*. Brooklyn, NY: Soft Skull Press.

Toqueville, Alexandar. 1840. *Democracy in America*. Vol. 2.

Wallerstein, Immanuel. 2004. *World-systems analysis: An introduction*. Durham, NC: Duke University Press.

White, Curtis. 1998. Writing the life postmodern. *Review of Contemporary Fiction* 16:1 (Summer): 112–21.

Wilson, W. S. 2005. Michael Hardt and Antonio Negri: Irreducible innovation. http://www.electronicbookreview.com 12-18-2005.

Chapter 7

Post-postmodern Discontent

Contemporary Fiction and the Social World

ROBERT L. MCLAUGHLIN

SETTING THE SCENE

Shelley's 1821 pronouncement, that "Poets are the unacknowledged legislators of the world" (Shelley 1974, 632), probably marks the high point of the literary artist's confidence in the ability of literature to engage with and have an impact on the social world. One can think of a few specific examples of such engagement and impact—Melville's *White-Jacket* (1850), influencing legislation banning flogging on U.S. navy ships, Stowe's *Uncle Tom's Cabin* (1852), crystallizing the debate over slavery, or Sinclair's *The Jungle* (1906), inspiring the creation of the Pure Food and Drug Act—but only a few. Otherwise, we tend to think of the social impact of literature as being more subtly epistemological and ontological: variously confirming or challenging our and our culture's values, raising consciousnesses, and occasionally transforming individual lives. If, however, one believes as I do—and, I think, as many fiction writers do—that art's social role is to question, challenge, and reimagine the ideological status quo, or, as Thomas Pynchon put it in a message of support to Salman Rushdie, "that power is as much our sworn enemy as unreason" (Words 1989, 29), then the kinds of influences (*impact* is probably too strong a word) literature can have in the social world can seem pretty vague and insubstantial. William Carlos Williams's famous lament, that T. S. Eliot's footnotes to *The Waste Land* had taken poetry out of "local conditions" and given it "back to the academics" (Williams 1951, 146), pointy-headed English professors in ivory towers, marks the opposite extreme to Shelley's confidence and represents, I

101

imagine, the anxiety of many authors: they desire their work to intervene in the social arena, but they fear that their work—and literature
in general—is increasingly irrelevant.

This fear seems to be well founded. Imagining a time past when
fiction, poetry, and drama were central to cultural life in the United
States may be false nostalgia; nevertheless, now, at the beginning of the
twenty-first century, they may never have been less central. The popular
public consciousness is concentrated on who is the latest "American Idol"
or on whom Donald Trump is firing on *The Apprentice* or whatever else
is going on on some of the other gazillion cable networks or on the latest
CDs and DVDs or on video games or on the infinite expanse of the
World Wide Web. Print media of any kind, much less literature that
aspires to serious intent, seems pretty dull in comparison. But, you might
object, what about the sheer numbers of books being published today
and the ease with which they can be purchased, thanks to the ubiquitous
Barnes & Noble and Borders superstores and Amazon.com and other
Internet stores? Surely that says something about the role of literature in
our culture. Well, yes, it does, but, to my mind, not much heartening. I
have argued elsewhere (see McLaughlin 1996) that U.S. commercial
publishers have always emphasized potential profit over artistic value in
the things they publish; nevertheless, in the days of the individual- or
family-owned publishing house, there was the possibility for eccentric
choices—that is, a decision to publish based on the publisher's or an
editor's affection and admiration for a book's artistic accomplishment or
for the prestige it might bring the firm, despite only a slim chance of
making money. There also was the possibility of eccentric publishers, like
Horace Liveright, who threw financial caution to the wind, publishing at
one time or another most of the major figures in American modernism.
But after the era of conglomeratization, now that the independent commercial publisher is almost extinct and what used to be publishing "houses"
are imprints of a very few huge multinational entertainment corporations, small, modestly performing cogs in the corporations' gears, the
chance for eccentricity, for anything of artistic merit to be published
without the possibility for profit, is slim indeed.

The era of conglomeratization has resulted in two interconnected
trends, both of which are bad news for serious literature. First, because
the many publishing imprints are owned by a small number of large
corporations and because these corporations stress profit over art, there
has been something of a homogenization of literature; the opening in
the cultural gateway has become smaller and smaller for the kinds of
books that are not easily accessible to a large audience of readers,

books such as poetry, drama, translations, or anything experimental. This is not to say that these kinds of books are not published, but that they have become more and more the charge of small noncommercial presses, nonprofit presses, and university presses, which can make them available but which lack the resources and the clout to make them compete for attention and impact in the cultural marketplace. The second trend is that as commercial publishers have come to think of the books they sell not as *books* but as *units*—products to be moved— they have concomitantly come to think of them as things to be *owned* but not as things to be *read.* Although many of us still like to think of the literary editor as a Maxwell Perkins wrestling a Thomas Wolfe manuscript into a masterpiece, more likely nowadays he or she is an MBA trying to cut the best deal on the latest potential blockbuster best seller, complete with audio rights, book club rights, and film rights— these are the areas where publishers make their profits, not in books per se. Practically every book from a major commercial publisher I read these days is rife with misspellings, typos, painful style lapses, incorrect "facts," and layout inconsistencies. Little care is put into editing the books, because there is little expectation that anyone will read them.

Granted, the foregoing is sweeping and probably overgeneralized, but it establishes the ideological and economic context for what many authors and readers are recognizing as an aesthetic sea change in literature, particularly fiction. Put simply, many of the fiction writers who have come on the scene since the late 1980s seem to be respond- ing to the perceived dead end of postmodernism, a dead end that has been reached because of postmodernism's detachment from the so- cial world and immersion in a world of nonreferential language, its tendency, as one writer once put it to me, to disappear up its own asshole. We can think of this aesthetic sea change, then, as being inspired by a desire to reconnect language to the social sphere or, to put it another way, to reenergize literature's social mission, its ability to intervene in the social world, to have an impact on actual people and the actual social institutions in which they live their lives. In the following I would like to look first at postmodernism as an aesthetic and a social phenomenon and next at the way the reaction against postmodernism has been articulated by two fiction writers, Jonathan Franzen and David Foster Wallace, who have overtly broken their fiction from their postmodern forebears to go in what they see as new directions. Wallace's work more than Franzen's offers us, I think, the opportunity to consider what we can call, for lack of a better term, post-postmodernism and its potential.

JOHN BARTH AND MISUNDERSTANDING
"THE LITERATURE OF EXHAUSTION"

In trying to assess exactly what post-postmodernism is reacting against, I think it is useful to return to John Barth's essay "The Literature of Exhaustion" (1967), which marked an earlier sea change, the transition from modernism to the next thing, and which can be regarded as a manifesto for the kind of literature that critics and scholars would soon be calling "postmodern." That this essay was misunderstood from the start is clear from the fact that in subsequent years Barth wrote two more essays, "The Literature of Replenishment" (1980) and "Post-modernism Revisited" (1988), seeking to clarify his ideas. Nevertheless, misunderstandings continue: in his study of David Foster Wallace, Marshall Boswell uses "The Literature of Exhaustion" to explain Wallace's rebellion against his "primary fictional father" (Boswell 2003, 9), a rebellion steeped in the desire to reconnect language and literature to the social world.

Boswell's take on the essay, which is not an unusual take, is that Barth cut the cord between the text and the world, smashed the mirror art traditionally held up to nature, and turned the referential function of literature in on itself. In Boswell's accounting,

> for Barth, the task of the *post*-modernist writer was not to develop additional new methods of rendering the act of perception but rather to examine the relationship between literary method and the reality it sought to depict. As he argued, the postmodern novel would employ literary conventions ironically, in the form of parody, thereby undertaking a self-reflexive inquiry into the ontological status of literary inquiry itself. (Boswell 2003, 12)

In other words, the process of representation, not the object represented, would be the subject matter of postmodernism. Boswell goes on, "... Barth's strategy follows Heidegger's existentialist critique of metaphysics, ungrounding certainties and producing in the reader both a sense of endless possibility and anxiety, since the text is now grounded in nothing beyond itself" (13). Boswell links Barth's position to poststructural language theory, especially Derrida: "In Barth's view, language always *replaces* the reality that it seeks to articulate. . . . To put it another way, language for Barth is inherently self-referential, which is to say it always refers back to itself rather than to the world" (26–27).

As I said, this is not an unusual take on Barth's essay and it can be a useful one, but in his rush to connect Barth with Derrida, Boswell misses some of the nuances of the essay. Early on, Barth divides contemporary artists into three categories: the technically old-fashioned artist; the technically up-to-date civilian; and the technically up-to-date artist. In the last category, he writes, "belong the few people whose artistic thinking is as hip as any French new-novelist's, but who manage nonetheless to speak eloquently and memorably to our still-human hearts and conditions, as the great artists have always done" (30). Shortly thereafter, he defines the artist of the first rank as one who "is the combination of that intellectually profound vision with the great human insight, poetic power, and consummate mastery of his means, a definition which would have gone without saying, I suppose, in any century but ours" (32). For all the essay's pooh-poohing of the old-fashioned, these are comments a new critic could embrace. Barth is certainly making problematic literature's referential relationship to the world, making the process of representation opaque rather than transparent—in fact, this is what I think he means by the old-fashioned artist: one who insists on the transparency of representation—but he is not severing the connection altogether.

In his two later essays Barth continues to insist on this connection. "The Literature of Replenishment" tries to clear up misreadings of his earlier essay and to connect its ideas to the scholarly work on postmodernism that sprang up between 1967 and 1980, but it also points toward the need for postmodern literature to find an audience, presumably as a way to intervene in the social world. Barth introduces this idea when he reminisces about the critical response to an early short story: "about my very first published fiction, a 1950 undergraduate effort printed in my university's quarterly magazine, a graduate-student critic wrote, 'Mr. Barth alters that modernist dictum, "the plain reader be damned": he removes the adjective' " (65). Later, while addressing the possible differences between modernism and postmodernism, he echoes Williams's complaint about *The Waste Land*: the problem with modernism's "relative difficulty of access" is that it has given rise to "a necessary priestly industry of explicators, annotators, allusion-chasers, to mediate between the text and the reader" (69). He goes on:

> If we need a guide, or a guidebook, to steer us through Homer or Aeschylus, it is because the world of the text is so distant from our own, as it presumably was not from

> Aeschylus's and Homer's original audiences. But with
> *Finnegans Wake* or Ezra Pound's *Cantos*, we need a guide
> because of the inherent and immediate difficulty of the text.
> We are told that Bertolt Brecht, out of socialist conviction,
> kept on his writing desk a toy donkey bearing the sign *Even
> I must understand it*; the high modernists might aptly have
> put on their desks a professor of literature doll bearing,
> unless its specialty happened to be the literature of high
> modernism, the sign *Not even I can understand it.* (69)

Barth fears for a literature that resonates only in English department classrooms and specialist scholarly journals: to have an impact in the world
beyond the campus quad, literature must reach the so-called common
reader. Barth comes to this conclusion about the postmodern author:

> Without lapsing into moral or artistic simplism, shoddy crafts-
> manship, Madison Avenue venality, or either false or real
> naïveté, he nevertheless aspires to a fiction more democratic
> in its appeal than such late-modernist marvels (by my
> definition and in my judgment) as Beckett's *Stories and Texts
> for Nothing* or Nabokov's *Pale Fire*. He may not hope to reach
> and move the devotees of James Michener and Irving
> Wallace—not to mention the lobotomized mass-media illit-
> erates. But he *should* hope to reach and delight, at least part
> of the time, beyond the circle of what Mann used to call the
> Early Christians: professional devotees of high art.
>   I feel this in particular for practitioners of the novel, a
> genre whose historical roots are famously and honorably in
> middle-class popular culture. (70)

Barth comes to the same conclusion (literally! He quotes himself!) in "Postmodernism Revisited," and here he offers a final
clarification of his initial ideas on self-referentiality. In an interestingly
postmodern twist he turns to Umberto Eco's explication of "The Literature of Exhaustion" for the clarification of his own idea. Quoting Eco,
he writes:

> The postmodern attitude [is] that of a man who loves a very
> sophisticated woman and knows he cannot say to her, "I love
> you madly," because he knows that she knows (and that she
> knows that he knows) that these words have already been
> written by Barbara Cartland. Still, there is a solution. He can

> say, "As Barbara Cartland would put it, I love you madly." At
> this point, having avoided false innocence, having said clearly
> that it is no longer possible to speak innocently, he will
> nevertheless have said what he wanted to say to the woman:
> that he loves her, but he loves her in an age of lost inno-
> cence. (Barth 1988, 22)

Barth sums up, "I like that, too: If for 'Barbara Cartland' we substitute
'the history of literature up to the day before yesterday,' it is the very
point of my essay 'The Literature of Exhaustion' " (22). Barth, then, is
suggesting neither a dead end for language and literature nor a severing of the referential relationship between language and literature and
the world. Rather, the used-upness he talks about is akin to the loss of
innocence of language or representation's loss of transparency. In the
postmodern era, language and literature make their own status as representation part of what they are about, but only part: the other part
is about our "still-human hearts and conditions."

Perhaps the best way to think about postmodern self-referentiality
is not as a denial of language and literature's connection to the world but
as their self-consciously pointing to themselves trying to point to the
world. Sure, we can all think of some examples of authors who have
severed the text-world connection, who submerge themselves completely
in the freeplay of language, who fit very well the description that Boswell
offers of Barth—Diane Williams might be mine—but I doubt if any of
these authors are among those we would consider among the most
significant or exemplary of postmodern authors. When I think of my
favorite postmodernists—Thomas Pynchon, William Gaddis, Robert
Coover, Don DeLillo, Ishmael Reed, Mary Caponegro, and, yes, John
Barth—it seems clear to me that, despite their wordplay, their awareness
of the conventions of narrative fiction, their anticipation of readers'
expectations, their blatant and subtle referencing of other texts, their
immersion into the luxury of language—in short, their continually breaking the fourth wall and refusing to let us suspend our disbelief—they
care deeply about the world. As an example, I offer Barth's most recent
book, *The Book of Ten Nights and a Night* (2004), in which some previously
uncollected stories from the 1960s and 1990s are brought together within
a frame that explores the value, if any, of art after September 11, 2001.
The problem, according to Barth's narrator, is "After Black Tuesday...
how to tell those or any such tales in a world so transformed overnight
by terror that they seem, at best, irrelevant" (5). Barth seems to be doing
more obviously here what he has always been doing: writing fiction about
fiction, but fiction that is placed in the social world.

FRANZEN, WALLACE, AND POST-POSTMODERNISM

So if we can agree that postmodernism, despite its wordplay for the
sake of wordplay, its skepticism toward narrative as a meaning-providing
structure, its making opaque the process of representation, nevertheless does not as a rule abjure literature's potential to intervene in the
social world, then why do we have a current sense of a sea change? Why
does it seem to us that younger writers—Rick Moody, Lydia Davis,
Bradford Morrow, Richard Powers, Cris Mazza, and A. M. Homes among
them—who are the heirs, one might think, of the postmodernists, are
doing something different, a something different that implies a critique of postmodernism? I turn to Jonathan Franzen and David Foster
Wallace for help with these questions, because they have been the most
articulate in expressing the post-postmodern discontent and in specu-
lating on directions for the future of fiction.

   Franzen lays out his ideas in his notorious 1996 *Harper's* article,
revised, softened, and retitled "Why Bother?" for his 2002 collection *How
to Be Alone,* and in another, angrier 1996 essay "I'll Be Doing More of the
Same," something of a dry run for the *Harper's* article, published in the
Review of Contemporary Fiction. He expresses despair over the novel's having lost its ability to bridge the personal and the social worlds and anger
at the two main causes for this loss. The first is the world of consumer
technology I described at the beginning of this chapter, particularly television. The myriad possibilities for technology-supplied pleasure leave
little time and little motivation for the comparatively more difficult work
of reading fiction. More than this, though, television, through its ubiq-
uity and ability to shape, structure, and interpret the world instantly for
its viewers, has in many ways usurped or short-circuited fiction's traditional purposes. Drawing on Flannery O'Connor, Franzen argues that
" 'mystery' (how human beings avoid or confront the meaning of existence) and 'manners' (the nuts and bolts of how human beings behave)
have always been primary concerns of fiction writers. What's frightening
for a novelist today is how the technological consumerism that rules our
world specifically aims to render both of these concerns moot" (2002,
68). Mystery has been replaced by the homogenous dream of consumer
technology; manners are irrelevant in a culture in which technology
makes more and more possible and desirable "an atomized privacy" (2002,
70). Franzen sees art as a response to a basic human emotion, "the Ache
of our not being, each of us, the center of the universe; of our desires
forever outnumbering our means of satisfying them" (ibid.). But consumer technology, superficially and illusorily, heals this Ache or, perhaps
better, represses it by making "each of us the center of our own universe

of choices and gratifications" (ibid.). This, then, is the crisis the novelist faces: "The novelist has more and more to say to readers who have less and less time to read: Where to find the energy to engage with a culture in crisis when the crisis consists in the impossibility of engaging with the culture?" (2002, 65).

The second reason the novel has lost the ability to bridge the personal and social worlds has to do, for Franzen, with academia. Like Williams and the Barth of "The Literature of Replenishment," he thinks that the absorption of the novel into the domain of English departments is bad for the novel and for the culture at large. As he bluntly puts it, "the single most tonic thing we writers could do for this country's literary life would be to publish half as many novels and teach twice as many literature courses, if only to displace an equivalent mass of theorists who have forgotten why novels get written and why people who aren't Ph.D. candidates might care to read them" (1996, 36). Ouch. What is wrong, exactly, with what these theorists are doing? Franzen explains, "The therapeutic optimism now raging in English literature departments insists that novels be sorted into two boxes: Symptoms of Disease (canonical work from the Dark Ages before 1950) and Medicine for a Happier and Healthier World (the work of women and of people from nonwhite or nonhetero cultures)" (2002, 78–79). (This is probably a good place to mention that, to me, Franzen's sense of what goes on in English departments, while not absolutely inaccurate, is exaggerated to the point of parody; that Franzen probably has not spent a lot of time in academia is further evidenced by the Chip Lambert-as-college-professor section in *The Corrections*.)

Two branches follow from this take on literature professors' sorting of novels and their implied uses. First, Franzen seems to think that the "Disease" has been overly simplistically diagnosed (the homogenization of culture and the deployment of power that has enforced it would seem to have less to do with the canon and lots more to do with contemporary consumer technology) and that finding a *cure* for the "Disease" is not necessarily the point of fiction (more on this later). Second, the comparatively recent emphasis on the literature of others beyond straight, white males, while indeed healthy in that it recognizes the diversity in our culture that the homogenous dream of consumer technology would seek to hide, can perhaps go too far toward the other extreme, Balkanizing our culture into separate, identity-based cultures. This tendency, combined with Franzen's other complaint about academia, the MFA program, which encourages insularity and homogeneity in style and subject matter, leads to a "retreat into the Self" (2002, 80). This retreat is both another manifestation of the upshot of consumer technology, atomized privacy, and an eschewing of the novel's traditional purpose of bridging the personal and the social.

Franzen's response to this crisis is twofold and essentially conservative. In "Why Bother?" he argues that the novel's social purpose, its ability to change the world, has been overemphasized. Indeed, despite his earlier complaints that TV has usurped the novel's role as social reporter, he concludes that the novel's value is not at all in its ability to represent or engage with a particular social moment. Rather, the novel's value is that it offers a way out of the loneliness engendered by the atomized privacy that results from contemporary consumer technology, but not by bridging the gap between ourselves and the social world. Instead, the novel reconnects us to fundamental human problems. Franzen uses Shirley Brice Heath's words: the novel gives us "a sense of having company in this great human enterprise" (2002, 83). This seems to be pretty much the same thing Barth meant by art addressing "our still-human hearts and conditions." The social function of the novel is both more personal and more essentialized than we usually think of it. Franzen argues:

> What emerges as the belief that unifies [novelists] is not that a novel can change anything but that it can *preserve* something. . . . Whether they think about it or not, novelists are preserving a tradition of precise, expressive language; a habit of looking past surfaces into interiors; maybe an understanding of private experience and public context as distinct but interpenetrating; maybe mystery, maybe manners. Above all, they are preserving a community of readers and writers, and the way in which members of this community recognize each other is that nothing in the world seems simple to them. (2002, 90)

We see what he means by fiction not offering us a cure for the difficulties of being human; rather, it reminds us of these difficulties and joins us to others who resist the "don't-worry-be-happy" siren song of consumer culture.

In "I'll Be Doing More of the Same," Franzen (1996) turns specifically to aesthetics and blames academia for the "growing critical infatuation with 'revolutionary' technologies and the 'subversive' side of pop culture" (36). He imagines that in the past the avant-garde's aesthetic experimentation "served a purifying purpose" (ibid.) for the literary mainstream. Now, however, the avant-garde, the experimenters, are the mainstream, the new literary establishment. With what result? "I see an academy (and foresee a national literature, produced by academics) lost in fantasies of transgression and subversion that are likely to confirm for young people, who have a keen sense of bullshit, the complete irrelevance of literature" (ibid.). I, for one, have trouble with this claim. Spending a lot of time in an English department and in bookstores and in reading popular book-reviewing fora, I do not see postmodern or, more generally, formally and stylistically innovative fiction dominating anywhere. It seems to me that most readers' expectations—inside and outside English department classrooms—are still mostly informed by the conventions of realism: linear plots, psychologically individuated characters, transparent representation. Regardless, Franzen concludes:

> The fact that critics and analytically minded fiction writers have lately discovered a "crisis" of form may not mean that printed fiction has exhausted itself, but simply that an era of (critically privileged) formal innovation is coming to an end, and that the time has come for form's dialectical counterparts, content and context, to return as the vectors of the new. . . . When the times get really, really awful, you retrench; you reexamine old content in new contexts; you try to preserve; you seem obsolete. . . . The day comes when the truly subversive literature is in some measure conservative. (1996, 38)

Clearly, though they are about the state of the culture, these essays are more about Franzen's coming to terms with himself as a writer of fiction in this culture; presumably, the ideas here influenced the writing of his 2001 bestseller, *The Corrections*. We might, then, expect an essentially conservative novel, eschewing postmodernisms, and in some ways it tries to be, but in others, perhaps unintentionally, it draws on the postmodern culture out of which it is written. The result, to my mind, is something of a mishmash. The central plot, focusing on the Lambert family, explores the despair produced by contemporary culture and possible responses to it, but it does so with familiar TV-movie-of-the-week-style narratives and characters, so familiar in fact that the epic-length claim on the reader's attention is hard to meet. The novel has an inconsistent attitude toward language, at times wanting to use it transparently, à la realism, at other times, drawing attention to it as language—whether in puns (the law firm of "Bragg Knuter & Speigh" [2001, 150]), in adopting extranovelistic discourse (the e-mail exchanges between Denise and Chip [431–36]), in parody (the "Corecktall Process" presentation [189–206]), or in breaking down the line between representation and the real (the story of Sylvia Roth, who reacts to her daughter's murder by drawing guns, and her husband, who reacts by choosing to create a world of language in which it never occurred [302–10]—I wish *this* had been the focus of the novel). The result is that the narrative voice continually shifts—and asks its readers to shift along with it—its attitude toward the social world it is representing and its attitude toward the process of representing that world. This could be interesting if one had the impression that it was being done intentionally, but here it seems the result of an author in flux, unsure of how he relates to the world and to his art form.

Wallace's take on writing fiction in the contemporary world is in many ways similar to Franzen's. Indeed, Wallace guest edited the issue of *Review of Contemporary Fiction* in which "I'll Be Doing More of the Same" appeared, and in a footnote to his introduction he wrote, "[Franzen] and I are friends, and sort of rivals, and we argue about all this stuff, and from the way I read his piece here it seems to me that I've won and convinced him I'm right" (1996b, 8). Like Franzen, Wallace sees television as both the biggest challenge to serious fiction's relevance in today's society and the cause of contemporary Americans' isolation and loneliness. Unlike Franzen, he does not write as if he is somehow above it all: "For younger writers, TV's as much a part of reality as Toyotas and gridlock. We literally cannot imagine life without it" (1997, 43).

In his most important critical essay, "E Unibus Pluram: Television and U.S. Fiction," which first appeared in the *Review of Contemporary Fiction* in 1993 and is reprinted in the essay collection *A Supposedly Fun Thing I'll Never Do Again*, Wallace imagines a complex symbiotic relationship between American fiction and television. He connects the rise of postmodern fiction to a reaction against the idealized version of America presented in 1950s' and 1960s' television shows, an America of loving families, social tolerance, justice, and unambiguous moral authority. Much of what made this fiction seem rebellious was its debunking of TV's myth of America through irony; that is, through insisting on the distinction between the myth presented on TV sets, the myth Americans presumably wanted to believe about themselves, and America as it really existed, an America of unthinking conformity, worship of money, institutionalized racism and sexism, and immoral foreign policy. As Wallace puts it,

> by offering young, overeducated fiction writers a comprehensive view of how hypocritically the U.S.A. saw itself circa 1960, early television helped legitimize absurdism and irony as not just literary devices but sensible responses to a ridicu-

lous world. For irony—exploiting gaps between what's said
and what's meant, between how things try to appear and
how they really are—is the time-honored way artists seek to
illuminate and explode hypocrisy. (1997, 65)

As postmodernism's main qualities, irony and self-referentiality,
percolated into the culture at large, however, they were claimed by
television and became its dominant mode of operation. Wallace writes,
"The fact is that for at least ten years now, television has been ingeniously absorbing, homogenizing, and representing the very same cynical postmodern aesthetic that was once the best alternative to the appeal
of Low, over-easy, mass-marketed narrative" (1997, 52). Thus TV has
become increasingly about TV and/or TV watching, and, in a reversal
of its earlier role as promulgator of American values, TV cynically mocks,
deflates, and debunks these values and their spokespeople: "the only
authority figures who retain any credibility on post-'80s shows . . . are
those upholders of values who can communicate some irony about
themselves, make fun of themselves before any merciless Group around
them can move in for the kill" (1997, 62). The epitome of all this for
Wallace is David Letterman, whose talk show is an elaborate parody of
talk-show conventions in which no guest and no idea escape the smirk
and eye-rolling of self-referential irony.
    One of the results of this dominant style in television is that "to
the extent that TV can ridicule old-fashioned conventions right off the
map, it can create an authority vacuum. And then guess what fills it.
The real authority on a world we now view as constructed and not
depicted becomes the medium that constructs our world-view" (1997,
62). The effect of this on the average TV viewer, the one whose loneliness and isolation are masked by the false communities TV offers, is
that she both adopts TV's worldview of weary cynicism to be part of the
TV "community" and avoids at all costs becoming the target of others'
cynicism: "the most frightening prospect, for the well-conditioned viewer,
becomes leaving oneself open to others' ridicule by betraying passé
expressions of value, emotion, or vulnerability. Other people become
judges; the crime is naïveté" (1997, 63). Thus techniques that were for
the early postmodernists the means of rebellion have become, through
their co-optation by television, "agents of a great despair and stasis"
(1997, 49). In a culture of irony and ridicule no assertion goes
unmocked, and if no assertion can be sincerely uttered and heard, then
nothing positive can be built. As Wallace puts it, "irony's singularly
unuseful when it comes to constructing anything to replace the hypoc-
risies it debunks" (1997, 67). The culture of irony and ridicule that

postmodernism has wrought, then, is essentially conservative, negating the possibility of change at the same time it despairs of the status quo.

So what does all this have to do with the contemporary fiction writer? Because the televisual culture has co-opted postmodernism's bag of tricks to deleterious effect, writers of fiction, especially those who see themselves as the heirs of postmodernism, need to find a way beyond self-referential irony to offer the possibility of construction. Wallace's conclusions, like Franzen's, seem conservative:

> The next real literary "rebels" in this country might well emerge as some weird bunch of *anti*-rebels, born oglers who dare somehow to back away from ironic watching, who have the childish gall actually to endorse and instantiate single-entendre principles. Who treat of plain old untrendy human troubles and emotions in U.S. life with reverence and conviction. Who eschew self-consciousness and hip fatigue. . . . The new rebels might be artists willing to risk the yawn, the rolled eyes, the cool smile, the nudged ribs, the parody of gifted ironists, the "Oh how *banal*." (1997, 81)

Wallace puts it another way—and reveals the difficulty of this conservative aesthetic—in his interview with Larry McCaffery: "You've got to discipline yourself to talk out of the part of you that loves the thing, loves what you're working on. Maybe that just plain loves. (I think we might need woodwinds for this part, LM.)" (McCaffery 1993, 148). The parenthetical aside is, of course, his preemptive ironic undercutting of his own sincere assertion and a signal, I think, that Wallace, unlike Franzen, is aware that neither America nor the fiction that seeks to represent it can return to a state of pre-postmodern innocence regarding language and the processes of representation. If the sea change in American fiction is an exhaustion of postmodern literature, a "used-upness" of self-referentiality's bag of tricks, then Wallace's response is not to retreat or retrench but, as Barth suggested in 1967, to write his way through it, or, as A. O. Scott (2000) puts it, "Wallace prefers to forge ahead in hopes of breaking through to the other side, whatever that may be."

We can see Wallace struggling to write through the postmodern dead end in much of his fiction, from the patricide of his postmodern forebears in "Westward the Course of Empire Takes Its Way" through filmmaker James Incandenza's struggle to "Make something so bloody compelling it would reverse thrust on a young self's fall into the womb of solipsism, anhedonia, death in life" (1996a, 839) in *Infinite Jest* to the many characters and narrators aching to make genuine personal connections amid the layers of language and language-based performance that make up our world in the stories of *Brief Interviews with Hideous Men*. One of these stories, "Octet," begins as a series of pop quizzes asking the reader how to handle certain narrative situations and ends as a plea from the desperate narrator for a way to be genuinely honest and truly connect with other people in a culture where language is hyperaware of itself as language and people are hyperaware of how they appear to each other and of what they risk in wanting " 'to be with' another person instead of just using that person somehow" (1999, 132). In another story, the last of the titular brief interviews, the hip, cynical, language-conscious narrator tells the interviewer about his encounter with a young woman, an apparent throwback, a "Granola Cruncher, or post-Hippie, New Ager" (245), who tells him the story of her abduction, rape, and near-murder by a serial sex offender. As she explains how she avoided being murdered by finding a way to spiritually connect with her attacker, to find the human being in him, the narrator's attitude toward her moves from contempt for her naïveté to an embarrassed admiration for her ability to meaningfully use "Terms like *love* and *soul* and *redeem* that I believed could be used only with quotation marks, exhausted clichés" (268) to loving her, the first time he has ever loved anyone.

CONCLUSION

So where does all this leave us in terms of the apparent sea change in contemporary fiction, post-postmodernism, and the role of literature in the social world? Self-referentiality by itself collaborates with the culture of consumer technology to create a society of style without substance, of language without meaning, of cynicism without belief, of virtual communities without human connection, of rebellion without change. However, as I argued earlier, postmodernism was never about self-referentiality by itself: postmodernism made the process of representation problematic; it foregrounded literature pointing to itself trying to point to the world, but it did not give up the attempt to point to the world. The sea change, I think, is a matter of emphasis. The emphasis among the younger writers I have talked about here, the post-postmodernists, is less on self-conscious wordplay and the violation of narrative conventions and more on representing the world we all more or less share. Yet in presenting that world, this new fiction nevertheless has to show that it is a world that we know through language and layers of representation; language, narrative, and the processes of representation are the only means we have to experience and know the world, ourselves, and our possibilities for being human. The better we understand them and how they operate, the better we can disengage them from the institutions that encourage the cynical despair that perpetuates the status quo and claim them for our own purposes.

Franzen and Wallace agree that literature has been and continues to be valuable as a way of critiquing our social world, finding ways to be human in it, and truly connecting with others. This is a good way to think about the agenda of post-postmodernism, but only if we understand that all of these things are mediated through language. This may seem obvious to readers, but the vast majority of Americans are not aware of the role language plays in constructing the roles they perform in this culture of despair. Post-postmodernism seeks not to reify the cynicism, the disconnect, the atomized privacy of our society nor to escape or mask it (as much art, serious and pop, does), but, by engaging the language-based nature of its operations, to make us newly aware of the reality that has been made for us and to remind us—because we live in a culture where we are encouraged to forget—that other realities are possible. That, it seems to me, is the social purpose the writers I have been calling "post-postmodern" have claimed for themselves. Will their work have a significant impact in the social arena à la Melville, Stowe, and Sinclair? Probably not, but most literature has not. We can hope that readers will discover this new fiction one by one or perhaps have it thrust upon them by some pointy-headed English professor and that they will let it speak to them and open their eyes and remake their world.

REFERENCES

Barth, John. 1967. The literature of exhaustion. *Atlantic Monthly* (August): 29–34.

———. 1980. The literature of replenishment. *Atlantic Monthly* (January): 65–71.

———. 1988. Postmodernism revisited. *Review of Contemporary Fiction* 8:3:16–24.

———. 2004. *The book of ten nights and a night.* Boston: Houghton Mifflin.

Boswell, Marshall. 2003. *Understanding David Foster Wallace.* Columbia: University of South Carolina Press.

Franzen, Jonathan. 1996. I'll be doing more of the same. *Review of Contemporary Fiction* 16:1:34–38.

———. 2001. *The corrections.* New York: Farrar, Straus and Giroux.

————. 2002. Why bother? In *How to be alone*, 55–97. New York: Farrar, Straus & Giroux.

McCaffery, Larry. 1993. An interview with David Foster Wallace. *Review of Contemporary Fiction* 13:2:127–50.

McLaughlin, Robert L. 1996. Oppositional aesthetics/oppositional ideologies: A brief cultural history of alternative publishing in the United States. *Critique* 37:3:171–86.

Scott, A. O. 2000. The panic of influence. *New York Review of Books* (February 10). http://www.nybooks.com/articles/232, accessed March 26, 2004.

Shelley, Percy Bysshe. 1974. A defense of poetry. In *The Norton anthology of English literature*, 3rd ed., vol. 2, ed. M. H. Abrams et al., 620–32. New York: Norton.

Wallace, David Foster. 1996a. *Infinite jest*. Boston: Little, Brown.

————. 1996b. Quo vadis—introduction. *Review of Contemporary Fiction* 16:1:7–8.

————. 1997. E unibus pluram: Television and U.S. fiction. In *A supposedly fun thing I'll never do again*, 21–82. Boston: Little, Brown.

————. 1999. *Brief interviews with hideous men*. Boston: Little, Brown.

Williams, William Carlos. 1951. *The autobiography of William Carlos Williams*. New York: Random House.

Words for Salman Rushdie. 1989. *New York Times Book Review* (March 12): 28–29.

Chapter 8

Toward the Edge of the Hermetic

Notes on Raising Fiction from the Dead

LIDIA YUKNAVITCH

ONE

Capitol thought, is matter moving through forms dead or alive?

—Kathy Acker

As always, I was awakened in the night by a dream. Somebody dead, a woman whom I admire, came.

In that liminal space between things, in the hours or pages spread out ahead of me, I saw that time had left her moorings and now spread laterally like a white web or the bones of an outstretched human hand. This was not a desperate image. Though mindless, it seemed to carry a precise logic, perhaps that of the body, or the imagination—the part of the mind that bypasses the mind.

Though the action was utterly unclear, I started out. I walked from the room which was my own to the city from different books. I used the image of the white web or bones of an outstretched human hand like a map. That city is formed like that; all streets, businesses, cultural movements, paths, human organisms, sewer shit and piss, politics, relationships and art, even rats radiate out from what is an unknowable center. Exactly like metastasizing cells.

There was something like a map, but there was no indication of a series of tasks to accomplish.

This map—this map was unlike what we mean when we say "map." When we ordinarily say "map," we mean something like "gimme directions," "how do I get there," "what is the route," "what steps do I follow and in what order." All of humans—the ones with education—know this. This is knowledge.

But this map was more like what it would mean if geography and the body were rejoined in a kiss. In that lipped spit hills would do their rising differently, and language, brought back to its free form, would again ocean the world. If I could traverse the distance of the bowl of textured and waxen lined skin of my belly from hipbone to hipbone with my outstretched fingers, if that crossing could be read not as a woman putting her hand to her flesh but reread as nomadic and wild with wind and sand and patterns of desert creatures, then that could be writing.

The words and voices and sounds of friends and colleagues and agents and editors came to me in great cacophonous waves. Echo effects of themselves. Nations of words. If you are not writing to reach the reader, this reader, an American reader, reader of all readers, reader of airport gift shops and grocery store lines, reader of Oprah book lists and *New York Times* lists and NPR interviews and Pulitzers and NEA's and Guggenheims and local specialness, reader of stuffing one's face at restaurants with meals costing more than the rents of the majority, reader of cruises and package vacations and world tours and five-star hotels, of appetizers and seven-course meals and different wines with different glasses for every bite, of gluttonous continued eating on to the desserts whose forms mimic the breasts and flesh swells of women or men in magazines, or reader of benevolent travel visiting indigenous cultures and listening to music without an idea in hell what the drumming means the sweat of the marimba or the body's undulations, eating some of the food but not all of the food and certainly not drinking the water and being sure to find toilets which are not holes in the ground, buying cloth and clothes and silver jewelry and hand-made stuff and woven thingees, reader of houses and cars and investments and retirements and pleasure, of educated classes, of pretty shoes and handbags, stylish glasses and leather furniture, pledger of allegiance to America reader, reader of snack food and junk food and sodas and fattish diets, reader of Weight Watchers and Slim Fasts and Jenny Craigs and Bow Flexes, reader of pill of the month prescription white coated haze-living, reader of super-model diet insider secrets and Hollywood couplings and severances and court cases, insuranced and clean reader, hair cut reader, reader with pets eating better than inner-city youths, television-eyed reader, mistake movie and news productions for reality reader, voting reader, 401K lane reader, reader with more than one bank account and retirement plans and investment opportunities and children in schools preparing readership, then who would you be writing to? And for what idiotic, self-indulgent purpose?

Though my mind, fed as it was with its messages, told me to go back and talk to the people in offices and restaurants, I jettisoned the chatter, believing instead that the body doesn't lie and might yet rise from its deadened existence. I set out.

TWO

Art becomes problematic precisely because reality has become non-problematic.

—Georg Lukács

The tasks had no order, nor did they "add up" to anything or create a "narrative." Unlike a "to-do" list, they free-floated across my mind, in and out of the gray folds of matter, or out before me like fireflies dissolving into distance and night. Glimpse. If I closed my eyes I saw them in retinal flashes and subconscious leaps. If I opened my eyes I saw the dull hum of what we see before us and the seductive objects of the world drawing us to them. Devouring senses away from a body and toward good citizenship. Consumerism. Level-headedness and excellent financial planning. So it was that I could not "set out" in the ordinary way. There were no origins, chapters, goals, telos, or mothers telling daughters how to become the thing that killed them.

My feet suddenly seemed extremely secretive and powerful, and I also realized how easily one can divert attention away from one's intentions through the eyes and face. In this way I was able to move closer to dirt and trees, to animals low to the ground, to sand, salt water, river flex, shorelines, and rocks. Other people saw what they saw, called me their "friend," acted out scripts or relationships, feigned reality. As much as it saddened me to admit it, I saw that representations of reality—movies, television, so-called art, talking heads, and moving lips—had overtaken reality, so far and wide that bodies were walking around and walking around and around and that's all bodies were. I sighed and tried really hard to listen to her.

When I was thirsty, I drank water. Probably it filled my mouth with toxins, but I did not become ill. When I was hungry I ate fish, and during the time when I put the meat into my mouth and for some time afterwards, I felt surges of water-life and sheen and quickening. I spoke to the fish with each bite; I let her enter my mouth and I came to her mouth and this was "eating." Some of the time I also ate berries and plants I recognized from books I bought and studied underneath the years of my education—books with glorious pictures, shiny pages, thick books with fake leather covers and the weight of a rabbit in your hands. Field guides, they are called.

One of the field guides turned me on. I had to touch my own skin and salt, I had to put my fingers between my legs and into the wet hot cunty mouth of myself and bring them again and again to my other mouth for sustenance or pleasure or violence. It made my tits hard and risen. My throbbing outbeat my heart by about a zillion years. It was like the drumming of the earth or its story tellers, and I almost forgot that my body and the ground beneath me were two different entities. Gushing and thick with sticky secretion I spread my legs as wide as they would go and opened my cunt to not anyone watching but the chaos of molecular and chemical fights that are reality, galaxies and highways of corpuscle, vein, or roads, circuitry and math. Pretty much music happened, generated from those crossings. I could tell, because the wind in the trees and the sound of my ass grinding into dirt and rocks and my blood thudding in my ears and my cunt throb and the distant sound of cars in the asphalt loops and the ringing of stars making their path from dark to light—living to dead—all made a similar pitch and thus a composition. I wished I had a pen but couldn't think where it was, because of course the missing element was words.

THREE

The Popular Novel that the public call healthy is always a thoroughly unhealthy production; and what the public call an unhealthy novel is always a beautiful and healthy work of art.

—Oscar Wilde

I felt an old rage running through me. I thought, hey, it isn't true what they've told us. You don't need anything to happen or depend on a conflict for a story to rise. You don't need a central character with motivations—you just need a body. A kind of Whitmanesque body, or a Rimbaudian one, an Ackerite or a Wildean or a Durasian or a Steinian or an Artaudian one. One of those. Then you can just let it . . . happen. I thought god damn it to motherfucking hell. I thought up a little ministory just for spite—I mean I became my writer me in a moment of rage and danger and in my head the novel I am currently writing ruptured up. The story is about a woman who suddenly refuses fake integration in favor of subversion, amnesia, passion, crime, promiscuity, suicide, and just plain silence. It goes like this:

This is the story of a woman so haunted by a random single photographic image that her entire life derails. Her hopes were lateral and plain. Her troubles were within the bounds of narrative. Forty years old, enough age to see that life is a story, the plots and characters already known, the crises and climaxes already written, the choices and outcomes there before you. Go ahead, believe in a god. Or don't. Transgress. Or be run-of-the-mill. Buddhist or Atheist or Christian or Immoral. Then at 4pm accidentally she has the liberal news media on the TV and there it is. A televised image caught to full stop, arrested into photo, a still shot of a blonde child at the moment her entire family is blown to bits.

She is not screaming.

Her close friend, the photographer, a woman, an artist at the top of her trade, an award-wining photo journalist, has captured the image of a child at the instant her entire family, identity, country, origin, place in time and space (you see here how all of this matters, the woman is a novelist, and so these ingredients matter, they are matter themselves, they will, as you have no doubt surmised, become the material for what must be, between the chaos of material that is an artist's brain, to the unquenchable desire that is the reader's hunger, eventually, an "instigating event" must present itself) has been obliterated. She is so moved by the photo for an instant she thinks this is the end of history.

This is not the end of history. It isn't, because in her lifetime she's seen the end of big wars or marriages or careers or dead infants, friends, lovers, fathers, mothers, innocent bystanders, tragic human dramas and the emergence of smaller ones, perhaps they are not even "wars" or "dramas" but we call them that. Perhaps they are ordinary people inside ordinary relationships fighting their way forward, the terrain of family and domesticity shell shocked by affairs and depressions, the landscapes of conflict and geopolitical movements given television production titles and graphics. Little sagas inside grand narratives, grand narratives revealed as a series of comic loops. Or let's focus—let's say there are countries, politics, geographies, ideals. Let's say love and life and all the scripts associated with being mean something. Let's say history holds now and again. One man or one woman touching another man or woman proves endlessly that history never was, or is, or anything between people. This is not history, neither the private life and love of one woman, nor the movement of nations, resistances, fires.

This is photography, narrative, art.

What happens is this: the woman novelist stops writing, eating, talking . . . the woman enters into a cataclysmic silence no one can talk her out of.

In other words, my writer self began to loop into her selves until the character self in my novel, plus the writer self looking in toward her, and the self writing this text all became indistinguishable from the words. I thought, this will confuse readers. They will lose their place.

FOUR

The time is now. Is it. The time. Now is it is.

—Gertrude Stein

I stopped.

I thought, this map has taken you to an otherwhere, not a some-where. I thought, you do not need to "go" or "arrive" either as a self or a character necessarily.

Now I understood that my actions had not followed an hourly pattern spliced by minutes. They had moved organically in rhythms and patterns like blood, corpuscles, breathing, or digestion. Or even matter in space or amniotic fluid. I understood—after the fact—since I had moved intuitively—that I had moved in bursts and ruptures, in sounds and motions sometimes more infinitesimally small than atoms, in the spaces between things, or in and out of motions like a train-hopper or a parasite—so that my journey had no origin or purpose or end.

This was a disturbing idea, of course, not so much to me but to others; I knew not to tell anyone, even though I wanted to. It was very painful not to tell.

I understood this had not only been a solitary journey but one without movement, plot, or payoff—there would be no proof of any-thing. No product. Nothing to give over from my outstretched hands to the masses or an agent—though if I could talk anyone into it, the smell at the tips of my fingers would be warm and sweet like skin and sweat and sand and exchanges with fish. I understood there would be no transcendence or applause, and that no one would remember my name or fill a room to hear me. I became fully cognizant of the cost—this moneyless motion. This undirected mistake. I thought maybe this was the worst of it, the horror of not making money for my efforts.

And yet inside that horror I discovered much larger truths, for instance, truths about being in my body and in the world and time and space and language and desire. I mean I fucking love it inside here. Wherever it is. I felt drifty like when you are stoned or altered. I thought a classic stoner or more seriously, a peyote thought, I thought, here's the real pisser . . . I thought, you don't need time. I mean, you don't need time in intervals, you need the body inside interval itself. That sensory perception. That.

This made me feel briefly like an untethered astronaut, then like a woman without a house, family, mother, father, husband, lover, or nation, then like a burning corpse, and finally like a body, which seemed sort of shamanic to me, which could be solely due to the fact that I'd been seeing a Jungian therapist for several years and my dead mother's gene pool carried American Indian material and my dead father's gene pool carried Eastern European material; at any rate, I became as free floating as a word or an image let loose from its meaning-making. I liked it enough to consider staying.

FIVE

All writing is pigshit . . . the whole literary scene is a pigpen, especially this one. All those who have vantage points in their spirit, I mean, on some side or other of their heads and in a few strictly localized brain areas; all those who are masters of their language; all those for whom words have a meaning; all those for whom there exist sublimities in the soul and currents of thought; all those who are the spirit of the times, and have named these currents of thought—and I am thinking of their precise works, of that automatic grinding that delivers their spirit to the winds—are pigs.

—Antonin Artaud

When I opened my eyes for a time I felt sort of pissy and rude. I thought, well fuck, if you don't need money, applause or time, then you for god damn sure don't need to feed the reader anymore. The reader is a big fat stuffed pig. They could probably live off of their own fat for quite some time should the feed slow or stop. They seem quite busy and contented consuming or mindlessly entertaining or numbing themselves. It's a lot of work, complacency. Earning enough profit to buy things and own them. Motherfuckers. Perhaps the relationship between us is finished for good. But my pissiness gave way to a heartthrob . . . I thought about how painful leaving a relationship is— like killing a part of yourself in order to save yourself.

SIX

Since the basis of my work is the very relationship between words and pictures, between the visible and the expressible, I am not bound to the forms ordinarily available to a novelist or a filmmaker. I am in that liminal space most closely related to desire and the unconscious. It is here, at this edge, desire and death reassert creative possibility away from society's death grip.

—Marguerite Duras

First I felt a panic. Because the last relationship I surgically re-moved myself from nearly killed me, and I've been in therapy for *years* in order to stay alive. I mean it hurts. Bad.

But being inside the text somehow lurched me out of that logic, and suddenly I became overcome with violent shivering and weeping.

Then I realized, it's just your body's coming through death.

It's just like when your daughter died.

It's just like divorce.

It's just like your brother dying.

It's just like your cancer scare, surgically removed until the next time.

It's just like finding your second husband with his cock deep inside another woman. Another woman. Another woman.

It's just like your lifelong friend describing being raped.

It's just like your other lifelong friend telling you it's AIDS.

It's just like the car wreck or overdose or disease or blast or murder or drowning or suicide or random accident.

It's just like a cluster bomb atomizing a family.

For real though, it's just like not when your mother died but when a woman writer much more meaningful to you did, and you felt your desired and imagined—violently—as violently as a child's—origins slip into the cleft of night. You looked hard for stars and remembered how bright the light of dead things can be. It made you hopeful. An image came and arrested inside you of a woman whose body is never "caught" by plot. Characterless void. A woman as white as dead stars, or like a white web or the bones of an outstretched human hand. A woman held by a blackness as black as a typed word, or space, or night, or nothingness. The physics and erotics of one woman's story.

It is coming to this. I have nothing to say if saying something means filling her mouth with nonsense. I may be a very underpublished girl. Is this the risk then?

Chapter 9

The Self-Deceiving Muse

Fiction and the Rationalistic Dictates of the Present

Alan Singer

ONE

The presentness of character in fictional narrative figures an inherently conflicted temporality. No one would dispute that plot conflict epitomizes tensions between moments in time as much as conflicts between persons. But our way of construing the thematic sense of narrative fictions, by putting an emphasis on the conflict of personalities, privileges the already formed dispositions of character. It transcends the disruptiveness of temporal immediacy, of *being present in the present*. A focus upon plot conflict inclines us to ignore the relative inchoateness of character in time. It inveigles us to lose sight of the possibility that character is too easily taken for granted as a repository of experience rather than a threshold of experience. Particularly from the vantage point of the novel of the present—since 1945—character is an increasingly vexed proposition. The present moment prompts us to consider how the novel has long harbored a notion of character that resists characterization insofar as it is responsive to the circumstance of presentness.

My purpose in reconsidering how the present bears on fictional narrative is to revise our notion of character in fiction and indicate its usefulness for modeling and remodeling human selves. By focusing on presentness as the salient quality of character, I wish to countenance a version of character that will appear to be paradoxical: a self that is inherently self-deceiving. Contrary to popular assumptions about self-deception, I will suggest that the condition of self-deception is both normative and imperative in fiction's aptitude for illuminating the meaningfulness of selves. I will propose that only from such a self-deceiving self can the ethical stakes of fiction be honestly derived.

The link between the presentness of character and its self-deceiving ethos is the ongoingness of temporality. Temporal change is the most immediate threat to ego identity. We are never more conscious of the frailty or instability of our ego ideals than in the midst of circumstances whose outcome we cannot predict. There is little disputing that a self-deceiver is motivated to hold a belief that promises to realize an idealized self: one that can sustain a self's beliefs through the vicissitudes of action. This bid for coherence between beliefs and lived experience, however, founders upon the simultaneous knowledge that the beliefs one is motivated to hold are often at odds with the facts. What is more, facts are quite often intractable to human will. The mind of a self-deceiver is thus torn between evidence that the world is one way and a desire that it be another way. The line that divides these visions of reality shifts as a variable of time that constantly threatens to divide character against itself.

An important threshold for recognizing a self-deceiving character is this assumption: a self-deceiver can know that what he or she believes is false, contrary to the facts. Self-deception thus presents us with an insuperable irrationality that makes the interpretation of character a seemingly impossible proposition. And yet the circumstance of a character seeming to believe what is false and acting accordingly, seeming to hold two contradictory beliefs, remains a fervent source of dramatic interest for us both in life and in fiction. Literary characters who exhibit symptoms of self-deception also give a defining contour to the history of the novel. Self-deceivers are so pervasive in the canonical texts of narrative fiction that the genre looks to be formally inextricable from the terms of their predicament: Don Quixote, Tristram Shandy, Emma Bovary, Stephen Dedalus, Conrad's Marlow, Ford's Dowell, Nabokov's Humbert Humbert, and so on. In one way or another all of these protagonists act at odds with what they know. They are self-deceivers in the sense that they seem to hold beliefs about their own motivations and acts that contradict their own accounts of motive and act. Thus, we are bound to conclude that self-deception—the epitome of irrationality—rationalizes the longevity of the genre as a métier of human self-understanding. In this susceptibility to paradox, the genre of the novel is painfully implicated in the predicament of its most exemplary and often its most tragically fated characters: their self-understanding awaits a plot resolution that entails a more capacious rationality than what is already compassed within their narrative universes.

While the paradox that seems to afflict the novel appears to deepen over the course of its history, philosophical debates about the status of self-deception vis-à-vis rationality have tended to underplay the paradox. Philosophers have achieved this result by putting argument on a path of inquiry that intersects with the novel's signature temporality. Certainly philosophical literalists have asserted that because self-deceivers believe and disbelieve a proposition *at the same time,* inquiry founders upon the "irreducibly paradoxical" nature of self-deception, proving further inquiry to be rationally "impossible."[1] But a recent turn in philosophical thinking has sought to obviate the preemptive characterization of the self-deceiver as merely irrational. In this new context of discussion carried on by Kent Bach, Alfred Mele, Robert Audi, Amélie Rorty, and others, rationalization is deemed an emphatically temporal phenomenon, for temporality entails a comprehension of how motivational biases of belief are fostered by changing circumstances of reflection.

Contemporary philosophical accounts encourage us to construe self-deception as a condition of presentness in the following sense: one's reasons for holding any particular belief in the present entail one's knowledge that such a self is beholden to another context of knowledge of which it is presently unaware. If one had different reasons, then one would possess a different criteria of salience for picking out elements of context in which one's beliefs seemed to be warranted. When we posit self-deception, we typically imagine that others would see things differently than the self-deceiver because they work within more relevant parameters of knowledge.[2] This is a presumption that a self-deceiver does not have all the relevant evidence by which to judge the advisability of the belief he holds and that the only way for him to be undeceived would be to vacate his irrational self. This is the virtually suicidal gesture of making the present collapse tragically into the past, a stance epitomized in Othello's words of contrition for the self-deceived murder of Desdemona, punctuated as it is by a self-dealt death blow: ". . . in Aleppo once/Where a malignant and a turban'd Turk/Beat a Venitian and traduc'd the state, I took by the throat the circumcised dog/And smote him . . . thus" (Shakespeare 5.2, 352–55). The power of Othello's words is their perfect coincidence with action, past with present. Can it be that the price of recognition of self-deception is so inexorably self-annihilation? More to the point, must it be the case that self-deception is mortally indebted to the past?

Our judging self-deception as a necessary sacrificing of the present to the past produces a somewhat irrational assumption that the only viable selves are rational with respect to a single evidentiary context for belief. In other words, a standard notion of self-deception cultivates a rather inflexible model of the rational self, one that I would like to suggest is irrational with respect to real pressures of our normal experience in time. The question of how one gains access to evidence that the self-deceiver is blind to cannot be answered in a way that squares with real temporality if we treat self-deception as a static condition. If we deny the presentness of the self by consigning it to a framework of judgment in which belief is an artifact of past experience, a self ensconced in a fixed repertoire of motives for belief, then self-deception is effectively a form of self-cancellation.

To the contrary, I suggest that self-deception should be viewed as an arena in which we can assess the unrealistic expectations imposed upon the self by its assimilation of inappropriate norms of rationality. By extension, I want to say that the novel, in which self-deception figures so formatively, can be seen as most vital in its ways of dramatizing how we might best exploit this arena. The novel's predisposition to represent eventful successiveness favors a character born of changing circumstances of self-recognition. In a philosophical account that buttresses this view, Kent Bach (1998) observes that self-deception needs to be understood in relation to an economy of attention. Bach makes clear to us that what we know is emphatically a function of our attentiveness and its volatile contingencies. The mind is, de facto, partitioned by virtue of its attention span, or by frames of reference that induce belief according to the limitedness of the scope of attentiveness they instantiate.

What is more to the point, Bach sees the paradoxical infinite regress to which we would be doomed if we had to posit an agency to take responsibility for the partitioning. Instead, he has recourse to an account of the attentional shifts of consciousness that can induce self-deception or govern an awareness of it that is fundamentally narrative. Bach asserts the essentially diachronic nature of rationality. Apparent paradoxes in self-deception are thus seen to arise from "some sort of gap between what one is at a moment and what one is over time" (1998, 187). If that gap is not taken into account, he implies, then a single moment in time privileges criteria by which one judges rational fit between act and world. The rationality Bach endorses, in contrast, like the genre of the novel itself, entails the necessity to transcend current moments in order to make salient evidentiary criteria—for belief in a particular course of action—that would not otherwise be apparent. As Bach says, rationality must be put "on a diachronic basis" (ibid.), in the sense that one's actions are seen to change the context in which judgment of their rationality applies. Bach desires to keep faith with the conviction that "if mental action, like directing one's attention, is included along with physical action, we *are* continuously faced with the problem of what to do next" (185, emphasis in original). This is the urgency of presentness per se.

On this basis, Bach can characterize a self-deceiver as a motivated and purposeful, but not intentional agent in his blindness toward a truth that, assuming other evidence precluded by his particular motive and purpose, would be apparent (1998, 165). A self-deceiver is able to act in a way that is blind to the "truth," because his view of the relevant evidence is prejudiced by motives and purposes whose validity entails a more relevant "truth" for him. Most commonly this would be his desire to see himself a certain way, to sustain an ego ideal, which any other "truth" would compromise. Hence, the man who wishes to see himself as not a cuckold will gather evidence from his observations of his wife's behavior quite selectively. Since Bach accepts that our attention is always inadequate to a range of relevant evidence available it makes less sense to stigmatize a self-deceiver's behavior as irrational than to grant the rationalistic dynamics by which evidence becomes accessible to an agent. Bach focuses therefore on actions whose truthfulness is not pegged to parity with the information one has intentionally. It is rather pegged to the lack of parity between the information inhering in the intention and the information made accessible through action. This privileges a presentness of mind that I am again bound to identify with the form of narrative fiction. After all, narratives starkly dramatize the question what to do next by their relentless successiveness. Without this plot momentum, character would cease to be a crucible of rationalization. Similarly for Bach, the meaning of an action is not determined by the intentions that led up to it but by the changes in construing relevant intentions that the act occasions in its sheer successiveness. Rationality in this context of self-deception is coordinate with the relative accessibility of evidence according to which the agent's intentionality would be ratified in his action. We can thus entertain the view that the disparity between information embodied in intention and the information embodied in action denotes an incommensurability not an unintelligibility.

In this respect Bach's position is coherent with Robert Audi's and Alfred Mele's idea that self-deception leads to rationalization and rationalization leads to self-deception. Rationalization in this case is understood "as a matter of appropriately responding to the reasons one has when one is suitably aware of them, and of some broadly instrumental relation they bear to something one wants" (Audi 1997, 146). Wherever ego needs underlie rationalization the occasion is favorable for self-deception. Whenever a self-deceiving intuition occurs it induces rationalizations that enhance its plausibility. I have already established how the psychological terrain of such experience is contiguous with narrative form, but it furthermore points up a threshold of value-making in fiction that is overlooked in the literary critic's emphasis on self-deceiving character as merely a flaw of reason. As I proceed to elaborate the ways in which self-deception deepens our appreciation of the project of rationality, I will be setting the stage for less obvious claims about the pressures fiction can bring to bear formally upon a self, unbeknownst to itself as a self-deceiver, particularly when working under an assumption that self-deception is non-normative. I will show that these formal pressures structure the very pragmatics of reading through which humanist claims for fiction encourage us to seek ourselves in literary experience in the first place. The pursuit of self-knowledge remains the most durable of motives for valuing art, but the self that is privileged in this idealism may be the most self-deceived of all.

We must first understand what the rationalizing needs of self-deceivers presuppose about the self in general. As Bach has already reminded us, such needs are largely defensive, born of desires that are menaced by an unrequiting world. In this context "desire" is not a strictly emotive state however. Alfred Mele stipulates "desires contribute to the production of motivationally biased beliefs" (2001, 24). Typically, as Audi theorizes it, a person is in self-deception with respect to a proposition p if and only if: (1) unconsciously he knows that not-p; (2) he avows that-p; and (3) he has at least one desire that explains why his belief that not-p is unconscious and why he persists in his avowal that-p. The challenge is to explain how the self-deceiver is disposed to avow that p even when presented with what he sees as evidence against p (1997, 132). Audi here figures a notion of character that is quite complementary to novelistic representation. Hypothesis testing is the métier of novelistic characters. They are marked as bearers of motivational biases that in the course of plot complication are skewed from contexts of rationalization but at the same time susceptible to the revisionary force of adverse circumstance. The difference between a literary character, qua self-deceiver, and the characterization of self-deception as Audi schematizes it, is this: a character who avows p knowing that not-p is not necessarily a character who feels bound to abdicate agency. Othello's suicide aside, in ordinary circumstances costs of erroneous decision making perpetually hang in the balance for those who persist in self-deceiving ways.

Accordingly we could say Audi shows us how to think of a self-deceiver as a self-enhancing agency, or an agency-enhancing self. For this reason the notion of self-deception I am adopting here is linked to an abandonment of three commonplace assumptions: (1) that self-deception is an analogue of deceiving others; (2) that self-deception presupposes an ideal self to be betrayed; and (3) that self-deception is antithetical to truthfulness. All of these assumptions decouple the act of self-deceiving mind from its ongoing activities. Indeed, Audi does not discredit the rationality of a reason upon which one acts, even if it is itself dependent on a self-deceived belief (1997, 151). What redeems the rationality of such decision making is its contributing to a reduction of cognitive dissonance. One acts "to achieve greater harmony among one's beliefs and attitudes" (ibid.). The imperative assumed here to reduce dissonance, to serve a self-protective need of a hypothesis tester, is clearly a form of narrative implicature.

Narratively speaking, it has typically been assumed that self-deception figures a character's loss of perspective, an implicit loss of self. Plato, in the *Phaedo*, characterizes the soul's imprisonment in the desires of the body as a skewed and preemptive line of sight, blinding us to preferable unrelativistic truth. The soul is "bewitched," it collaborates with its own "imprisonment" within an unshakable and ungovernable viewpoint. But in the context of the present it might be apt to say that self-deception is a modus operandi for a character's acquiring new lines of perspective. It fosters an increasingly complex articulation of perspective out of an awareness of one's misperception of the adequacy of any original perspective.

David Sanford (1988) formulates this version of self-deception as the "contention that . . . being self-deceived consists in one's misapprehending the structure of one's attitudes, in one's taking the having of one attitude to explain the having of another when the true explanation is something else" (169). Sanford adduces the example of a father who wishes to maintain his belief that his son has not resorted to thievery of the father's valuable stamp collection.

In Sanford's nomenclature the dispositive beliefs here are "anticipating" and "ostensible" (159). The father anticipates the inevitability of concluding his son's guilt if he countenances the evidence. Belief in the inadequacy of the evidence is hence an ostensible reason for discounting it. The terms *anticipating* and *ostensible* beliefs refer to states of mind that hinge upon perspective shifts. Anticipating and ostensible beliefs inevitably force a reckoning with the fact that "one's ostensible reason always functions differently from the way one takes it to function" (156). They assume a human propensity to take a desire for one thing to be a desire for another. They assume that whatever attitudes we hold are in turn held hostage to our ability to anticipate how they will survive our need to justify them under changing conditions of action. The reversal of the "direction of dependence" between reasons and beliefs is itself evidence of ways in which the structure of one's attitudes follows the form of one's desires amidst a world of frustrating circumstance. This is understood in much the manner of Sanford's troubled "father." Anticipating the reason he would have for abandoning his belief in his son's innocence, the father adopts a belief that preempts any damaging suspicion. His self-deceiving rationalization in this case depends upon his not knowing what he has done. And yet I would argue that our very awareness of the reversibility of the relation between reasons and beliefs portends the possibility of knowing that one does not know something. And this is the strongest incentive for our thinking about self-deception as not simply predicated on making invidious judgments about human character.

An attunement to reversals of perspective that is crucial to Sanford's account of the rationality of self-deception takes us back to the narrative implicature of self-deceiving mind and to the condition of presentness without which such reversals are inconceivable. Sanford prompts us to see a resemblance between "misapprehending of the structure of one's attitudes" and reversals of narrative plot insofar as both occasion a testing of the stakes of one's knowledge (169). Both dramatize the urgency of the question what to do next by emphasizing the reversibility/ revisability of the present moment. One is never more present to oneself than in the circumstance of knowing that there is something one does not know. The self-deceiver knows this more than the man of unproblematic self-knowledge by virtue of his being tethered—albeit unconsciously—to a context other than the one he acknowledges as the operative motivational bias of his belief. His misapprehension of the structure of his attitudes is implicitly "apprehensive" or "anticipatory" with respect to another motivational context threatening to be made present in an ensuing moment of time. It could be said, therefore, that the presentness of the self-deceiver is more alive to the past and the future than the subject of nostalgic retrospection or hopeful fantasy could possibly be.

This is to say that self-deception attunes us to complexities of presentness that we might otherwise rationalize or narrate away in an unself-conscious enlistment to the most confident Enlightenment fables of self-understanding. The prevalence of the theme of self-deception in the history of the novel may even be the source of the novel's energies with respect to an Enlightenment subject that conferred formal integrity on the genre in the first place.

Herbert Fingarette (2000, 64), in a classic text on self-deception, proceeds from the premise that we only really understand self-deception when we deemphasize the relation of consciousness to knowledge and emphasize its relation to action. This proposition has its basis in a decidedly non-Enlightenment idea of character. Fingarette thinks of character not in terms of the inviolable intentionality of the autonomous Enlightenment subject but in terms of self-avowals that a subject can make within changing circumstances of time and place. Fingarette's hypothesis is built upon a premise that human identity is bounded by the framework of avowal, an act of identification. But the subject is formed out of what he calls an identification "as." The force of "as" here relates the identificatory subject to any number of possible contexts of self-avowal, in stark contrast to what Fingarette dubs an identification "with." Identification "with" denotes a nature that is only exemplified rather than instantiated in its actions. One "identifies with" what is already decided. Thus, Fingarette does not presuppose an "already well formed self" (70).

It would be fair to premise that in narrative "identity as" is virtually epiphenomenal of plot reversal, as long as we do not use that premise as a springboard for leaping to the postulate of a self that is indeterminately in flux, a perpetually self-reinventing persona. This would likely lead to madness or mere lying. Rather, reversal figures a self that is constrained to choose terms of self-recognition in relation to a range of successive perspectives within which he or she might find a better purpose for himself or herself. In other words, counters of reversibility suggest that "identity as" might be a formal feature of the novel that most predisposes the genre to the theme of self-deception. It intimates how self-deception, with respect to the artifice of character, is potentially "remedied" by the structural form of the novel because of the special attunement to presentness that the novel's complicity with self-deception entails. I am alleging, in effect, that the theme of self-deception has a beneficent corollary in the cognitive qualities of the reading experience, which the formal devices of the novel command.

TWO

Now I want to examine the exemplarity of these formal devices with respect to a novel that is almost totemic for the theme of self-deception. Flaubert's *Madame Bovary* (1965) is, at the same time, a watershed for a historical view of the novel that sees in its formal particularity a discipline of cognitive attentiveness. Flaubert's credo, that "ideas are actions," expressed in correspondence with Louise Colet,[3] captures a vital concern for this author and anyone who knows susceptibility to self-deception: Flaubert fears that cognitive responsibilities governing our attentiveness to the world and concomitantly the authenticity of our standing within the world are in constant jeopardy from our most lax habits of mind. Such after all is the ethical tension that, by the most conventional accounts, charges the scene of self-deceiving mind. The classic self-deceiver, asserting belief in what she knows to be counter to the facts of her experience, is abdicating cognitive vigilance that would hold her accountable to herself. Emma Bovary is, culturally speaking, iconic of this cognitive abdication. Nevertheless I have to point out how Flaubert's aesthetic practice requires going beyond a simple analogy between irony and self-deception if we are to appreciate how his self-deceiving characters tell us something important about the ethical work of the novel.

Flaubert dramatizes the "ethical tension" discussed earlier—and which strikes me as the *sine qua non* of narrative emplotment—in two ways. At the level of characterization we are insistently reminded that Rodolphe and Emma are striving to see themselves in one another's eyes. They are indeed looking to see before either one of them can be objectively seen, that is, seen without a self-deceiving screen of imagining how they might be seen at their best. But neither wants to see the spectacle of his or her own hypocrisy. In other words, anticipating and ostensible beliefs come into play. Each wishes to be seen as an object of romantic desire; each anticipates evidence of reciprocity; each countenances ostensible evidence that they are above the lustful intent that their anticipation embodies, which their decorous speech belies. But this decorous speech serves as an ostensible reason for their believing in romantic consummation.

Next I want to emphasize how Flaubert's reader is implicated in the same formal dynamic as his characters, but with a difference. My proposal here will be that some remedy for the problems of self-deception is proffered in the formal devices of this particular novel: by Flaubert's maximizing the reversibility of the direction of dependency of reasons and beliefs that obtains between character and reader. Flaubert's text plays upon this reversibility in a way that invites our broadening the scope of rationality to include self-deception. Rationality in this regard begins to focus the challenge of our attentiveness to what we do not know as a productive self-discipline.

As Amélie Rorty (1988) proposes in an essay that lends some unexpected dignity to a deceptive self, the self-deceiver is caught sustaining two pictures of reality in a relation of superimposition to one another. Rorty observes that "only a presumptively integrated person who interprets her system-of-relatively-independent-subsystems through the first *picture of the self*, only a person who treats the independence of her constituent subsystems as failures of integration, is capable of self-deception. Not everyone has the special talents and capacities for self-deception. It is a disease only the presumptively strong minded can suffer" (25, emphasis in original). Rorty seems to think that what motivates the self-deceiver—in the urgency and earnestness of her compulsion to integrate—invites a degree of self-consciousness that would be unthinkable without panoptical attentiveness. Capacities of critical reflection are thus entailed by the possibility of self-deception, where a presupposition of an integrated self actively contends with discrepant subsystems of desire and knowledge. After all, the presumptively integrated self cannot be its own integrator. Hence, it must know more about itself than it can give account of in the immediacy of its giving account. This is an inescapable warrant for critical self-reflection. The ideal aspired to here, the demand that must be served, denotes a resource of rationality that might not be tapped by mere rational self-assertion. I want to consider the possibility that the special talents Rorty extols as features of this rationality are nurtured by Flaubert's aesthetic practice to make us readers "suffer" Rorty's notion of strong-mindedness.

In the famous agricultural fair scene of *Madame Bovary*, Flaubert's alternation of the action between above and below ground, his use of overlapping phrases and "rhyming" actions, in order to cue shifts of perspective, assures our questioning whether or not time has passed in the scene, whether or not his scene's space is continuous. Flaubert thus induces an unusually high standard of attentiveness. Presentness becomes a condition of reflective scrupulousness for his reader. To sample the pattern of Flaubert's practice, we need only begin a reading of the agricultural fair scene at its start. Rodolphe voices a sentiment that "a day comes" (1965, 103) when happiness is realized. But his utopian aria is interrupted by a councilor holding forth in a ceremony underway beneath the lovers. The councilor is proclaiming that agricultural laborers are "men of progress," whose happiness comes about by waiting out the storms of political change. The councilor's phrase "men of progress," his paean to forward-thinking human enterprises, punctually chimes with Rodolphe's progressive view of happiness in the ensuing moment of narration: "A day comes . . ." when true love reveals itself by opening the horizon of one's despair. For emphasis, Rodolphe puts his hand over his eyes, blinding himself to his blind judgment.

The councilor resumes below with allusion to the blindness of men imprisoned in old-fashioned thinking. He ends by heralding progress as a "duty," to serve the good of all. "Duty" is the next word out of Rodolphe's mouth. He confesses being "sick of the word" (ibid.). Between these different acts/scenes a deceptive continuity of action/thematic meaning is in play.

Each of these strategic overlappings exhibits a shifting dependency of reasons and beliefs as a fulcrum of knowledge that ultimately divides characters from reader. While the self-deception on display here is merely descriptive of the characters' terminally developed personalities, it constitutes for the reader something like a further development of the critical capacities that Rorty hints are inherent to self-deceptive practice. By showing us a deceptive continuity of time and action, a perpetual present in overlappings of similar but distinct actions and dialogue, Flaubert foregrounds the presentness of our own decision making. Flaubert is alerting us to the way that the remarks of the councilor, Rodolphe, and Emma are consistently expressing thoughts that could be taken quite differently if one shifted one's perspective. The present is the possibility of such shiftiness. Because the interdependency of reason and belief is an operative variable of meaning here, we must put some pressure on it. For example, the councilor's paean to the progress of agriculture obtrudes between two appeals by Rodolphe to the coming of a new day. In the first appeal, Emma's hopeful belief in the possibility of her happiness appears to be aroused by reason of Rodolphe's confession of the torments of his own soul. Not coincidentally these torments flow from the "world's point of view" that judges his passions harshly. As I have already suggested, point of view—owing to its intrinsic instability as revealed in self-deception—is a crucial stake of Flaubert's aesthetic practice here. Rodolphe presents his torment as a belief that the world's bad opinion of him gives reason for him to demur seducing Emma. But by the same token, Rodolphe's self-sacrifice would be reason for his belief in Emma's surrender to his passionate need as a just reward. On the other hand, Emma's willingness to believe in his unhappiness is a reason for her entertaining the possibility of fulfilling her own romantic fantasy, as if her own generosity toward one so needy as Rodolphe would be reason enough to believe in the necessary consummation of their love.

But after the interruption of the councilor's paean to progress the argument has progressed to a different vantage point. The new day coming when "one is near despair" is occasioned, according to Rodolphe, by a realization that: "you feel the need of . . . giving everything, sacrificing everything to this person" (ibid.). This was the sentiment that we previously surmised bolstered Emma's reason for wanting to believe in the absolute generosity of a true lover suffering the scourge of social judgment, especially when this generosity was indulged as her own best self-image. Now it is purveyed as Rodolphe's belief, and in turn revealed to be his reason for presuming upon Emma's vulnerability to lovely sentiment. Of course Rodolphe's espousing the belief that one would give oneself helplessly is a good reason for sustaining his faith in Emma's susceptibility to seduction. But it reverses the direction of dependency of a belief stated earlier as a reason for selflessness. We recognize that he is now seeing his own personal need as the reason for his belief.

The deceptive continuity between Rodolphe's gesture of putting his hand over his face with the councilor's invocation of "blindness" in the next overlapping again reveals a reversal of the direction of dependency of reason and belief, but now in a way that hinges on the reader's assumption of a "duty." I want to suggest that this is a duty not unlike that alluded to by both Rodolphe and the councilor, for it is a duty that links the councilor's invocation of blindness to our possibility of seeing beyond the critical blindness that both Rodolphe and he epitomize. So it is a duty we cannot shirk, as Rodolphe admits to doing, without risking complicity. The motion of Rodolphe's hand, characterized as the gesture of "a man about to faint," reveals a reason that is immediately belied by the narrator and, in that way, instantiates a scruple about the relevant duty. The reason that we are told the gesture "suits" is Rodolphe's declaration that the recognition of love—selfless desire!—is like a bedazzlement one experiences "if one went out from darkness into light" (ibid.). Following the action of Rodolphe's hand with the kind of attentiveness that I have said self-deception induces, the narrator observes that the gesture is only completed when, lowered from his eyes, his hand is allowed to "fall on Emma's" hand (ibid.). So we can see that what looked like a reason that would determine Rodolphe's belief in himself as selfless is in fact dependent on a belief in Emma's vulnerability. That vulnerability is, in turn, a plausible reason for the self-dramatizing gesture, which would denote a belief on Rodolphe's part in his own pathos. Without pathos he has to confront something like rapaciousness as his own reason for acting.

This brings me back to our duty as readers and to a warrant for treating self-deception as a rationalistic tool in a way that ultimately diverges from the characters' fates in Flaubert's novel. The effect of Flaubert's aesthetic practice depends on actualizing the presentness of the reader as producing a self that serves only a self's relation to what it does not yet know about itself. Just as Rodolphe, in his anticipation of Emma's response, is prompted to entertain a range of ostensible reasons, and just as his ostensible reasons are thwarted by moments of uncertainty that require him to adapt his anticipating beliefs, so Flaubert's reader is herself anticipating what ostensible reason for sympathy or ironic contempt will be forthcoming vis-à-vis Rodolphe and Emma. Alternations and overlappings of the below stairs and above stairs action figure a presentness that is perpetually challenging self-knowledge for the reader even as it is conjuring a false appearance of simultaneity and stasis. So any idea that the self of the reader is able to escape uncertainties of the present more successfully than the selves of the characters would seem self-deceived in the most conventional sense. Flaubert is interested in something more: fostering from presentness a reader's proficiency in recognizing self-deception as a modality of selfhood. This is something the characters know without knowing it. Lack of self-consciousness about what informs their self-consciousness disposes them to repetitious behaviors, makes them prisoners of their facticity. A reader can transcend that facticity, but in a manner that is not prone to the stasis of repetition: a possibility that transcendence typically invites us to believe in, as much as facticity does.

Fingarette emphasizes that only where we see a self-deceiver making an avowal to know, exhibiting a volitional self-consciousness, is she realizing a human capacity to make avowals—upon which any defensible concept of identity subsists. To avow is to establish one's "personal identity in some specific respect" (2000, 69), some specific "identification as." The importance of the phrase "in some specific respect" is for Fingarette the guarantor of some comparative judgment by which one will own up to a specific relation to the world by disavowing an alternative. It authorizes "one's existence as a particular person" (71). Certainly, if self-deception entails disavowal of what would thwart one's avowal, then it is likely to open our eyes to the fact that we actively could see otherwise.

Presentness, like Fingarette's "identification as," entails active consciousness. The character who does not know what she knows can come to knowledge only through a decision to instantiate herself by an avowal of what knowledge she possesses, however contingent on shifting evidentiary grounds it may turn out to be. This is a notion of human identity as exclusively active. I would argue that while we see the activity of Flaubert's characters in their reversals of the direction of dependency between reasons and beliefs, we do not see our own complicity with them until we are forced into the same circumstance of decision making. We are led to this in the experience of reading Flaubert's text wherever contextual parameters require an avowal of reading them from another viewpoint. I have staked my argument on the claim that this is what Flaubert's structuring of the agricultural fair scene accomplishes. In a sense, narrative fiction generally involves an activity of adapting to new evidentiary grounds for one's avowals of what one knows one knows.

As I have already noted, Fingarette calls for a "de-emphasis of the relation of consciousness to knowledge, and the emphasis of its relation

to action" (64). With this admonition Fingarette means for us to see
the self-deceiver in tandem with agency-enhancing practices that I
maintain have been the métier of the novelist since the genre's inception. Now we might even suspect the disingenuousness of Flaubert's
confiding to Louise Colet his anxiety that not enough is happening in
Madame Bovary, for the agricultural fair scene shows us how "ideas are
actions," inasmuch as readers can be reminded of their agency in reading novels as a particular condition of being a human character.

If we can see how the characters' words are actions because they
constitute a fulcrum of reasoning across which the stakes of identity
seesaw back and forth (as a result of the shifting of evidentiary grounds
for motivational biases), then perhaps we can see more. We are made
aware that we see all this by means of our participation in protocols of
hypothesis testing. Flaubert's alternation of viewpoints—challenging our
orientation to what motivational biases may affect our sympathy for
fictional characters whose own motivational biases are so labile—tells us
something about an intrinsic fictionality of our own character. We are as
dependent as Flaubert's characters on apprehending a way in which any
misapprehension of our attitudes does not therefore presuppose a "fixed
system of the self," one possessed of a finite repertoire of avowals. Rather,
it denotes a repertoire constantly in need of expansion or new
justifications. Self-deception is curiously instrumental to such an enterprise. Indeed, the reader of the novel form historically has always been
vividly present to the text in this capacity, but she has not always realized
or accepted the duties of this human predicament. Flaubert insists upon
spelling out our doing our duty in a way all novels do not. Flaubert's
insistence is redeemed by our ineluctable recognition that the human
self that reads novels would certainly benefit from assuming such duties,
from spelling them out. Fingarette's theory of self-deception is predicated on the proposition that self-deceivers resist spelling out the conditions under which they act, the terms of their engagement with the world
(39), because they are focusing upon other forms of engagement. But
this is not due to their passivity. They are agents, not victims, of self-
deception, because they are bound by the necessity of instantiating themselves in avowals that preclude some instance of spelling out.

What is more relevant, for my purpose, is that Fingarette links self-
deception to the willing suspension of disbelief that is proverbially
operative in artworks: "The so-called 'suspension of disbelief' essential
in the arts is in fact the focusing of attention on the artistic content of
the work, and the systematic avoidance of focusing attention on its
aesthetically non-relevant properties, even while still taking account of
them" (175). The mobility of motivational biases that underwrites our

recognition of the emotional, psychological reality of fictional characters is likewise the means by which our willing suspension of disbelief
is enabled. It is the indexical marker of our presentness as readers. In
other words, presentness in this context is another name for the quality
of attentiveness that the imperative of decision making imposes. One
feels the pressure of it when in the course of instantiating oneself through
one's avowals one is confronted with unstable ratios of information vis-
à-vis what one knows and what one wants to know, what one has reason
to believe and what one believes for reasons he can circumstantially
muster. Thus to be present is to open the perspective that knowledge
of self-deception is a normative duty of what Audi calls "conscientious
consciousness" (1997, 150). This consciousness is marked by its vigilance with respect to the prospect that other evidentiary and motivational grounds exist.

The present perfect and/or present tense of narration, which
coincidentally is the verb tense of the last line in Flaubert's novel,
signals our responsibility to changing conditions of self-avowal, the very
threshold of self-deceiving mind. Flaubert's closure in *Madame Bovary*
coheres with my proposition that the way of being in narrative time
requires a responsiveness to conditions of self-deception—what
Fingarette might call locating the self in avowal—as a *sine qua non* of
ethical character. For in the narrative of *medias res,* in the presentness
of reading, we know the inescapability of knowing that we need to
know more. Being mindful of self-deception potentiates powers of mind
that are inescapably bound to the circumstance of presentness where
such knowing presses urgently upon the levers of ethical obligation.

To speak of ethical obligation in the shadow of Flaubertian form
is to realize how swiftly that shadow moves in relation to contemporary
narrative experimentation in novels. As I indicated at the commence-
ment of this argument—and particularly in novels since 1945—character becomes increasingly a site for intensification of presentness, and in
that respect a marker for a transformation of novelistic form. If, as I
have suggested in my reading of Flaubert, the novel has "long harbored
a notion of character that has resisted characterization" then it might
be fitting to conclude with a quick survey of novelists for whom this
notion portends a convergence of ethical obligation and aesthetic innovation. Since I have made self-deception a predicate of such a characterization of the novel, as well as the characters it harbors, I would take
Samuel Beckett, John Hawkes, and Joseph McElroy as exemplary practitioners of the novel for whom knowing is an expressly transitive bur-
den of narrating. What makes them exemplars is their common stake
in compositional strategies that call a reader to account for the present-

mindedness of misreading. This is more than plot reversal and certainly more than a typological illustration of the phenomenon of self-deceiving mind. What these innovators always presuppose in their formal enterprise is a reader's characterization as one who must deny the lucidity of evidentiary grounds for reading correctly in order to read correctly. Self-deception and rationalization, as I have suggested throughout this chapter, become reciprocal mandates of self-realizing ambition.

The Beckett of the last short novels, *Company*, *Worstword Ho!*, and *Ill Seen, Ill Said*,[4] deploys what I have elsewhere characterized as a "parsimonious syntax," whereby the eliding of syntactical elements (articles, prepositions, etc.) seems to render one's sense of narrative lucidity an artifact of a yet unrecognized error. I have asserted that the strategy of parsimonious syntax has the effect of instantiating a "self in error."[5] But error, in this case, is not a malignant unintelligibility; it is a warrant for rationalization. Particularly in *Ill Seen, Ill Said*, Beckett complements his syntactical strategy with the conjuring of an invisible interlocutor whose admonitions to the reader to go slow and be wary of error render presentness and contextual refiguration consonant with one another. The admonitory refrain of the voice demurring error in Beckett's narrative devolves exclusively to the reader's fate as one who could know how much the authority of one's reading was a function of *spelling out* (to use Fingarette's phrase) of the conditions of one's knowledge claims.

John Hawkes and Joseph McElroy give us even more contemporary evidence that the possibilities of formal innovation in the novel depend—for the sustenance of its contemporaneity—upon a narration of the self through the labyrinth of self-deception. Hawkes, I believe, is too glibly acknowledged as an innovator by dint of his enthusiasm for unreliable, self-deceiving narrators. I think, in fact, that the rhetorical pyrotechnics, for which his self-deceiving first-person narrators are renowned, obscure a more consequential innovation: Hawkes's willingness to allow catachrestic figuration to complicate a reader's prioritization of evidentiary contexts for discerning boundaries between a narrator's imagination and realities which that imagination both constrains and is constrained by. It is on this basis that Hawkes's fictions, particularly works like those that make up the triad *The Blood Oranges*, *Death, Sleep, and the Traveler*, and *Travesty*, present us with the predicament of a narrative voice that we suspect of self-deception in the conventional sense that I have been challenging but whose self-deceiving gestures risk contamination to the reader. It is a contamination that is more virulent than mere knowledge that things are otherwise than the narrator is willing to admit. The excesses of imagistic elaboration that at times threaten to arrest Hawkes's narrative actualize a prospect for thinking that every elaboration of the figurative register portends our reckoning with the necessity of knowing more than we know.

Joseph McElroy's most recent novel, *Actress in the House* (2003), offers the most vitally contemporary gloss upon self-deception as a mode of human creation in which presentness is the *sine qua non* of aesthetic value. Such brief mention as I have space for here can hardly do justice to McElroy's innovation. But the hallmark of his métier is decisive for furthering the thinking I have attempted to provoke in this chapter and for grounding my own desire to keep faith with *fiction's present*. McElroy's novel proceeds by a kind of recursive syntax wherein point of view frequently appears to be unmarked unless one learns to read retrospectively. But the retrospect is neither backward looking nor nostalgic. Rather, it appears to be improvisational. A moment from *Actress* is exemplary: McElroy has his protagonist, Becca Lang, physically poised in the narrator's thought of her. She is sexually present to the narrator. But in a syntactical instant she is traversing space and time beyond the boundaries of any individual body:

> Becca was at the bureau drawers for a moment, the Sunday-night sour expression passed across the fine wide mouth, she was no pet to tend, and yet, almost naked in white underpants you could see the pale and shadowy behind through. That is what she was. She herself in the cab going downtown to the movie yesterday had betrayed a certain knowledge of Dutch Guyana. The once and "former" Suriname the super hailed from. (McElroy 2003, 310)

Each word does not so much fit the sentence as each makes the sentence fit a world whose dimensions we are still learning to compass as we read. We go back in time at least twice from the moment at the bureau, to the moment in the cab, to the moment in history, as if we are deceived at every point where we think we know what time it might be. Though the retrospect seems linear, we are really going forward on a trajectory of speculation about how best to incorporate what we do not comprehend at the moment, such as the fact that the "super" is custodian of Becca's residence. McElroy has always been a writer seeking to make thinking an ever-more transitive enterprise by means of such contextual transits back and forth on divergent trajectories. In *Actress*, the entire plot is predicated on what may be false perception: that an actress on stage has been *actually* slapped rather than merely represented to be so victimized. In McElroy's fiction, the prospect of being so self-deceptively mistaken is the prospect of becoming connected to the world in ways that the stigma of mere error absolutely precludes.

What all these fictions of the present have in common then is a vital rapport with the quandary of knowing one's self through the detours of self-deceiving mind. They better acquaint us with pressures that temporal experience brings to bear as we learn to bear temporality's duration. The forms of the novel that are most responsive to self-deceiving mind—rather than the novels in which self-deceiving mind is merely character-ized—may be the most scrupulous witnesses to fiction's present.[6]

NOTES

1. See Audi (1997, 131, ch. 6).

2. Alfred Mele gives one of the most persuasive glosses on "jointly sufficient conditions" for self-deception in *Self-Deception Unmasked* (2001, 117–21).

3. See excerpt from letter dated January 15, 1853, in the *Norton Critical Edition* (313–14). Excerpted from *The Selected Letters of Gustave Flaubert* (1953).

4. All three works were collected by Grove Press in a single volume, *Nohow On: Company, Ill Seen, Ill Said, Worstward Ho* (1995).

5. See my *Aesthetic Reason: Artworks and the Deliberative Ethos* (2003, 91).

6. The author wishes to thank the English Department of Penn State University for giving a first audience to this talk. He also wishes to acknowledge the invaluable editorial suggestions of Professor Robert Caserio.

REFERENCES

Audi, Robert. 1997. *Moral knowledge and ethical character.* New York: Oxford University Press.

Bach, Kent. 1998. (Apparent) paradoxes of self-deception and decision. In *Self-deception and paradoxes of rationality,* ed. Jean-Pierre Dupuy, 161-89. Stanford, CA: CSLI.

Fingarette, Herbert. 2000 [1969]. *Self-deception.* Berkeley: University of California Press.

Flaubert, Gustave. 1965. *Madame Bovary.* Edited and translated by Paul De Man. New York: Norton.

Hawkes, John. 1970. *The blood oranges.* New York: New Directions.

———. 1973. *Death, sleep and the traveler.* New York: New Directions.

———. 1976. *Travesty.* New York: New Directions.

McElroy, Joseph. 2003. *Actress in the house.* New York: Overlook Press.

Mele, Alfred. 2001. *Self-deception unmasked.* Princeton, NJ: Princeton University Press.

Rorty, Amélie Oksenberg. 1988. The deceptive self: Liars, layers, and lairs. In *Perspectives on self-deception,* ed. Brian P. McLaughlin and Amélie Oksenberg Rorty, 11-28. Berkeley: University of California Press.

Sanford, David H. 1988. "Self-deception as rationalization." In *Perspectives on self-deception,* ed. Brian P. McLaughlin and Amélie Oksenberg Rorty, 157-69. Berkeley: University of California Press.

The selected letters of Gustave Flaubert. 1953. Edited and translated by Francis Steegmuller. New York: Farrar, Straus and Giroux.

Shakespeare, William. 1942. *Othello.* In *The Complete Plays and Poems of William Shakespeare.* New York: Houghton Mifflin, the Riverside Press.

Singer, Alan. 2003. *Aesthetic reason: Artworks and the deliberative ethos.* State College: Penn State University Press.

Chapter 10

Notes on Fiction and Philosophy

Brian Evenson

In a very real way, what readers see in a work of fiction is determined by the models they employ as they approach it. There is little possibility that the reader will have an unmediated experience with a text simply because no reader is, ultimately, unmediated; we read from contexts, from positions, and as we read we consider books we have read before, books we have heard about, movies, classes we have taken, people around us, the dog down the street, and so on. Probably our biggest difficulty with acknowledging fiction's present involves the insistence of the models of the past, which, like Melanie Klein's part objects, we have internalized and which seem to speak to us from within with a voice of authority. Thus, to move to an understanding of late twentieth- and early twenty-first-century fiction, the first step is to move out of the fourth century BC: to let go of the Aristotelian notions that still dominate most thinking about fiction in writing workshops today. Indeed, one of the paradoxes of the institutionalization and burgeoning of writing programs in the United States has been that most of these programs are much less interested in pointing to fiction's present—let alone fiction's future—than in preserving fiction as an eternal past tense. Discussions of setting, plot, character, theme, and so on, their parameters derived from Aristotle, seem hardly to have advanced beyond New Criticism's neo-Aristotelianism; and when a workshop student says "I didn't find the character believable," usually the model for believability is firmly entrenched in nineteenth-century notions of consistency that have probably less to do with how real twenty-first century people act (not to mention nineteenth-century people) than with specific, and often dated, literary conventions.

I am of the opinion that the most authentic service a writing program can do for writing students is to give them an aesthetic base, introduce them to different philosophies and aesthetic ideas—current as well as past—making available to them different models for understanding fiction. For just as what readers see in a text is determined by the models they bring, consciously or unconsciously, to bear on said text, so too the writer's ability to construct and revise his or her own text is determined by the differing philosophical and aesthetic ideas he or she has both consciously or unconsciously internalized. What is important is not so much finding the *right* model—there is not one—as allowing writers to locate themselves within a field that contains varied philosophical and aesthetic possibilities, and to see their own position as always potentially fluid. Indeed, if there is a future in fiction, I think it lies in the active dialogue that can occur between fiction and philosophy/theory, a dialogue in which each prods the other toward new possibilities, where each poses questions that the other is compelled to answer.

With that in mind, I want to begin with a philosophical notion and consider what questions it poses for a fiction writer, how it provokes in a writer what might seem to a philosopher a somewhat eccentric response. I want to start with Heidegger and a concept from one of his lesser-known works and apply a gentle and at times nonphilosophical pressure to it. In doing so, I am less interested in either presenting myself as Heideggerian or giving a serious philosophical critique of Heidegger than in simply seeing where one idea can take us, seeing "what happens next."

In his book *Holzwege* [Woodpaths] (1950), Heidegger suggests:

> "Wood" is an old name for forest. In the wood are paths that mostly wind along until they end quite suddenly in an impenetrable thicket.
>
> They are called "woodpaths."
>
> Each goes its peculiar way, but in the same forest. Often it seems as though one were identical to another. Yet it only seems so.
>
> Woodcutters and foresters are familiar with these paths. They know what it means to be on a woodpath. (3)[1]

For Heidegger, thought is a path proceeding through a dark wood (echoes of Dante here), an unpredictably winding path that can be made neither straight nor wide without impairing its ability to function as path. For Heidegger, to think Being is to be "highly errant," to accept a wandering of sorts in which thought nonetheless does not eschew its path (1950, 185). As he admonishes in "The Thing" (1971),

"Stay on the path, in genuine need, and learn the craft of thinking, unswerving, yet erring" (186). Following a woodpath is unswerving errancy, for by staying on the woodpath we travel toward we know not where, winding about, entering and leaving unexpected clearings, seeing exposed to us at each turning a different portion of the forest.

Heidegger's notion is an intriguing one, and analogous notions abound throughout his work, a work that is crucial to any number of schools of twentieth- and early twenty-first-century philosophy. But on a practical level, the woodpath is likely to raise simple questions for a lay reader, questions that for a writer can serve as an aesthetic provocation. For Heidegger, the woodpath is something that winds to and fro the forest, ending "quite suddenly in an impenetrable thicket." This is an idealized version of the woodpath—if an actual woodpath seems to end suddenly in an impenetrable thicket, then it is likely one has lost track of the path. In other words, to have ended in an impenetrable thicket is as much a function of the way in which one understands the woodpath as it is a function of the path itself. We are perhaps led to the thicket by our own error, by having lost the trace, by having accepted as trace what is offered as mere decoy or distraction. It indicates a problem in our understanding of what the path is. The idea that the path leads to impenetrable mystery is the sort of idea that would come neither from the forester nor the woodcutter familiar with the forest but from a city dweller lost in the woods.

"Woodcutters and foresters are familiar with these paths. They know what it means to be on a woodpath," Heidegger suggests (1950, 3). However, again there is a space that we might wriggle into. Heidegger does not acknowledge that foresters and woodcutters "know what it means to be on a woodpath" in radically different ways.

The forester is, by one definition, an inhabitant of the forest. By another, he is a person trained in forestry or forest lore, someone who cares for the forest. In both these senses taken together, the forester as inhabitant and the forester as one who cares for the forest, we do not seem to be too distant from Heidegger's better-known idea of dwelling. The thinker as forester dwells as the guardian of Being. For Heidegger in "The Thing," such "Guardianship of Being is not fixated upon something existent. The existent thing, taken for itself, never contains an appeal to Being" (1971, 184). For this reason the thinker does not attempt to guard Being as one might guard an object defined by value. Rather, guardianship is a "watchfulness for the has-been and coming destiny of Being" (ibid.). Admits Heidegger, such thinking is both a wandering and a following of a path: "As a response, thinking of Being is highly errant and in addition a very

destitute matter. Thinking is perhaps, after all, an unavoidable path,
which refuses to be a path of salvation and brings no new wisdom"
(1971, 185). The forester, too, is a wanderer of sorts, highly errant
and, in a sense, destitute. He looks not to get out of the forest (for
he has no idea of salvation) but only to care for the forest. His task
takes no reward as a claim, asserting itself only as a scrutinizing and
continuous movement through his environment.

Certainly this is a valid notion of a certain kind of artist, and it is
perhaps not surprising that Heidegger, with his own intense interest in
poetry, seems so taken with this notion of care. But as the underside of
any notion of care comes a notion of hurt, and it is this latter notion
that strikes me as more relevant to fiction's present because so often
ignored in literature's past. In traveling from place to place, the forester crushes plants underfoot, pushes back vines, and removes dead
wood. Following in the traces that animals have made, he makes the
path his own, cultivating a smoothed-out corridor that, though it moves
through the forest discreetly, cuts through it nonetheless.[2]

This notion of hurt invites thoughts of the other sort of person
who Heidegger claims knows the woodpaths, the one who his commentary largely ignores: the woodcutter. When the woodcutter enters the
wood, he is in search of something that he can take out again, either
firewood or wood of finer quality for building purposes. He learns the
path of the forest so that the forest will offer up to him what he needs.
The woodcutter is not an inhabitant of the forest in the sense that a
forester is. He is he who takes. But, nonetheless, he knows how to
follow the same paths the forester follows. If needs be, in search of
wood the woodcutter's axe will cut a path into the supposedly impenetrable thicket. He has no qualms about taking what he needs and
reappropriating it for a new context.

I should say that one of the reasons Heidegger discusses the forester a great deal and the woodcutter almost not at all is that such a
method of cutting one's own path is for him a divergence that limits
one's understanding of Being. For Heidegger (1971), it is "all the more
strictly true that each man gets farthest if he goes only as far as he can
go on the way allotted to him" (95). One pursues a path and by means
of this pursuit reaches "into the abyss, to attend there to intimations
and signs" (ibid.). The Being revealed lies in the truth that comes
about in following the path itself.

I would agree that truth comes from this process rather than as
an end result, both for thinkers and, more importantly in terms of our
context, for writers. If we make a beeline for the impenetrable thicket
and clear the thicket to open up its mystery, then by so doing we

destroy its mystery, disperse its truth. The process of unveiling itself is more important than that which lies behind the veil. In fiction I would argue that style constitutes the veil, and that in fiction there is ultimately nothing behind this veil.

Nevertheless, there is nothing that demands that the writer stay upon a path that has been "allotted to him" (by what agency or power so allotted, Heidegger does not say), nor that he or she should be circling around a particular thicket. The thinker does not have to stay upon a given path—Heidegger, with his own departure from the path of traditional thought, is one of the philosophers who knows this best—and by cutting new paths he potentially discovers new thickets that he might choose to leave untouched. The woodcutter's axe opens spaces that have been ignored by past errancy, reveals paths that have been hitherto blocked up.[3] The writer who cuts his own paths shall find truth in the process of that cutting if he understands such cutting as a process rather than as directed toward a goal. I would argue that the woodcutter both knows how to pursue a path and knows that when the usefulness of the path comes into question he can strike out on his own and start cutting, and that the woodcutter is more of an apt figure for the contemporary writer than is the forester.

Beginning with a lesser-known Heideggerian notion, we have started to provoke ourselves elsewhere by focusing on some of the things in which Heidegger is less interested. This is an act of bricolage, an attempt to borrow what is needed to get somewhere new, but it also is something that, for me, comes quite directly out of the fact that I was reading Heidegger for the first time around the same time I was reading Austrian writer Thomas Bernhard, with the collision of the writer and philosopher provoking new possibilities. Bernhard's work is in part a response to Heidegger; some of his books deliberately pose problems or questions that Heideggerian philosophy would have difficulty answering, and these problems are simultaneously philosophical and aesthetic. This, I think, is as it should be. Indeed, if your fiction poses problems for which a particular philosophical stance provides perfect answers, then your work is not really posing problems; you are serving instead as a missionary for a theory.

Having moved from the forester to the woodcutter, in place of Heidegger's *Holzwege* as an exemplary term we might substitute the title of one of Bernhard's books: *Holzfällen* (Cutting Timber).[4] The thinker comes to cut, to move beyond the forest of Being. This woodcutter thinking taken to its limit is the philosophy Nietzsche calls in *Twilight of the Idols* philosophizing with a hammer. It is a philosophizing that intends to clear a space for things to come, and I think it is practiced by contemporary fiction writers much more frequently than by contemporary philosophers per se.

Such philosophizing is nihilism in the sense that Heidegger defines it in his Nietzsche lectures: "that historical process whereby the dominance of the 'transcendent' becomes null and void, so that all being loses its worth and meaning" (1982, 4). Nihilism in its most extreme form has no lesser goal than razing the forest of Being. But such is an extreme form of nihilism, the nihilism of the woodcutter gone mad, striking out at all around him: if we shift our metaphors, this is the artist as killer.[5] Still, there are subtler forms of nihilism. To cut timber (*holzfällen*) is not necessarily to decimate a forest. We also cut wood to glimpse or come to a place where a woodpath will not allow us to go. We cut wood to gain a passage into the depths of the woods, or a passage through the wood to a landscape lying outside the wood. In gaining passage, we destroy some of the forest, but such path-making moves beyond the forest—we organize the forest in our own way instead of allowing ourselves to be organized by it.

In Bernhard's novel *Correction* (1979), Roithamer takes as a project inflicting his will upon a forest. With money from an inheritance, he decides to "build his sister a cone, a cone-shaped habitation, and not only that, but most incredible of all, to erect this giant cone not where such a house might normally be located, but to design it and put it up and complete it way out in the middle of Kobernausser forest . . . all at once the road through the Kobernausser forest was actually being built, a road that would go to the exact center of the forest at an angle he had calculated for months" (11). Instead of moving about on woodpaths, Roithamer cuts directly to the center of the forest and there prepares to establish his sister in the perfectly shaped cone. He tells his sister nothing of this, his plan being to surprise her with the cone, a cone that will bring her, he feels, "the highest, supreme happiness" (246). Yet when he speaks to her of it, "the effect of the Cone on my sister was devastating . . . from that moment on, everything led to her certain death" (267).

Roithamer's solution is to understand the forest by clearing a space in its center and there establishing not himself but an object of personal value: his sister. The Cone is a dwelling place for his sister, the center of all his efforts, all of his (lowercase b) being. In fact, he puts his entire being into the project to such an extent that when his sister suicides, leaving the Cone empty, Roithamer kills himself in turn.

One might argue that when we attempt to establish at the center of our understanding of Being that which is constructed of values, we put ourselves in a position that quickly concedes defeat. To try to insert something to fill an absence is to offer it up to the void, to constitute its destruction as a thing. While Heidegger suggests that "What matters to preparatory thinking is to light up that space within which Being itself might again be able to take man, with respect to his essence, into a primal relationship" (1971, 55), Bernhard might argue that no such space exists, ready-made to be lit, and no such essence exists to light it. All thinking, to some degree, is a clearing away—lighting is only secondary to this clearing. What is cleared and thus revealed is Nothing, an "absence of a suprasensory, obligatory world" (Heidegger 1970, 61–62).

One wields one's axe to move to the center of the forest, there to chop up the inscrutable thicket of Being. One clears the clearing and moves beyond it to a place beyond Being, if one has the courage to move beyond (1970, 100). Roithamer is unable to move beyond. By attempting in a post-transcendent world to set up as transcendent those things that can no longer be considered transcendent (even if they once were), one in essence denies their thingness, their historical and/ or tangible reality. Roithamer's sister, separated off as she is by her brother in a building of perfect geometrical proportions, must die. No longer a thing, she becomes an idea now devoid of meaning for having been elevated to transcendent status. If placed in the Cone, she becomes first only a speck in the void and then nothing at all.

But it is precisely in this evanescence that nihilism begins to understand itself as nihilism. What has been in the past the very center of Being, upon which all else has depended, has now become not merely a corpse but an absence, a source of absencing. We cannot say that it is nothing so much as that it *makes* Nothing. To bring something into the circle is to destroy that thing. It is a vortex, a black hole, an abyss.

Nihilism's clearing of a space is altogether different from the Heideggerian clearing (lighting: *Lichtung*). Nihilism clears the space to make nothing—it cuts down the trees of being to open a void. If it does build in the space cleared, it builds that absurd notion of being that is most amenable to nothingness. Heidegger's clearing is another process entirely. It is not something that one clears for oneself but something one stumbles upon: "In the midst of beings as a whole an open place occurs" (1971, 53). Says Heidegger, "We never come to thoughts. They come to us" (6). We do not find them when actively searching but stumble upon them while errant. They are the site at which Being is revealed to a greater or lesser degree. "That which is can only be, as a being, if it stands within and stands out within what is lighted in this clearing" (53).

In *Correction*, on the contrary, the clearing becomes a place constructed for the encounter with death. Roithamer enters into the clearing to commit suicide. The clearing of Being is where one hangs oneself, thus negating the possibilities of the being.

Roithamer is that thinker who carries a shoulder-slung axe, carving his path to the center of being. There he clears a space and then cuts himself to pieces. Having no ability to see the future, he turns upon himself, unto his own destruction. Nietzschean nihilism, however, does not allow itself to fizzle out in the clearing of Being. Rather than becoming caught in the clearing, Nietzsche moves through it—not because he can see the future but because he no longer thinks in terms of either future or past. He is not moving from one point to another; he is just moving. He keeps cutting, striking paths with the axe, paths that twist free of the forest and destroy the forest itself. Indeed, the Nietzschean figure at its extreme becomes more a trajectory than a human being, pure movement.

It is perhaps time to add another piece to the collage, time to return to theory, to see where Roithamer's cone might lead us, though I shall do so only briefly. One direction might be Deleuze's and Guattari's notion of the line of flight that cuts a path through striated space, through organized space, the alternative to lines that segment us, dividing our lives into neat and careful packages and repeated events. For Deleuze and Guattari, one is a conjunction of molar and molecular lines that shape and stratify one's organism. School is a segmenting line, as is habit, as is work; culture becomes a line as well, a channel that directs our actions. Serving as a rupture to this segmentation is the line of flight, something that cuts through habit and segmentation and, at least momentarily, delivers the self to an intense freedom. Such a line of flight "carries deterritorialization to the absolute, intensity to the highest degree" (Deleuze and Guattari 1987, 132). Subjectification, however, "attempts to impose on the line of flight a segmentarity that is forever repudiating that line" (134), a struggle that is literalized in the narrator Rudolph's struggles in another Bernhard book, *Concrete* (1982).

Though I began by declaring that there is no unmediated relation to the text, Deleuze and Guattari suggest as an alternative an active, conscious slicing through a mediation that is constantly trying to fold us back into it: we cut a path through our segmented and mediated lives, and in so doing we open ourselves to the possibility of destruction and thus to an experience that can impact us beyond (or outside, to move toward Maurice Blanchot's thought) mediation. From here we are on the verge of a theory of writing as velocity and trajectory, a theory of art based on velocity, where the despair of nihilism has been replaced by a sort of relentless rush, where harm is neither directed at oneself or outward but has become simply pure intensity, where Being is no longer an issue. We enter into the work, both as writer and reader, breathlessly, giving up our beings in favor of speed, of a nullity that moves beyond Being—a speed that for the duration of the work substitutes itself for our being. What that means in terms of actual writing strategies contemporary writers are just beginning to explore.

There has been something at once arbitrary and highly personal in my choices of writers and philosophers, and in the choice of what I have chosen to borrow from each. I could have taken other approaches, could have chosen other concepts or clusters of concepts from Heidegger that would seem as contemporarily relevant—perhaps even more so— as Deleuze and Guattari. Or with Bernhard I could equally have chosen to talk about Wittgenstein, who I believe is as much at the heart of the critique in *Correction* as Heidegger. And Bernhard himself, with his patterns of intense repetition and non-paragraphing, is interesting to consider in view of narrative theory. Indeed, stylistically he poses problems that narrative theory does not quite know how to resolve. But the point is that all these possible approaches to fiction, as well as the aesthetic positions at which I have hinted, are unavailable to me if I remain, as many workshop programs encourage students to do, exclusively grounded in new criticism and Aristotelian notions.

Good fiction, I would argue, always poses problems—ethical, linguistic, epistemological, ontological—and writers and readers, I believe, should be willing to draw on everything around them to pose tentative answers to these problems and, by way of them, pose problems of their own. For innovative writers, I believe, philosophy is always best an errant affair, a personal and an intense wandering, a series of tools that one can employ, move beyond, come back to; it is our ability as writers to stay curious, to borrow, to bricoler, and to adapt and move on that keeps us from becoming stale.

I also would argue that the future of fiction lies in writers' ability to complicate notions such as Deleuze's and Guattari's in ways that I cannot yet foresee, ways that might lead back, among other places, to other Heideggerian notions. I begin to get a hint of such a direction in the work of Antoine Volodine, whose ability in *Minor Angels* to assemble a novel-length text out of dozens of discrete "narracts" that both do and do not hold together seems to be pointing toward structures that are at once errant in a Heideggerian sense and have short bursts of Deleuzian velocity. Or, in Eric Chevillard's *Palafox* (2004), in which the character's physical form seems to be constantly shifting so that it is never graspable, never stable: post-human in a disturbing sense, which reintroduces the notion of the sublime in a way that responds to both Kant's original notion and Lyotard's twentieth-century response to it. As a writer, my fascination with such writers is likely to lead me into new spaces—and, indeed, my fascination with Volodine is based in part on my willingness to see in him impulses sympathetic (but also disruptive) to philosopher Giorgio Agamben's notion of "whatever being." And this too will, I feel, eventually be responded to both by literature and philosophy, the conversation between the two fields enriching each other, and enriching writers of both, in ways that none of us can afford to do without.

NOTES

1. This translation of the forward is that provided in Heidegger, *Basic Writings* (1977, 34).

2. Indeed, the thinker, it might be said, is he who follows animal tracks through the forest of Being. There is something bestial about thinking. From here, one might perhaps move to Deleuze's and Guattari's notion of becoming animal, but that is beyond the purview of this chapter.

3. Heidegger's approach to Greek philosophy intends to do just this—he wants to open up pathways to early Greek thought that reveal their relation to our own paths, a relationship long obscured.

4. The American title of the work is translated not as *Cutting Timber* (which the British translation uses) but as *Woodcutters*.

5. Or, in the words of Eric Chevillard, "The ten fingers of the pianist compose the two hands of the strangler" (1993, 50).

REFERENCES

Bernhard, Thomas. 1979. *Correction.* Translated by Sophie Wilkins. New York: Alfred A. Knopf.

———. 1982. *Concrete.* Translated by David McLintock. Chicago: University of Chicago Press.

———. 1989. *Woodcutters.* Translated by David McLintock. Chicago: University of Chicago Press.

Chevillard, Eric. 1993. *La nébuleuse du Crabe.* Paris: Editions de Minuit.

———. 2004 [1990]. *Palafox.* Translated by Wyatt Mason. New York: Archipelago Books.

Deleuze, Gilles, and Felix Guattari. 1987. *A thousand plateaus.* Translated by Brian Massumi. Minneapolis: University of Minnesota Press.

Heidegger, Martin. 1950. *Holzwege.* Frankfurt am Main: V. Klostermann.

———. 1970. The word of Nietzsche. In *The question of technology and other essays,* ed. William Lovitt, 15–88. New York: Harper and Row.

———. 1971. *Poetry, language, thought.* Translated by Albert Hofstadter. New York: Harper and Row.

———. 1977. *Basic writings,* edited by David Farrell Krell. New York: Harper and Row.

———. 1982. *Nietzsche. Volume four: Nihilism.* New York: Harper Collins.

Volodine, Antoine. 2004 [1999]. *Minor angels.* Translated by Jordan Stump. Lincoln: University of Nebraska Press.

Chapter 11

James, Cather, Vollmann, and the Distinction of Historical Fiction

ROBERT L. CASERIO

ONE: THE IVORY TOWER

The field of English studies has become used to celebrating, for more than a decade, the importance of borderlines and in-between conditions. "A contingent, borderline experience opens up in between colonizer and colonized. This is a space of cultural and interpretive undecidability produced in the 'present' of the colonial moment": the gist of Homi Bhabha's (1994, 206) sentence has established itself as a critical commonplace. And not only the present of the colonial moment confers borderline experience: whether understood as history's present, or as fiction's present, or as plain "now," temporality confers a borderline experience on us all. Every passing moment solicits comprehension of our immersion in an in-between element. Saturated as we are by attention to in-betweenness, however, when a topos prevails as much as the borderline-borderlands has, one might be excused for wanting to hear something new about it, even something of a challenge to it. There is a considerable challenge in Dorrit Cohn's recent book *The Distinction of Fiction* (1999). Arriving in the form of a contribution to narratology, and without intending to address postcolonial poetics or any undecidable aspect of presentness, *The Distinction of Fiction* emphatically reverses the celebration of borderlines. It intends not to undo borders, not to find them undecidable, and not to find them nefarious. Cohn wants to reestablish impermeable aspects of borders. The territory whose borders she wants even in some ways to seal is fiction's; and she wants especially to limit border crossings between historical narrative and fictional narrative—so much for mutually porous relations

159

between fiction and the historical present! Drawing inspiration from modernist historical novelist Alfred Döblin's insistence that "the historical novel is, in the first place, a novel; in the second place, it isn't history," Cohn claims that there is a "great divide" (162) between fiction's territory and history's. The claim, inasmuch as Cohn formidably defends it, might give us pause. If the distinction of fiction inheres in fiction's resistance to history—either to history's past moments or to its present ones as historical narrative makes them available to us—then we cannot continue to mingle historical and aesthetic concerns as unqualifiedly as we have in the last generation of scholarship. And if we respect the claims of Cohn's argument, then we will be reminded that our deconstructive inheritance, of which borderline thinking is an offshoot, never intended us to get rid of divisions and distinctions but to struggle with them no less than with their in-betweens.

What might such a struggle mean for fiction's present, for a "now" whose quicksilver character appears perennially to have nurtured novelistic inspiration? Surely a discursive capture of the present's in-betweenness might qualify for what Cohn calls "signposts of fictionality" (109–31). But for Cohn fictionality's signposts do not depend on in-betweenness. She sees fiction as a discourse defined and constituted by its limitary difference from another, contrastive discourse: history. With historical narrative as her constant foil, Cohn identifies fiction with freedom. "The process that transforms archival sources into narrative history," she writes "is qualitatively different from the process that transforms a novelist's sources into his fictional creation" (114). In fiction, the transformational process depends upon liberties taken by fiction with time and with knowledge—liberties that are precluded in the nonfictive realm of historical discourse. Fiction's way of taking liberties with historical discourse is fiction's freedom from history, even from history's present moment. When Cohn asserts that "artful perturbations of . . . temporal structure show fictionality" (116), one only need think for confirmation of how the writing of history has yet to set as a standard for itself the temporal perturbations of Ford's *The Good Soldier* (1915). Fiction's juggling with time is a compelling mark of a stubborn difference between itself and nonfiction. Even more compelling, in fiction "the minds of imaginary figures can be known in ways that those of real persons cannot" (118). The transparent minds Cohn expounded in her earlier famous book are transparent just because they are not real. Narrators of fiction assume "optical and cognitive powers unavailable to a real person" (127). Only fiction, not history, can present past events—even real historical ones—through the eyes of a figure on the scene of the past in the very present of the scene, as if there were no gap or lag between a subject's immediate inward experience and a record of the experience. But while fictional narratives cultivate an impossible immediacy, they also rely on a distinct mediacy, inasmuch as they separate narrators from real authors. In fictions, narrators and their real authors and their narrators are not the same; in histories they decidedly are one. Again we see, in contrast to fictional storytellers, the constraints under which Cohn's historians labor. Historians must maintain a stable character of "objective subjectivity" (118); fictional narrators need subscribe to no stable single-mindedness. Unlike a historian's narrative procedure, which is highly restricted by its sources, a novelist's relation to his or her sources is free indeed. And a reader's relation to fiction is correspondingly free. It is so free in fact that Cohn pairs it with stress: "Reading fictional narrative . . . burdens its performance with uniquely stressful interpretive freedom" (130).

Cohn's essential motive for erecting territorial signposts of fictionality, and for renewing the fiction/history boundary, might well be her assertion and preservation of interpretive freedom. Her book does not make any separate plea for the value of that freedom, just as it does not expound an encomium on the liberties that fictional narrative takes with truth. It is for the sake of a disinterested vocation to set scholarly things right that Cohn delineates fiction's domain. But she also takes for granted, apparently, an immediate attractiveness of the emancipatory diction, which she attaches to her signposts. Is not that attractiveness one to which English studies especially responds?

However one answers that question, certainly Cohn's limitary project promises to make sense of persistent efforts by fiction writers, such as Henry James and Willa Cather, to theorize their own signposts of fictionality. It is odd that James and Cather do so, given their persistent realistic representation of their contemporary worlds—their fictions' present temporal settings—in historical terms. Odd as it is, however, both James and Cather in the declining years of their careers write into their work self-reflexive dramas that anticipate Cohn's divide between fiction and history. James's great unfinished *The Ivory Tower* (1917), which Ezra Pound rightly identifies as a modernist *ars poetica* of fiction, is named for an artful receptacle into which is sealed, with the approval of the novel's protagonist, the unknown background of the protagonist's inheritance. The protagonist's subsequent undoing of the seal, in order to discover the real history of the inheritance, was to have been the climactic moment in the novel's projected but unwritten pages. But James imagines his novel as itself the receptacle, and as therefore a break with its historical environment. How is the dividing and disjoining break— more a disconnect between the ivory tower and life than an in-between

of the two—to be understood? Is it James's admission that even historical fiction is fiction, not history?

   To arrive at answers one must take a closer look at *The Ivory Tower*.
Its protagonist, Gray Fielder, inherits, in the form of a stupendous
bequest, the world order of high capitalism. Although, according to
James's notes, Gray suspects "black and merciless things that are behind
the great possessions" (295) amassed by capitalist accumulation, he
chooses to keep his suspicions in suspense. If merciless things belong
to the past of great possessions, then an administration and use of the
latter might not be merciless in the present. Because Gray wants to see
if fruits of capitalism can work for ends that are both pleasurable and
morally decent, he experiments with the present, allowing it to function as a screen of indeterminacy in relation to the past. Indeed, he
appoints a man he admires to manage his inheritance, in hopeful trust
that the manager will demonstrate how accumulated riches in their
present state need not be a sign—a "conclusive sign" (318)—of continuing nefarious exploitation. Gray understands that such a conclusive
sign might be sealed in the tower, in an epistolary text that is a history
of the background of his fortune. But Gray refuses to read that text,
preferring to suspend his suspicions and to trust his screen. After all,
the letter in the tower, written by a business enemy of Gray's benefactor,
might be merely a spiteful slander on the origins of Gray's inheritance,
and on capitalism itself. And if the present truth about the character of
capitalism's accumulations is indeterminate (perhaps that character is
merciless, perhaps merciful, perhaps both and neither), should a single
past perspective on those accumulations be accepted as a substitute for,
or as a determinant resolution of, their present indeterminacy?

   For better or worse, however, Gray's suspicions get the upper hand.
Black and merciless things behind his possessions threaten to come to
the front of them. What happens in the present outside the tower corroborates the history of treachery within it. James's notes for his novel
argue that the present history of capital will repeat its past history; that
present and past are twins in immorality and in lack of mercy. But, then,
if James offers the novel's ivory tower as a figure for history's determining impact upon the present, and if he invites us to think of that receptacle also as a figure for novelistic art (for the well-wrought urn of fiction),
then does not James thereby suggest a twinning of past and present, and
of artifice and history? Such a suggestion, whereby history inside the
bounded enclosure of art is no different from material history enacted
outside that enclosure, would appear to confute Cohn: it amounts to a
parable that erases distinctions between artifice and life, between fiction
and history. Yet the fact of the containing receptacle is paramount to

James's imagination. He clings to the object, the elaborate artificial box, because it stands for a boundary between past and present, and between revelatory discourse and indeterminate immediacy. Aiming his narrative at some conclusive sign of the present's unresolved meanings, seeking a significance that is "determinant" ("my cherished word," James notes [319]) within whatever resists such search, James images the ivory tower— the very name he gives his fiction—as a crucible of determination. The crucible cannot function, cannot deliver what it contains, without instancing limitary constraints in the course of delivery. The crucible resolves what is indistinct into a form of distinction.

Such resolution, as James sees it, opposes an inevitable license granted to "massed ambiguity" (267) by capitalist world order. Ambiguity is a freedom from determination's constraints, and Gray's experiment with his fortune courts an escape from distinctions into interminable ambiguity, existence free of defining limits and meanings. Such boundless liberty from definition feeds, as well as characterizes, the economic order Gray inherits and spurs Gray's financial manager to appropriate an ever-increasing share of Gray's funds. Liberty from definition also characterizes the present and the past, until a moment when an aspect or emphasis in the present gives a shape to the past, or until a moment when an aspect or emphasis in the past gives a shape to the present. The explanatory text within the tower is not available as truth until a present action makes relevant, and corroborates, what is locked away in the tower. Until that authenticating and objectifying corroboration, the ivory tower contains only a hypothesis about past and present, only a provisional explanation for history's determinants. For a suspenseful stretch of time, therefore, the truth of history in James's text appears to be both inside the tower and outside it, because each side of the divide hypothesizes each side's narrative as the true story of the present. But ultimately only one side is substantiated as actual truth. The tower text, originally doubted as distorted fabrication, takes on the authority of actual truth thanks to Gray's experiment upon the character of his historical present. Such a gain of authority, a veritable transubstantiation of a hypothesis—a speculative fiction—into truth, is made possible only by a "disconnect" between past and present, inside and outside, provided by James's artifice, by his bounding and enclosing receptacle. If the tower compels James's imagination, then that is because, I suggest, it stands for formal separations and articulations, for resistance to any breakdown of distinctions.

In naming his novel for the art object within it, James offers his novel as a self-reflexive phenomenon: it is itself a container, wonderfully self-enclosed, like the object it contains. James's container offers

Gray's story as, in contrast to the eponymous object, open to the present moment of historical and personal time. But that openness is a feint. James's fiction is twice bounded: the tower figures a limitary enclosure within the text as if art did not seal off the text from the very historical present it purports to mirror. James's historical moment marks his text, certainly; yet that marking would not be legible if his text and his present were products of undifferentiated intermingling. The novel would be incapable of determining the bearing of the present, were the novel not a self-contained container. James's hero, no less than his tower, figures that self-containment, which becomes Gray's liberty from his inheritance. Without the distinct detachment from context instanced by the tower's receptacle for its sealed letter, and without Gray's potential for being himself sealed and detached from the present, Gray would become as free, and as insatiably and willfully indeterminate, as his money-possessed circle of new acquaintances. Self-contained, an ivory tower of a person, Gray becomes what he is because of his struggle to internalize, utilize, and exorcise the capitalist present's intrusive, willfully indeterminate history. Analogously self-contained, the ivory tower of James's fiction becomes what it is because of its (and its author's) same struggle.

Given such an ethos of self-containment, and given James's purpose to insist on distinctions in the face of their erasure, James would seem to incline to the idea that historical fiction is fiction, not history. If we now turn to Willa Cather, and take her *Shadows on the Rock* (1995 [1931]) into account, it appears that Cather also confirms that historical fiction is fiction, not history. Despite the novel's attachment to the history of Quebec during the period 1697–1698, at every turn Cather seems to divest the novel of historical, even of worldly, attachments. The name "Quebec" corrupts "an Indian word meaning 'the closed-up place' " (Vollmann 1993, 899). Cather seems to have jumped at the possibility of exploiting the closed-up place of the rock as her version of an ivory tower.

It is startling to see Cather, whose other novels belong to the canons of historical realism, use the historical subject matter of *Shadows on the Rock* to keep history at bay. While Cather relies on Parkman and Jesuit histories for her very material, she simultaneously is rejecting the historical past, the historical present, and historical discourse. The young heroine's love for Quebec's fogs comes from their making the rock's denizens feel "cut off from everything and living in a world of twilight and miracles" (50). Who among critics has not noticed this cutting off? The result of the notice has been a derogatory critical equation of Cather's twilight and miracles with a Disney-sentimental animation. On the showing of *Shadows on the Rock*, the practice of the history-fiction distinction looks like an irresponsible escape from reality and from the application of fiction to historical needs.[1] But there is something rigorous in what Cather is up to, just as there is rigor in what Cohn is up to. Cohn sees fiction itself as a territorial disciplinary injunction to maintain a territorial separation of fiction from history. In the novel's opening announcement, that because it is late October the last summer ships are returning to France, the description of "retreating sails" resonates with the sealing off of Quebec from Europe for a long season. "Now for eight months the . . . colony would be cut off . . . from the world" (3). The first character to focalize the sailing/sealing is an apothecary, a medical man, whose pharmacy cannot reverse the dismemberment: "this severance grew every year harder to bear" (3). It does not grow harder for the apothecary's daughter, Cecile. She appears to thrive on the sealing that cuts off one thing from another. One of the novel's first self-reflective moments (an ivory tower moment) involves Cecile's response to the story of a miracle told by an Ursuline nun. The nun intends to apply a moral to the miraculous narrative: "And now," she begins, "from this we see"—but Cecile severs the story from joining up with history, from the world of practicable applications: *"N'expliquez pas, chère Mère, je vous en supplie!"* The sudden breaking out into French emphasizes the disruptive artifice Cather has undertaken to pursue. "But it is the explanation of these stories," the storytelling nun protests, "that applies them to our needs" (32). Nevertheless, in this novel, Cather, like Cecile, runs away from the application of fiction to historical needs. Cather resists those needs, whether they derive from fiction's present (in depression-era 1931, a need for proletarian realism) or from a present historical or political urgency (the rise of fascism).

Because running away from history does not suit the temper of our literary criticism, why bother with such flights, no matter what authorities produce them? One reason to bother is the indubitable fact of the forms Cohn anatomizes. Having thought for decades about them, and having addressed relevant counter-arguments (from Derrida's and Foucault's to Hayden White's), Cohn persuades one that fiction's optical and cognitive powers are not easily portable across the borders of other discourses. Like Cohn's, Cather's use of fiction's special arts defends them against any easy translation into nonfictive discourses, or against any easy appropriations of them by history. But it must be admitted that the more one looks into *Shadows on the Rock* the more one feels that Cather's practice of the distinction of fiction has a shocking aspect. Drawn out and fleshed out by a James or a Cather, the components of Cohn's "distinction" take on a life of their own. In Cather, the life they assume is feverish. The apothecary in *Shadows on the Rock* is an anti-hero because his author's self-disciplining formalism, especially in light of its compulsion to divide history from fiction by enclosing the latter, comes to seem sickly, or at least unwilling to be medicated. We know, from biographers as well as from critics, the story of Cather's obsessive-compulsive fantasy about her loss of a hand. A fearful threat of dismemberment, the critical tradition goes, incites Cather to use writing to reassert her healthy control over emotional and artistic break-age.[2] But such a critical line appears to be wrong. Cather writes to be more broken rather than less, to suffer breaks rather than repair them. Every fictional sealing, every evocation of bordered enclosures in her, courts cutting. Now fiction's cutting away from, or breaking off from, the world's other discourses, at least as Cather instances a modernist version of the break, seems less than sanative. What hath the Jamesian ivory tower wrought? An ostensibly historical novel closes itself off from the historical presence it evokes! Gray Fielder holds himself open to his present, provisionally at least; Cather, in comparison, seems compul-sively bent on self-sealing. But suppose Cather, even at her most self-sealing moment, is not an exception but a novelistic norm. Ought not an equivocally sane character of fiction be recognized as such by Cohn's dispassionate analysis? Why not use Cather to recognize fiction's im-medicable tendency and then to reassess, perhaps less dispassionately than Cohn, the great divide?

The middle book of *Shadows on the Rock*, Book Three, brings us closer to the formal patterning's reiterated character. By this point in the text Cather has erected numerous equivalents of James's ivory tower. Various containers—everything from a magical "crystal bowl full of glowing fruits of colored glass" (48) to a newly opened crèche—have reiterated the severed, sealed-off state of the rock. Anything not so sealed appears by now to be anomalous and untrustworthy. When Book Three begins by introducing a new character, a young bishop, who immediately is marked by the narrator as temperamentally unstable, we are to understand the bishop's instability as a negative: the character is unstable because he is not self-contained. The next episode reiterates the value of self-containment. Cecile has heard of a miraculous conver-sion: a sailor has found faith after swallowing powdered bone derived from the skull of a Jesuit martyr. But her father, the apothecary, who calls himself "the guardian of the stomach" (103), refutes his daughter's inclination to violate bodily continence. Only a self-containment whose boundaries are strictly guarded can effect miracles. Accordingly, a miracle of strict, indeed, harshly violent, self-containment enters Book Three. It takes the form of the story of the Montreal anchoress, Jeanne Le Ber, who for years has willfully immured, indeed, entombed herself, in a church cell, to universally inspiring effect. Of course the story of Jeanne is inserted by Cather without any attachment to the surrounding narrative; only after a disjunction of thirty pages will Jeanne's tale be applied to, or explicated in terms of, the narrative's story line. Disruption is the seal of Jeanne's importance.

Self-containing kinds of disruption matter for Cather, not self-rupturing kinds. After we are told about Jeanne's self-containment, a woodsman comes to the apothecary shop, seeking help: he has undergone a stomach rupture. It cannot be repaired. With a failure to medicate this break the narrative, having attended to an unsealed rupture, opens for the reader a secret it has all along contained: the apothecary and his daughter plan to return to France. Will they thus undo their severance from the world? They mean to persuade a young priest friend to return with them, but the priest arrives to tell two tales of consecrating confinement within the rock's boundaries. One tale is about Jesuit martyr Chabanel, who overcame his terror of New France by a stabilizing vow to permit the wilderness to enclose him, no matter what the price. The second tale is about the young priest's vow to repeat Chabanel's career. The apothecary, stunned by these revelations of self-enclosure, searches for a metaphor wherewith to comprehend. Perhaps, the apothecary thinks, the young priest's vow is "the box of ointment which was acceptable to the Saviour" (125). From this salvific box we move to the next. Cecile falls ill, but she has a vision of boxed-in immurement that cheers her: all the outside world, even the "merciless forest . . . seemed to her like layers and layers of shelter, with this one flickering, shadowy room at the core" (127). Inside layers and layers of bounding shelter against history, the shadowy core is Cather's fiction itself.

In what I have just redacted, I have traversed only thirty-five of the novel's pages. An ivory tower patterning of the narrative figures and refigures itself in terms of bounds, and it does so right up to its termination. In the novel's last sections, the governor of Quebec dies after vividly dreaming of the enclosed space of a childhood house. The enclosure in the dream protects him from invasion by a faceless giant. The dream itself also is an enclosure. And when after the governor's death his heart is removed from his body and is sealed in a leaden box, the casketed heart comes to the apothecary shop, which is itself a double for the dream house. In the novel's final pages the apothecary recognizes that in his present moment he is more "wholly and entirely cut off" (213) from the past than he was on the novel's first page, and he becomes convinced that there also is an impassable divide between the past and future. As for the present, it is curiously blank, set apart from dying past and hidden future, a specimen of self-containment that evokes fiction's self-presence rather than history's. The narrative maneuvers us into accepting such temporal and discursive divisions.

However obsessively Cather is working her narrative structures, it is clear that she recognizes her monomania on behalf of severance. Jeanne Le Ber is a portrait of the author-artist: out of her enclosure she issues beautiful embroideries and inspires heartening legends. But later the narrative comes round to a more worldly inspection of her. When it does so, she has momentarily ventured out of her saintly ivory tower. We then are told that her face has petrified with sorrow. This drama-tization of authorial coming out is an alternative picture of the self-containing and self-contained distinction of fiction from history; of what the distinction does to its objects. The transparent minds are "hoarse, hollow"—mere skull and bones—and their utterances carry "the sound of despair" (147). And the authorial mind appears to con-fess itself well-nigh crazed by a formalist version of obsessive-compulsive disorder. As for the reader whose attention is caught by the procession of Cather's ivory tower episodes, he learns indeed what Cohn means when she says "reading fictional narrative . . . burdens its performance with . . . stressful . . . freedom." The freedom is stressful because, how-ever interpretive, it is scarcely free. With Cather in front of us those free agencies promised readers by "the distinction of fiction" are hard to tell apart from a reader's submissiveness to an ever-repeating set of con-straints. But more constrained than the reader of *Shadows on the Rock* is its writer. She exhibits her free inventiveness as self-conscious, self-enclosing, and even self-punishing imprisonment.

Shadows on the Rock confirms an impossibility and unreality that Cohn identifies with fiction. Only fiction can penetrate the enclosure of a dying man's dreams. It can be thus penetrating only after it constructs the enclosure. But even as Cather's novel attests to the rightness of Cohn's anatomy of fiction's special arts, clearly the novel reverses one of the foundational contrasts on which Cohn rests the signposts of fictionality. Whereas Cohn argues that historical narrative is identical to constraint and fictional narrative identical to liberty, Cather exercises herself in *Shadows on the Rock* in order to make us match fiction with constraint, and to match history—the thing that is shut out from the novel, even as it inspires the novel—with free agency. Cather equally exercises herself to show how the constraints that characterize fiction are as haggard or gruesome as they are pretty or magical. With Cather brought to bear on Cohn, one wishes that Cohn had not taken for granted the attractiveness of the emancipatory diction she attaches to her signposts.

We must make something of Cather's mixed confirmation and contradiction of Cohn. Not only a neglected or contemned novel by Cather is at issue. For one thing, modernism is at issue: woven throughout modernist fiction, with James as a prime instance, is the very distinction Cohn painstakingly articulates. For another thing, disciplinary distinctions that make fiction available to separate study, apart from other kinds of discourse—history, for example—are at issue. Also at issue is what characterizes a relation between distinct discursive entities. Even as fiction and history are distinct from each other, nevertheless they influence each other, as Gray Fielder's story shows.

Under Cather's influence I suggest that we might understand Cohn's distinction between fiction and history as one that has been made necessary by historical forces and conflicts. It is not art's intrinsic autonomy, forever unfolding, that separates fiction from history. The great divide results from an undergirding symbiosis of the divide's antagonists. Historical perplexities, no less than fictional forms, stimulate the need to distinguish fiction from history. But only in the light of such a distinction can fiction, as we saw with James, become what it is by utilizing and exorcizing history's nefarious intrusions; only in the light of an analogous distinction can a moral agent gain sufficient self-possession to resist a nefariously shaping historical present. Accordingly, Cather proposes, I think, that the distinction between fiction and history needs to be maintained as a promise of the solution of historical perplexities. How perplexing that a Chabanel should bind himself to a vow to live among peoples he detested (as his own historical relation tells us), because any alternative struck him as a satanic suggestion! Yet such binding constraint becomes a paradoxical historical agency in history. It also becomes a paradoxical mechanism of agency in producing fiction. A solution to such perplexities and paradoxes has nothing to do with unconditioned freedom of the kind Cohn equates with fiction and with reading fiction. Toughly analytic though Cohn be, she is a utopist. As Cather rather than Cohn makes us see, forms of fiction are painfully identical to constraints, immurements, and inhibitions. Inasmuch as fiction might contain intimations and resolutions of historical problems, writers and readers of fiction must come to terms with boundaries, with patient suffering, and even with limitations of agency. All of these are involved, pace Cohn, in distinguishing fiction from other discourses.

In actual history, a figure like Chabanel shows us how an agent's immurement in an oath can maintain him in time's river, and enable him to influence it. In fiction, a figure like Gray Fielder can show us how history can be discovered inside an ivory tower of art, or come to reside in that tower, by being kept out of it. To work out what I mean,

I will take one more look at Cather, and then solicit fiction's present, in the work of William T. Vollmann, for ultimate help. If we look at the relation of *Shadows on the Rock* to Cather's previous books, we can see how history is in her novel by virtue of being kept out of it. Immediately after the thirty-five pages of box-after-box construction summarized earlier comes another episode about someone suffering rupture. Here, gruesomely, the earlier episode about ingesting bones turns into an account of bones coming out of a person. A strange fellow named Blinker, whom Cecile has taken under her wing, has suffered a decomposition—a "suppuration"—of his lower jaw. "Pieces of bone came out through his cheek" (129). Now, suddenly, something else comes out: Blinker explains his history. In France he was a torturer's apprentice. He was "brought up to that trade" (131). He carries inside him, he tells the apothecary, the faces, the voices, and the words of the tortured. He is moved to open up his history by the contagious effect of a similar story, one told by the apothecary about his former life in France. One of the apothecary's family retainers, a knife grinder, had been tortured to death for a petty theft. Explicating this tale, the apothecary faults the law as the torturer. "The Law" tortures in order, he says, "to protect property . . . [the Law] thinks too much of property" (75). The novel suggests that the only possessions that are free, and free of the law, are ones that are separated, or suppurated, out of the history of property and law's abetment of it. How fortunate that the apothecary and his daughter are prevented from returning to France! "Wholly and entirely cut off . . . a helpless exile in a strange land" (213), suffering the division of new times and places from old, the apothecary is blessed because he has been cut off from the historical regime of property. Where there is property, free agency is not worth having. The apothecary's separation from history, an analogy to Chabanel's vow, helps him overcome the economic and political order that would otherwise submerge him.

In Cather's *The Professor's House* (1973 [1925]) thinking too much of property causes a breakup of the intense love between Roddy Blake and Tom Outland. Blake, behind Outland's back, sells off the collection of containers—beautiful jars and bowls—that represents the two comrades' discovery and exploration of Cliff City. The city, situated atop the closed-up space of Blue Mesa, is presided over by a "beautifully proportioned" tower—this one is red—that "held all the jumble of houses together and made them mean something" (201). Blake and property spoil what Blake and Outland have held in common. Outland's reparative response to the spoliation is of course not a reassertion of property rights. He takes up exile on the mesa "in a world above the world" (240). "It was possession" (251), he says, but not of the owning kind. Cut off from ownership, he feels he has found everything rather than lost it. And he has no need to further record the history of the place, especially his "own." He squirrels away his previous mesa diary and refuses to consult its instance of history, let alone continue it. Screened off from history, Outland lives entirely in a self-enclosed present. But the record of the rock-top experience is carried forward by the exile's author. In a collapse of differences that we expect fiction to maintain among author, narrator, and character, historical Cather becomes her own Outland. *Shadows on the Rock* is its author's Outland-ish (and apothecary-like or Chabanel-like) spiritual exercise on a mountaintop. The force of the exercise, more detached even than Gray Fielder's (and something like an interior exploration of his state of detachment and suspense), with an almost-heated-to-madness intensity of structuration, derives from the shadowing sources—the historical sources—below it and outside it. They have been left out, or squirreled away, but they have not been left out of account, because those sources justify the flight from property—hence from present history—that Cather enshrines on her sealed-off rock of freedom.

The sources are peculiarly American, because they are Native American; and they are peculiarly non-American, because they are communist. Given this riddling origin, no wonder Cather chooses for her shrine a specific Canadian site: a geographical narrows to which the United States is attached but which also is not part of us. As for her native American non-American historical sources, they are easy enough to name. Of course, a preeminent name is Francis Parkman, but we would not have Cather's career and her fictive shadows on the rock of history if it were not for Lewis Henry Morgan's *Ancient Society* (1985 [1877]), and his *Houses and House-Life of the American Aborigines* (1965 [1881]); and of course *Ancient Society* depends upon Morgan's *League of the Iroquois* (1996 [1851]).[3] Morgan contends that private property commences with the dissolution of democratic and egalitarian gentile structures, of which the Iroquois are the supreme example. Had Americans modeled themselves on Iroquois economic principles (as well as on Iroquois federal principles), history and property might have met their match. Marx and Engels, Engels especially, were inspired to make them meet their match because of Morgan's book about the ancient gens. In Marxism, the Iroquois share the stage with Hegel. A world-historical irony is that the United States went on fighting for property against "outland" revivals of the economic order of its aboriginal peoples. The irony is more salient when we consider that, following Morgan, Parkman makes the victories of the Iroquois against the Huron, the Jesuits, and the French a gateway to the ascendancy in North America of English freedoms. "Liberty may thank the Iroquois," writes Parkman, "that the plans of her adversary [her adversary being the Absolutism of the Jesuits and the French] were brought to nought, and a peril and a woe averted from her future" (1963 [1867], 552). If, despite Parkman's magnanimity, the Iroquois have gone thankless by Liberty, then have they also been snubbed by Cather? Her Quebec of 1697–1698 derives from Parkman's epic. Even though the Iroquois wars are coming to an end by 1697–1698, it seems wrong that the Native Americans have scarcely a presence in her novel. And yet they are there, inside the ivory tower, whose beautiful proportions debar the history of property, and thereby conserve Native communism. That tradition, contained in Outland's and Cather's beautifully proportioned towers of red rock and grey rock, constitutes a different narrative history from that in James's tower. Yet its warning against the present history of possessions, and against an unconstrained liberty of acquisitiveness, is the same as James's. James's protagonist would have discovered in his tower the corroborative truth that was to make him free—and free of property. But James imagines such freedom as impossible without a prior constraint and a prior constraining separation from history. The prior constraint might be any shaping force of domination in the present. The counter to such constraint, imitating it yet combating it, is art's formal distinctness, art's self-contained autonomy, hence its difference from history. James seems to have thought that only by way of a poetics that disconnects fiction from history can fiction subsequently return to history. Cather conforms her fiction to James's apparent conviction. The conformity gives evidence of the accuracy of Cohn's insistence that even historical fiction is distinctly different from history. But Cather's conformity also goes beyond Cohn, because James and Cather identify fiction with limitations that take priority over freedom.

If only the beautiful proportions of James's and Cather's towers did not, in the name of the distinction of fiction, conserve a disciplinary torture of formal constraint! Surely the torturous constraint is altogether possible to break. Perhaps the contrast between fiction and history is itself wholly vulnerable if Cohn's contrast does not survive beyond James's and Cather's examples. Why not find a novelistic instance that definitely erases a history-fiction divide? Vollmann's *Fathers and Crows* (1993) might be that instance. It is a sublimely baggy monster of a historical novel about Champlain's founding of Quebec, about the Jesuits, the Hurons, and the Iroquois. In *Fathers and Crows*, all the history is in the fiction—and, given the crowded near-thousand pages of it, all the history in it clearly is out of the containing fictional box.

TWO: STREAM/DREAM OF CONSCIOUSNESS

But with all the history out of the box, where is the fiction?

In leaving *Shadows on the Rock*, I thought to find a text from fiction's present where history and fiction intermingle, where the past is present by virtue of being the fiction writer's historical inquiry, which he or she publishes as a historical "novel": a supreme example of Cohn's generic in-between, in which the writer's freedom and the reader's freedom are a perfect match. Yet the more one considers *Fathers and Crows*, the more Vollmann seems to confirm the divide between history and fiction by standing fully, voluminously, on history's side of it. The "novel" is framed by reports of visits by Vollmann to Montreal, where his Quèbècois friends debate the history of Canada's multiple national identities. Is this novel really an autobiography, wherein the author's life and travels preface a vast historical meditation on contemporary conflicts? The text is certainly a history. "This book," the opening pages say, "is the story of how the Black-Gown [the Jesuits] and the Iroquois between them conquered the Huron people" (7). The Huron people, unsuccessful participants in a North American arms race in the seventeenth century (which foreign power could arm which native people first, in order to acquire the latter as allies?), found themselves near extinction. They received no word of thanks from either Liberty or Absolutism. Now Vollmann complexly gives them their due. His text is laced with commentary and footnotes by anthropologists and historians, whom Vollmann repeatedly enlists to shore up his historical accuracy. Three volumes of Parkman are in the near background; thirty-seven volumes of Jesuit *Relations* are in the foreground. Although the title page announces that the volume is the second of a series called *Seven Dreams*, the fictionlike liberties that dreams take with reality are here overwhelmed by a resolutely documented narrative.

But the novel does adopt a persona named William the Blind, and a gap between fictive William and actual Bill is a signpost of fiction. Cohn helps us identify the fiction, and the Dream element, by isolating a crucial formal component of historical fiction. The formal component is a moment-to-moment present-tense sequence of subjective impressions that we vulgarly call "stream of consciousness." Stream of consciousness is a supreme illusion invented by fiction to represent interior life. On the far side of fiction's border, historians cannot—will not—make use of the stream. But why might novelists use it in historical fiction?

Cohn's answer is canny, and once again motivated by her belief that the distinction of fiction and the freedom of the reader of fiction are a complementary pair. Fiction writers do not enlist stream of consciousness to represent history but to represent fiction. Everyone knows that we do not talk inwardly like Molly Bloom. Juxtaposed with historical elements, stream of consciousness plays up historical fiction's promiscuously mixed but still separate collage of fabrication and fact. For Cohn, the mixture permits a reader to feel the liberty of exercising separate interests—in fiction, in history—without any need to unite them, and without any constraint on liberty. Historical novels make history and fiction available for speculation and pleasure, and exercise us in noticing (in one and the same volume) differences between history and fiction. Exercising both sides of the divide, even while maintaining it, reading historical novels strengthens the agency of a reader's comparative and contrastive capacities. If Vollmann gives us stream of consciousness in *Fathers and Crows*, then we will be in touch with the fictive part of his history. And we will have an occasion to exercise our discriminatory agency and freedom.

Is not such exercise an essential site of fiction's present: a novelist freely choosing to juxtapose his materials, drawing them from diverse times and discourses, redrawing them at will to shape a discursive in-between "now"? At an early page of *Fathers and Crows*, one steps into a stream of consciousness that Vollmann also figures as a stream of time ("the Stream of Time . . . that must eventually freeze over in allegories . . . although in my book it remains a determinedly downpassing creek" [5]). Here is a joining disjoin of history and fiction, with history's fortunes unfolding downstream, and downpage:

> The Black-Gowns prayed to the Huron: LET US LOVE YOU—and the Huron were destroyed. If you pray to a prostitute: let me love you—then maybe you or she will be destroyed. If I pray to Sainte Catherine [Tekakwitha]: let me love you—well. . . . That is the Sixth Point. . . .
>
> To love Christ properly (taught the Black-Gowns), you must despise yourself. The more you dissolve yourself in the river of Him, the more you will be Him in all His Love and Power. This may be so, and it may not be so. But do you need to despise yourself in relation to other human beings?
>
> Consider that moment (not a great deal downstream . . . that little rivulet called Time) . . . when Père Chauchetière was pleased to see that certain Savagesses had begun to adopt austerities. . . . Père Chauchetière had never sought to communicate these things to the Savages, believing them still to be too lowly of purpose and understanding to benefit

(remember that these were Iroquois!), but GOD shaded three
Savagesses with his black wings; they formed a society to
commence a sort of convent, at which Père Chauchetière
was forced to intervene, saying my dear children, I cannot
permit this because your grace is not sufficiently tested at
which they threw themselves down before him, . . . pleading
and wailing and gashing their foreheads on the stones like
undisciplined infants. (14–15)

How is one to read a prose composed of such streaming elements, and
what attitudes is one to take toward the latter? Are we, like Père
Chauchetière, also "to intervene"? What is the point, the first point of
the river passage, let alone the Sixth Point? Is the use of you-narration
part of the history, or a signal of fictionality? The questions will have to
be searched, researched, the points claimed, reclaimed. Agency will be
exercised as a necessary *articulation* of what rushes along in the water.
The stream is more than one: it is actual Canadian fleuves, the St.
Lawrence above all; it is metaphorical literary rivers: Twain's Missis-
sippi, the roman fleuve, Joyce's riverrun. Readers will have to distinguish the multiple things rushing by to keep their heads above water,
and to keep them there freely and pleasurably, even as they maintain
the fiction-history divide—or even as they countenance a fiction-history
dissolve. But a reader's upright agency is threatened by thronging
questions. One sinks in this river—which has all the fluid undecidability
of a present moment—at the very instant of putting a toe in the water.
Who is Sainte Catherine? Is she Huron? What Iroquois women are
here? Why is the narrator (or is it Bill? or William the Blind?) praying—
and praying erotically? And why does he contemplate a destruction by
prayer of what he says he loves? Is he kidding? In what light is one to
"Consider that moment" in which the moment-to-moment present of
the eddying stream gathers force? The prospects for freedom and pleasure are not encouraged by the fact that *Fathers and Crows* is soon to
introduce a character named Born Underwater. She is to be one of the
text's enduring figures, but her name is ominous. We must assume, in
order to follow Vollmann's text, that one's ability to make and maintain
distinctions will get a reader through, will strengthen the agency that
can bear one's reading swimmingly along. Because Cather did not feel
borne along swimmingly by history, she undertook to enclose herself in
constraints. What is at stake in Vollmann's ever-expanding streams of
consciousness, and the agency whose practice those streams might in-
cite, is the hope that fiction and history work together to overcome
their divisive constraints.

For better or worse, however, distinctions are the settings of limits. If Vollmann pushes against them—the title page announces that the work is "compounded and confounded from diverse relations"—then does his text exhibit the success of the push, or does it show that the anti-limitary project is another case of the Blind leading the blind? One signpost of fictionality in narrative is, we have noted, perturbations of chronology. There are considerably less temporal perturbations in Vollmann than is suggested by pages fourteen and fifteen. But of the most prominent analepses that structure *Fathers and Crows* one at the book's very midpoint celebrates a breakdown of borders, a successful practice of an in-between. This analepsis is called "Temperance." It narrates the life of the Jesuit Roberto de Nobili, a missionary to India, who—to the scandal of his Jesuit superiors—told the Indians of the subcontinent that "you can be a Brahmin and a Christian too" (475). Temporarily punished, but then reinstated, de Nobili, who himself exchanged his black gown for a saffron robe, made 4,000 converts. The narrator remarks, "So, if [conversion] had to be done at all, it could have been done that way in Canada. It could have been done" (477). Had it been done, the Huron would not have suffered as they did.

It was not done; "could haves" are curiously fictional; the tone of the narrator's sentences is hard to gauge; and paging through *Fathers and Crows* one can scarcely find "Temperance": for, although set at the novel's midpoint, "Temperance" is only eight pages long. Inasmuch as *Fathers and Crows* is nonfiction, all of its history might mean to promote the temperance it pictures at its heart. But how curiously enclosed or contained temperance is in this text, as if in an ivory tower. Unlike Chabanel, de Nobili figures a liberty from limits; yet despite de Nobili's success as an "in-betweener," his evoker, William the Blind, is inspired to allegorize him in terms of a formal confinement. Such confinement might express how temperance, besides being a mean—a golden in-between—depends upon discipline, upon self-contained resistance to rivers of time and desire that carry along, or have their source in, insatiable, intemperate drives. What is limitary, and not what is anti-limitary, resists inrushing historical agents of riverine imperial domination. Meanwhile, perhaps Vollmann figures de Nobili's virtue by extraordinary narrative containment because he acted on a continent far from North America. What matters for Vollmann's choice of subject matter is limitations set for him by an American continental container (however loose and baggy) rather than by another.

Because the markedly fictional stream-of-consciousness segments of *Fathers and Crows* are intermittent, and relatively short in duration, their contrast to more realistic and historically documented segments becomes heightened. If Vollmann wants to unify fiction and history's mutual workings, then he therefore must find a structural way to subdue any contrast between fictional stream and historical fact. He finds a way in self-reflective aspects of his male protagonists. Champlain and the Jesuits (especially the martyr, Jean de Brebeuf) are portraits of William the Blind the artist-novelist. Like Champlain, the novelist also is an explorer. His rivers of time are likenesses of geographical rivers Champlain set himself—for property's sake, of course—to measure and map. And Champlain's frustrations in the text—"Was there no end to anything? When would he reach the final measurement?" (427)—are a historical novelist's frustration as he tries to reach final measurements for a staggering array of historical and material givens. Champlain's search for a latitude that will put him on a direct line from Canada to China echoes the fiction writer's search for a latitude wherein facts and fiction can align themselves and be at one. But the character that is even more an authorial projection is the Jesuit Brebeuf. His practice of St. Ignatius's spiritual exercises is proto-novelistic. Loyolan exercises make ethical and spiritual deliberations depend upon the work of imagination. Each exercise produces, simultaneously, a historical fiction and an intervention in the stream of history. No wonder Vollmann disrupts forward chronology in *Fathers and Crows* to insert a life of Ignatius. Ignatius is one of the fathers of the novel form. Vollmann's treatment of him is a metafictional literary history. A historical fiction about the past, *Fathers and Crows* also harks back to the past of fiction, to the novel form's origins in mental and imaginative exercises that accompanied militant spiritual and material empire. Fiction's present derives from world-historical exercises aimed at the simultaneous acquisition of souls, territory, and wealth.

By making map-making explorers and imagination-exercising priests serve as his doubles, Vollmann undermines differences between history and fiction. History making and history writing and fiction making and fiction writing are the same activities; and their productive agents are alike. There need not be any antagonism between them. All work equally in the streams of time and consciousness. Throughout *Fathers and Crows*, Vollmann describes his characters as "making the Exercises" when they reflect upon what they do or will do. The reader too "makes the Exercises" while reading. When one sees that *Fathers and Crows* structures the reader too as explorer and as Jesuit we see that the reader's exercises, whatever they do articulate, do not articulate a disjunction between the fictionalizing of facts and the historicizing of them.

And yet Vollmann's solution to the problem of fiction's distinction, serviceably constructive as it is in many directions, advances the

problem distinctly once more. The will—of blind Will or Blind Bill—
to explore a solution finds its limits. Champlain and Brebeuf double
the author's exploratory and spiritual agency. The agency, however, in
historical terms and contexts, is destructive. *Fathers and Crows*, unlike
Parkman's history, is not about the saving of Liberty by anyone. That
might be Vollmann's blindness. But his book is a story of how Exercises
of an agency that could not distinguish between reality and fiction
conquered the Huron people. All together the agencies of property, of
arms races, of technological development in the 1600s, no less than the
spiritual agencies, seem not to distinguish between reality and fiction,
between fact and invention. Hence, those agencies are unconstrained.
Without constraint, outside the confines of fiction or of reading fiction,
history is a fullness of violence. Henry James calls his art of fiction the
religion of doing. Vollmann identifies even his own explorerlike and
imaginative art with the disaster of doing. This is why "Bill" at page
fifteen thinks that, under the sign of agency's paramount value, even
prayer can destroy its object. So the values of *Fathers and Crows* are
highly contradictory. Vollmann must chronicle and replicate a colossal
commitment to historical agency. And he must at the same time be
critical of that agency and radically contain his own. His artistic agency
must be separated off from the disastrous history that impels it. He
needs an equivalent of James's ivory tower, of Outland's blue mesa, and
of Cather's rock.

He finds his equivalent in something like Cather's heated obses-
siveness, but his version of it is harder to countenance, or to bear. His
withdrawal from the historical destructiveness with which agency is allied propels, not surprisingly, a retreat of his fiction into a sphere of
passions. Fiction's transparent minds provide a locus for the retreat.
The stream of consciousness encloses passions of the mind. But passions that interest Vollmann in his retreat from agency are intensely
tortured ones. Their character perhaps results from the way historical
conditions have driven agency inward, and turned its energies inside
out. In *Fathers and Crows* the Iroquois's candidate for sainthood,
Catherine Tekakwitha, a product of Jesuit inspiration, has gained the
narrator's love. She is a model of self-torture. In loving her, and not
loving his male doubles, the narrator expresses horror at the torturous
historical constraints upon agency; and at the same time he expresses
his alliance with passion at any price, rather than with history's en-
tanglement of exploration and action. If the price of passions that lose
the name of action is mortifying self-discipline, then so be it. There is
a decided resemblance between Vollmann's use of the Iroquois Catherine
and Cather's use of Jeanne Le Ber.

A story of inevitable constraints, rather than inevitable liberties, is the critical tale I have essayed.[4] Whether we consider James and Cather in fiction's past or Vollmann in fiction's present, fiction's attempt to engage with history, once confronted with wills to power and property that authorize history, pushes fiction back into its self-contained realm. This might make those of us in the present who want to bridge a history-fiction divide suffer pains of intellectual or disciplinary constraint. Yet the inhibition of agency entailed by such suffering is not without value. As we see it in James, Cather, and Vollmann, the inhibition is loyal to an impulse to counter a North American agency that long has overexercised itself, at the expense of passivity, and of valuable passions other than a passion for sheer agency or a passion for amassing accumulations (art being among such alternative passions). Lest I seem too narrowly inspired, however, by ivory towers, I want to evoke from Huron and Iroquois traditions an illustration of a necessary operation of constraints upon us, whether we locate such constraints in history's realm or in fiction's. Morgan and Parkman appear to have reminded Vollmann, the author of *Seven Dreams*, that the Huron and Iroquois regularly celebrated dream-guessing rites. The custom of the rites was for a dreamer to go door to door requiring neighbors to guess what the dreamer had dreamed of, and then to give the dreamer the dreamed-of object. Whatever accumulation or gift exchange is marked by the custom, certainly the dream feast suggests an all-but-impassable riddling. Between the "Can you guess?" and any answer is a great divide. An answerer goes immediately to the boundary between the invention of truth and knowledge of truth. And although the boundary at first looks like a carnival escape from compulsions, in the dream-guessing rite the yielding of answers and property—one must answer, one must give—evokes the phenomenon of limitary constraint. If at first a riddler accepts any response, then at rite's end he or she is limited by truth and is allowed to retain only a true answer.[5]

In *Fathers and Crows* history perhaps repeats, for author and reader, the dream rite's command: "Can you guess what I've dreamed about? Tell me! And give me what I've dreamed." Whatever the answer, history reluctantly tells what it has dreamed of in the past, or what it dreams of in the present. Although history, like the riddler, at first takes any answer the present gives it, response to history's dreaming ultimately is fixed at a boundary between knowing the truth and inventing it. Slipping the boundary, as Vollmann suggests, even where he self-laceratingly repeats the slippage, has been destructively problematic. Consider, for an example of the problem, how Champlain and the Jesuits believed they knew what both the Huron and history dreamed of: Huron conversion to French "goods" in the forms of French arms, French fur trading, and Catholicism. Explorers and priests were happy to give those goods in response to the riddle of "savagery." Their giving, complacently attached to their own dreams of enhanced agency for Frenchmen and "savages" alike, ignored any distinction between French and Jesuit imagination and the impenetrability of others' historical dreams. And why not ignore that distinction if one assumes that any difference between self and other, or between fact and desire (whether acquisitive desire or religious desire), is indeterminate? Gray Fielder's money and his financial manager's conduct inherit the self-same blurring of determinate boundaries that simultaneously initiated early modernity and Western empire. Of course, what seventeenth-century French agents "gave" to Huron dreamers in fact coerced the Huron nation to submit to French and Jesuit dreams, that is, to fictive inventions—including an invention of property—that Europeans did not care to recognize as fiction. The Huron generously answered to such dreams, fatally; but Huron revenge lies in the essential ignorance of their sly-seeming exploiters. The stream of time's forever self-enclosed and secret dreaming makes fools of those who seek to master it by inventing ways to overleap the distance between fact and fiction. The dream rite perhaps allegorizes constraints that condition both knowledge and invention—even the most generous-minded knowledge and invention as well as the most nefarious.

Cohn gives no account of historical causes for her distinction that constrains the intermingling of fiction and history. And her study of the distinction is, at least in light of James, Cather, and Vollmann, overly optimistic about liberties and a freedom from pain she believes the distinction entails. The novelists, despite James's, Cather's, and Vollmann's differences from each other, are more alike, and more unlike most contemporary academic critics, because their historical meditations have made them deeply uncertain about the value of the absence of constraints. The present is a dream rite, baffling us contemporaries, demanding that we yield up its secrets, even though it will scarcely disclose them. Novelists attempting to gloss the present in their fictions must be wary of unconstrained response. To solve the riddle might mean a fatal overleaping of boundaries. At the same time that the present asks fiction to guess what the present is dreaming about, the present and the past also suggest that fiction limit itself, that it be tempered by self-contained form, in order to respect limits upon agency and indeterminacy. If literary tradition can be trusted, then contemporary fiction writers—like Gray Fielder in his suspenseful financial experiment, like Cather's characters in their self-enclosure, and like de Nobili in his temperance—might well doubt indeterminacy's expansive freedom, even if such indeterminacy appears to be an inspiration for novelists and readers, or a doorway to fiction's "in-between" inwardness with contemporary reality. A choice of constraint rather than freedom, or of boundedness as a best form of freedom, is not easy to come to terms with. James, Cather, and Vollmann powerfully ask that we come to terms. In responding to those novelists I consent to their divide between fiction and history, because that division has at stake an important bearing on the history of the novel, on historical discourse, and on history as we live it. Given my consent, however, in the last analysis my disagreement with Cohn also is an admission that she is right: the distinction of fiction holds. Fiction's self-contained, bounded distance from history perhaps constitutes its most adequate relation to the present.

NOTES

1. Skaggs (1990) acknowledges the traditional critical complaints about the novel's escapism and defends Cather by arguing that Cather meant *Shadows on the Rock* to be a miracle play in novel form. Unfortunately, Skaggs's defense tends to reinstate a sentimentality it means to oppose. Following Skaggs, and as if to continue compensating for the novel's low reputation, recent appreciations of *Shadows on the Rock* tend to become uplifting meditations. I hope I read against the grain of uplift. For a discussion of recent criticism, see note 4.

2. See O'Brien (1987, 384).

3. Given Cather's interest in the Southwest, it seems likely that she would have known Morgan (1965 [1881]) and just as likely that she knew his other famous books. But current criticism drops Morgan out of sight (see, for example, Harrell 1990), as if Morgan (1965 [1881]) would not have been in Cather's mind at the time of the discovery of Mesa Verde. Meanwhile, although Tooker (1985) claims that Morgan (1996 [1851]) "remains the best single description of the Iroquois culture" (xvi), it appears that matching Cather with Morgan is now a sensitive matter. Millington's (1999) conjunction of Cather and Boas is more prudent in light of Trigger and Washburn (1996), who celebrate Boas as the first who "emphasized as anthropologists had never done before the dignity of Native peoples and of the ways of life they had evolved before the arrival of Europeans" (96). Boas's initial work, *The Central Eskimo*, was published in 1888 by the Smithsonian. Despite failures of emphasis in previous anthropologists, one might claim that readers of problematic texts do not necessarily replicate the failures of those texts and sometimes in the course of being inspired by such texts correct their ideological deficiencies rather than mechanically repeat them. I do not see Cather as such a mechanical reader. Skaggs (1993) points out Cather's verbal borrowing from at least three of Parkman's histories of French influence in North America but does not explore how Cather shifts what she borrows into ideological registers more progressive than Parkman's.

4. Recent criticism of *Shadows on the Rock* emphasizes the liberty and agency of its author and its characters. Stouck (1999) celebrates the freedom of Cather's border crossing. In effect, Millington (1999) also does so, by emphasizing discursive convergences, hence a blurring of borders, between Cather's fiction and "modernist" (Boasian) anthropology. In Harris (1999), skepticism in Cather's hands turns out to mean optimism, hence a promise of enlarged agency; and Moseley (1999) maps all the characters in *Shadows on the Rock* as heroic Jungian agents. My emphasis on nefarious aspects of agency sorts somewhat with Romines (1990), although the latter's feminism is made uncomfortable by the very figures of constraint that Romines traces.

5. For a spectrum of descriptions of the dream rite, see Parkman (1963 [1867]) on the Huron (154 ff), Wilson (1960) on the Iroquois (227–33), and Trigger (1976) on the Huron (83 ff).

REFERENCES

Bhabha, Homi. 1994. *The location of culture.* London: Routledge.

Boas, Franz. 1964 [1888]. *The central Eskimo.* Lincoln, NE: University of Nebraska Press.

Cather, Willa. 1973 [1925]. *The professor's house.* New York: Vintage/Random House.

———. 1995 [1931]. *Shadows on the rock.* New York: Vintage/Random House.

Cohn, Dorrit. 1999. *The distinction of fiction.* Baltimore. MD and London: Johns Hopkins University Press.

Harrell, David. 1990. Willa Cather's Mesa Verde myth. In *Cather studies,* vol. 1, ed. Susan J. Rosowski, 130–43. Lincoln and London: University of Nebraska Press.

Harris, Richard C. 1999. Willa Cather and Pierre Charron on wisdom: The skeptical philosophy of *Shadows on the rock.* In *Cather studies,* vol. 4, ed. Robert Thacker and Michael A. Peterman, 66–79. Lincoln and London: University of Nebraska Press.

Ignatius of Loyola. 1989. *The spiritual exercises of St. Ignatius.* Translated by Anthony Mottola. New York and London: Image Books/Doubleday.

James, Henry. 1917. *The ivory tower.* In *The New York edition of the novels and tales of Henry James,* vol. 25. New York: Charles Scribner's Sons.

Millington, Richard. 1999. Where is Cather's Quebec? Anthropological modernism in *Shadows on the rock."* In *Cather studies,* vol. 4, ed. Robert Thacker and Michael A. Peterman, 23–44. Lincoln and London: University of Nebraska Press.

Morgan, Lewis Henry. 1965 [1881]. *Houses and house-life of the American Aborigines.* Chicago and London: University of Chicago Press.

———. 1985 [1877]. *Ancient society*. Tucson: University of Arizona Press.

———. 1996 [1851]. *League of the Iroquois*. Secaucus, NJ: Citadel Press/Carol Publishing Group.

Moseley, Ann. 1999. The hero within: Heroic archetypes in *Shadows on the rock*. In *Cather studies*, vol. 4, ed. Robert Thacker and Michael A. Peterman, 97–117. Lincoln and London: University of Nebraska Press.

O'Brien, Sharon. 1987. *Willa Cather: The emerging voice*. Oxford: Oxford University Press.

Parkman, Francis. 1963 [1867]. *The Jesuits in North America*. Boston and Toronto: Little, Brown and Company.

Pound, Ezra. 1968. *Literary essays of Ezra Pound*. Edited by T. S. Eliot. New York: New Directions.

Romines, Ann. 1990. The hermit's parish: Jeanne Le Ber and Cather's legacy from Jewett. In *Cather studies*, vol. 1, ed. Susan J. Rosowski, 147–58. Lincoln and London: University of Nebraska Press.

Skaggs, Merrill Maguire. 1990. *After the world broke in two: The later novels of Willa Cather*. Charlottesville and London: University Press of Virginia.

———. 1993. Cather's use of Parkman's histories in *Shadows on the rock*. In *Cather studies*, vol. 2, ed. Susan J. Rosowski, 140–55. Lincoln and London: University of Nebraska Press.

Stouck, David. 1999. Willa Cather's Canada: The border as fiction. *Cather studies*, vol. 4, ed. Robert Thacker and Michael A. Peterman, 7–22. Lincoln and London: University of Nebraska Press.

Tooker, Elisabeth. 1985. Forward. Lewis Henry Mogan's *Ancient society* [1877]. xv–xxviii. Tucson, AZ: University of Arizona Press.

Trigger, Bruce G. 1976. *The children of Aataentsic: A history of the Huron people to 1660*, vol. 1. Montreal and London: McGill-Queen's University Press.

Trigger, Bruce G., and Wilcomb E. Washburn. 1996. Native peoples in Euro-American historiography. In *The Cambridge history of the native peoples of the Americas*, vol. 1, *North America: Part 1*, ed. Bruce G. Trigger and Wilcomb E. Washburn. 61–124. Cambridge: Cambridge University Press.

Vollmann, William T. 1993 [1992]. *Fathers and crows*. Harmondsworth, Middlesex: Penguin Books.

Wilson, Edmund. 1960. *Apologies to the Iroquois*. New York: Farrar, Straus and Cudahy.

Chapter 12

Fourteen Notes Toward the Musicality of Creative Disjunction, or Fiction by Collage

LANCE OLSEN

ONE: CONCLUSION: AMPHIBIOUS AESTHETICS

If we are witnessing at the creative peripheries of our culture the pro-liferation of a postgenre composition that questions the need for dis-cussing such apparently singular species as, say, *science fiction* and *postmodernism*, we also are witnessing the proliferation of a postcritical writing that questions the need for discriminating between such appar-ently singular species as *theory* and *fiction*. We are witnessing—and have been for at least the last thirty or forty years—what Steven Connor (1997) discusses as the slow "collapse of criticism into its object" (227). We are witnessing, that is, the advent of performative critifictions dedicated to effacing, or at least deeply and richly complicating, the accepted differ-ence between privileged and subordinate discourses. The collage imagi-nation at the core of such a gesture is one committed to liberating juxtaposition, mosaic, conflation, fusion and confusion, Frankensteinian fictions, cyborg scripts, centaur texts, and the narratologically amphibi-ous writings that embrace a poetics of beautiful monstrosity.

TWO: RONALD SUKENICK, 1972

We have to learn how to look at fiction as lines of print on a page, and we have to ask whether it is always the best arrangement to have a solid block of print from one margin to the other running down the page from top to bottom, except for an occasional paragraph indentation. We have to learn to think about a novel as a concrete structure rather than as an allegory, existing in the realm of experience rather than in the realm of discursive meaning, and available to multiple interpretation or none, depending on how you feel about it (1985, 206).

THREE: MILORAD PAVÍC, 1998

In his essay "The Beginning and the End of Reading—The Beginning and the End of the Novel," Milorad Pavíc distinguishes between two kinds of art: *nonreversible* and *reversible*. Nonreversible art, such as traditional fiction, is unidirectional; instances "look like one-way roads on which everything moves from the beginning to the end, from birth to death" (1998, 143). Reversible art, on the other hand, such as architecture and sculpture, is prismatic, multidirectional, and rhizomic; instances of these "enable the recipient to approach the work from various sides, or even to go around it and have a good look at it, changing the spot of the perspective, and the direction of the looking at it according to his [or her] own preference" (142). Pavíc endorses the latter variety, affirming that his goal in collaged works such as *Dictionary of the Khazars* has been "to make literature, which is a nonreversible art, a reversible one"—one that pits itself against the deep-structure propulsion of narrative by rupturing its seemingly inflexible arc from birth to death while celebrating the strength of the human imagination (143).

FOUR: FRIEDRICH NIETZSCHE, 1874

One day sitting at his writing desk in his Basel flat Friedrich Nietzsche will look at the pages of the manuscript on which he is working and grasp with resounding disappointment the architecture of every phrase is wrong his house of signs a ruin not the *what* of saying the *how*. He will look at the sheet of paper before him and all he will see is how every blocky paragraph is the color of ashes just another sentence in a language filled with them because every writer in his country has become a journalist wearing a blend-in essence and in the next breath it will come to him that writing isn't expansion but compression a texturing into fragment saying in seven sentences what everyone else says in a book saying in seven sentences what everyone else *doesn't* say in a book employing the figure of aphorism and the form of collage to construct a particle philosophy for a particulate world bringing together what is shard and riddle and chance engineering with his flesh.

FIVE: RONALD SUKENICK, 1975

This novel is based on the Mosaic Law, the law of mosaics, or how to deal with parts in the absence of wholes (1975, 122).

SIX: QUOTATION AS CHANCE

Both the structuring and the reading of collage fiction often involves an aleatoric component that recalls not only the Cubist work of Braque and Picasso but also the Dada and Surrealist work of Duchamp and Breton: interest in the found object, the ready-made, the chance encounter. It also recalls Lévi-Strauss's notion of *bricolage*, as Gregory L. Ulmer points out, foregrounding concepts of already-extant messages, severing, discontinuity, and heterogeneity. Ulmer goes on to argue that collage is a form of citation "carried to an extreme . . . collage being the 'limit case' of citation" (1983, 89), and Derrida reminds us that "every sign, linguistic or non-linguistic . . . can be cited, put between quotation marks; in so doing it can break with every given context, engendering an infinity of new contexts in a manner which is absolutely illimitable" (1977, 185). Collage, then, through the very process of cutting up and cutting off, opens up and opens out. By appropriating and quoting out of context, the form releases new and often unexpected contexts, recontextualizations that can surprise the author as well as the reader.

SEVEN: LITERAL AND METAPHORICAL COLLAGE

The notion of collage can be used literally or it can be used metaphorically in fiction composition. That is, as Ulmer and Derrida indicate, collage fiction can be deeply appropriative in nature, cutting up previous texts to create new ones, as in, say, the work of Eliot and William S. Burroughs. But it also can be used as a structuring principle for new textual units—not only as a juxtapositional combination of ready-mades, then, but of just-mades, as in, say, the work of Milorad Pavić or Julio Cortázar.

EIGHT: RONALD SUKENICK, 1994

You need to understand that understanding is an interruption. Understanding is always an interruption of which you understand in the form of the cryptic. You need to interrupt yourself (1994, 74).

NINE: PATCHWORK BODY

Collage fiction draws attention to the sensuality of the page, the physicality of the book, and therefore draws attention to writing as a
postbiological body of text. This point is evinced, for instance, in Steve
Tomasula's novel *VAS: An Opera in Flatland* (2002), and Shelley Jackson's
Web-based hypertext, *My Body* (1997). Replete with three-color graphics, foldout pages, wild typographic play, diagrams, doodles, drawings,
and disparate citations, the former involves an expansive comic plot
about a man named Square living in a (literally) two-dimensional sub-
urban world with his wife, Circle, and their daughter, Oval, and Square's
struggle over whether or not to undergo a vasectomy. But it is the
structure of that plot—that is, the body of the text about the text of the
body—that makes Tomasula's collage fiction an unforgettably unique
reading experience. In the latter, the reader chooses which parts of
Shelley Jackson's critifictional autobiography to read by clicking on
various parts of her body in a schematic sketch. The sound of lungs
inhaling and exhaling in the background provides musical accompani-
ment to much of the reading experience.

TEN: SHELLEY JACKSON, 2003

*In collage, writing is stripped of the pretense of originality and appears as a
practice of mediation, of selection and contextualization, a practice, almost, of
reading. In which one can be surprised by what one has to say, in the forced
intercourse between texts or the recombinant potential in one text. . . . Writers
court the sideways glances of sentences mostly bent on other things. They solicit
bad behavior, collusion, conspiracies. Hypertext just makes explicit what everyone does already. After all, we are all collage artists.*

ELEVEN: COLLAGE FICTION AS CONTINUUM: A

Just as there are many modes of realism, there are also many modes of
collage fiction. If we imagine a narratological continuum of textual
possibilities, then we discover at one end scholarly works with their will
toward intellectual authority through collaged citation, or, slightly farther on, my critifiction *Girl Imagined by Chance* (2002), which blends
authentic citation with false, questionable, and pure fiction to generate
a lyrical structure whose intent, among other things, is to explore notions
of cultural memory and textual authority.

TWELVE: COLLAGE FICTION AS CONTINUUM: B

Near the middle of our continuum, we discover particulate fictions that assume but do not require a reading strategy that arcs from beginning to end. Here I am thinking of a novel such as David Markson's *Vanishing Point* (2004), with its interlacing of art historical, literary, musical, and other arcana in brief prose blocklettes, or Joe Wenderoth's epistolary novel, *Letters to Wendy's* (2000), in which a deliciously unstable narrator composes a series of easily interchangeable prose-poem missives to the fast-food chain. Farther on still appear books that employ both text and graphics in collaged arrangements, such as Kathy Acker's avant-punk *Blood and Guts in High School* (1978), Eckhard Gerdes' avant-samizdat *Cistern Tawdry* (2003), and Eduardo Galeano's politico-surrealist *The Book of Embraces* (1989), whose narraticules (most only a few lines long, none more than two pages of prose) are sometimes political in nature, sometimes philosophical, sometimes fictional, and almost always highly metaphorical, meditative, and elusive; none contributes to an overarching plot, but each speaks and adds to the rest.

THIRTEEN: COLLAGE FICTION AS CONTINUUM: C

Beyond these are books such as Max Ernst's *Hundred-Headed Woman* (1929) that employ no or virtually no text whatever, and, at the far end of our continuum, we discover bookless do-it-yourself collage texts such as Marc Saporta's *Composition #1* (1963), which arrives as a bundle of loose pages in a box along with instructions to shuffle and read, or Web-based hypermedial compositions requiring a reading strategy uninterested in or even actively antagonistic to notions of beginning, middle, and end. In this limit-case category, I am thinking of such work as Stuart Moulthrop's *Reagan Library* (1999) and Talan Memmott's *Lexia to Perplexia* (2000).

All these modes share, to one degree or another, a belief in the musicality of creative disjunction because . . .

FOURTEEN: VICTOR SHKLOVSKY, 1917

And art exists that one may recover the sensation of life; it exists to make one feel things, to make the stone stony. The purpose of art is to impart the sensation of things as they are perceived and not as they are known. The technique of art is to make objects "unfamiliar," to make forms difficult, to increase the difficulty and length of perception because the process of perception is an aesthetic end in itself and must be prolonged.

REFERENCES

Acker, Kathy. 1978. *Blood and guts in high school.* New York, NY: Grove Press.

Connor, Steven. 1977. *Postmodernist culture: An introduction to theories of the contemporary.* Cambridge: Blackwell.

Derrida, Jacques. 1977. Signature event context. *Glyph* 1: 172–97.

Ernst, Max. 1981. *Hundred-headed woman.* Translated by Dorthea Tanning. New York, NY: George Braziller.

Jackson, Shelley. 1997. *My body.* http://www.altx.com/thebody/body.html.

———. 2003. *Stitch bitch: The patchwork girl.* http://www.mit.edu/comm-forum/papers/jackson.html.

Galeano, Eduardo. 1991. *The book of embraces.* Translated by Cedric Belfrage. New York, NY: Norton.

Gerdes, Eckhard. 2003. *Cistern tawdry.* New York, NY: Fugue State Press.

Markson, David. 2004. *Vanishing point.* Emeryville, CA: Shoemaker & Hoard.

Memmott, Talan. [n.d.] *Lexia to perplexia.* http://tracearchive.ntu.ac.uk/newmedia/lexia/.

Moulthrop, Stuart. 1999. *Regan library.* http://iat.ubalt.edu/moulthrop/hypertexts/rl/.

Olsen, Lance. 2002. *Girl imagined by chance.* Tallahassee, FL: FC2.

Pavíc, Milorad. 1998. The beginning of the end of reading—the beginning and the end of the novel. *Review of Contemporary Fiction* (Summer): 142–46.

Saporta, Marc. 1963. *Composition #1.* New York, NY: Simon & Schuster.

Shklovsky, Viktor. 1998 [1917]. Art as technique. In *Literary theory: An anthology.* 17–23. Malden, MA: Blackwell Publishers.

Sukenick, Ronald. 1975. *98.6.* New York, NY: Fiction Collective.

———. 1985. The New Tradition. In *In form: Digressions on the act of fiction.* 201–13. Carbondale, IL: Southern Illinois University Press.

———. 1994. *Doggy bag.* Normal, IL: Black Ice Books.

Tomasula, Steve. 2002. *VAS: An opera in flatland.* Barrytown, NY: Station Hill Press.

Ulmer, Gregory L. 1983. The object of post-criticism. In *The anti-aesthetic: Essays on postmodern culture,* ed. Hal Foster, 83–110. Port Townsend: Bay Press.

Wenderoth, Joe. 2000. *Letters to wendy's.* Athens, GA: Verse Press.

Chapter 13

Mount Rushmore

Four Brief Essays on Fictions

MICHAEL MARTONE

WASHINGTON

Freud fucked us up, this Father business. The Mother business as well. He, Sigmund, is the inventor of the modern novel, is *the* novelist of the twentieth century, the founder of the form. He is the Father, that again, of the notion of Character and even more importantly the notion of the character of Character, this business of depth, this business of three dimensions, this business of complex. The forefather of the epiphany of The Epiphany and the transformation of transformation of Character that follows. He, Freud, elicits in me a kind of envy, yes, Envy, that I have not, in all my years, invented or, in all my years to come, will never invent, any Character as real as Ego, as real as Id. There! There are fictions for you. So contagious as to jump the page, reformulate the brain chemistry so completely as to deny the efficacy and accuracy of Brain Chemistry to explain the brain. His invention of the Subconscious, the Unconscious naturalizes inside us (Inside Us!) the idea of the Subconscious, the Unconscious (See!) as if these fictions are not fictions. I like the bib of slag spilling down the General's chest, a graphic demonstration that the head of the Head of State was always in state there inside the mountain. See the limestone wigged helmet of the figurehead on the brow of the cliff ship! The lithic waste is the cascading, foaming bow wake. George is a kind of Venus in drag and Penis in person, the titanic member being the progenitor of his Country, sure, but also Love, I guess, or at least that compelling drive of Sex, emerging from the sea of solid rock.

191

JEFFERSON

He was the writer. Well, Lincoln, too, wrote, signed on to write Jefferson's sequel. And Jefferson is the one whose backstory has legs. The heritage of his transmitted DNA decoded as avidly as the Declaration is parsed for intention. My favorite plot twist? The branch of Hemmings's children by Tom who passed into Ohio, refusing to cotton up to the analysis of their genes, preferring White-ness over Jefferson-ness. How odd our desire that this one have a life that is narrative not simply anecdote. And irony too. Backstory and, there on the escarpment, he's got George's back. The inventor of political parties, the originator of difference. The Great Deconstructor has the least "face." No distinguishing marks save that distinction of no distinguishing marks. Okay, red hair, but this is a monochromatic mountain. Jefferson pulls duty, in two dimensions, flat visage on the screwy two-dollar bill. J is our K of presidents. Anonymous and somewhat known with the suggestion there are things one wants to know. And inside Jefferson is Madison, the symbiote inside the big brain, the watch in the pocket. Madison writes Jefferson; Jefferson writes *America*. *America* is the Great American Novel.

ROOSEVELT

Reading left to right: Roosevelt. The Modernist whose medium is stuff, stuff like mountains, like canals, like painting battleships white and sending them on a performance piece around the world. Probably his idea to create the thing itself, this wacky stunt in South Dakota. Or at least it was in the air he breathed, expelled. His is the spitting image of the contemporaneous Zeitgeist, the modesty of the placement of his visage tips-off the self-consciousness of the facade. The least equal of these equal giants but nonetheless the Great Sculptor of the ideal of giants. The last of firsts but the first of lasts. There is real artistry in the rendering of the pince-nez. The glasses are there but not. A transparent reproduction of Transparency. Transparency the dominant ideology of the age, our age. The trick of Realism, its tricklessness. See, these busts bloomed on the mountaintop, a spontaneous generation like maggots appearing on rotting meat. WYSIWYG is what you see and what you get from this point on. No bull. The eye is drawn to those eyes, magnified by the invisible glass. What are you looking at? The writing of novels, I think, is so beside the point isn't it. One writes novels to write the author of the novel. The book itself does not last, is not carved on the side of a mountain, is not printed on money. Funny, the New Critical transparency was to focus on The Work and not The Author of The Work. But it is always *Marvel's* "To His Coy Mistress." Every work comes with that apostrophe of possession. The Author ain't dead. The Author ain't even ain't.

LINCOLN

The most dead one. How did Washington die? Jefferson? Roosevelt? Lincoln's death was the one dramatized, in a theater no less, by an actor acting and acting. History is scripted. The show goes on. Literally, the show goes on. *Our American Cousin* performed daily like clockwork. The clocks all set for ten after ten. What ever happened to pageants? The great theatrical recreations of historical events by ordinary citizens, descendants of the participants in the original events, on the sites where the original events first transpired? Sure, the Mormons perform each summer, on another mountain in New York, the visitation of the angel to the Prophet Joseph Smith. Now there is a novel! But the art form of the pageant, the Pre-Postmodern art form, seems to have waned. Perhaps. Perhaps, pageantry continues but is only now disguised as Real Life, Story and History the same. The recent War in Iraq was staged. It was held in theater. How did the President watch the performance? Not that much differently than I did, I bet. Like a King in Shakespeare watching a play on stage upon the stage. Like the Subjects of a King watching the pageantry of royalty, of war. My favorite part was the soldier, wounded in the hand, waiting for the evacuation by helicopter, who had the word HAND written on his forehead, talking to his mother, a half a world away by satellite phone, talking to his mother in real time (Real Time!) while I watched. That was my favorite part. Lincoln's forehead was a stage. In the movie *North by Northwest*, all of the presidents look on when the actor Cary Grant playing the role of Roger Thornhill playing the role of Mr. Kaplan performs a staged performance of his (Cary Grant playing Roger Thornhill playing Mr. Kaplan) death all witnessed by the back projected image of the mountain, there, through the window by the barber shop quartet of stone. At the moment of the assassination The Real World approaches harmony with the Fiction of the World. *Sic Semper Tyrannis!*

Chapter 14

Recognition as a Depleted Source in Lynne Tillman's *Motion Sickness*

SUE-IM LEE

Recognition is the fuel that runs the engine of the realist novel. Unwitting Isabel Archer requires years of heartache—and many hundreds of pages of narration—to realize that she had been made "a convenience" (James 1979, 528) by those she trusted the most and, upon arriving at the proper recognition of the base nature of Madame Merle and Gilbert Osmond, completes her portrait of a lady. Poor Dorothea Brooke enters a marriage on an entirely mistaken idealization of her suitor Causabon of Middlemarch, spending her marriage in misery and mistreatment at his hands until she accepts the implications of her misrecognition. In Dickens's and Hardy's novels, too, mistaken identities and mysterious lineage provide crucial pivot points of tension, until proper recognition of respective identities—the mysterious stranger that Pip meets in the marshlands, the true parentage of Oliver Twist, the repentant vagrant who returns to become the mayor of Casterbridge— settles the score and completes the drama at both novels' conclusions.[1]

In fact, it may be more accurate to say that *mis*recognition is the fuel that runs the engine of the realist novel. How many unhappy romances and friendships, disastrous marriages, failed businesses, and faltering careers rest on individuals exercising acts of misrecognition? And what can solve the dilemma of misrecognition except the eventual promise of proper recognition, a promise delivered at the end of the novel? As the initial misrecognition gives rise to misunderstandings, dashed hopes, and irreversible life decisions, the protagonist's movement toward the final port of arrival—toward proper recognition— parallels the development of the plot. More significantly, the foundational convention of the novel—the developmental character—

195

requires the epistemological *boundaries* set forth by the initial misrecognition and the eventual, proper recognition, for we map her "progress" by her increasing proximity to attaining proper recognition.

The novel's logic of developmental character, hence, takes place in a unique epistemological condition—one in which misrecognition is ultimately a correctable phenomenon, and proper recognition is an acquirable skill, a fruit of experiential labor. This chapter argues that one of the fundamental challenges to the novel comes from contemporary fiction that explicitly questions the novel's epistemological condition. That is, a mark of fiction's present is its treatment of recognition as a *depleted* resource, a resource that once delivered the promise of proper recognition but that no longer can. Recognition becomes the subject of ambivalence and distrust, and concomitantly, the epistemological condition of the novel becomes the subject of nostalgia and scrutiny. I offer an analysis of Lynne Tillman's novel *Motion Sickness* (1991) as exemplifying the treatment of recognition as a depleted resource in contemporary fiction, and I suggest that the unique combination of desire and distrust for recognition articulates a particular moment in fiction's present—a moment when the memory of the novel rings strong, whilst being countered by poststructuralist and postmodern suspicion of recognition.[2]

This conflict that marks fiction's present can be mapped within the very definition of the word "recognition." "To recognize" can mean: (1) "To know again; to perceive to be identical with something previously known" and "To know by means of some distinctive feature; to identify from knowledge of appearance or character"; (2) "To perceive clearly, realize" (Recognition 2000). The first set of definitions denotes "recognition" (the act of recognizing) as the act of knowing by *knowing again*—to know in reference to what one already knows, to know by association. The second definition, however, denotes something entirely different; one knows (perceives, realizes) *without* recourse to knowing again (the exemplar quotations for this definition are: "Linnell has made us recognize a new beauty in the heather"; "Kepler first recognized the fact that the eye is a camera" (ibid.). Hence, within its definition, "recognition" carries the seeds of the paradox constituting one of the key philosophical and theoretical challenges of the late twentieth century: How can knowing be at once a "knowing again" and "knowing afresh"? After poststructuralism mapped "knowing" as fundamentally an operation bound within preexisting codes and systems, how can recognition claim an "outside" from when one may know afresh? Such skepticism has a profound effect on the literary envisioning of intersubjective encounters: How do characters recognize each

other? How do I recognize others? How do they recognize me? Ultimately, what are the criteria for discerning the difference between
misrecognition and proper recognition? If I cannot discern the difference, then are they one and the same phenomenon?[3]

The distance between knowing again and knowing afresh, an ir-
reconcilable gap in poststructuralist theory and postmodern fiction, is
seamlessly spanned in the convention of the realist novel. We think of
the novel's narrative environment "bookended," as it were, by the two
definitions of the word. The protagonist's initial misrecognition demonstrates the knowing again, while her "realization," "perception," or
clearer "knowing" by the narrative's end demonstrates the knowing
afresh. The interim—the unfortunate repercussions of misrecognition—
constitutes the story's tension, until finally the protagonist is delivered
to the port of knowing afresh—until Isabel Archer realizes the truth of
her situation "as distinctly as if it had been a picture on the wall" (James
1979, 508).

Precisely such a port of arrival—a knowing as concrete and as
fresh as a picture on the wall—is desired by Tillman's protagonist, and
in some parts *Motion Sickness* explicitly invokes the specter of Isabel
Archer in dramatizing its protagonist's epistemological wanderings. Thus
while Tillman imbues her protagonist with a desire that belongs to, and
is delivered in, the narrative environment of the nineteenth-century
realist novel, the epistemological condition of *this* late twentieth-century
novel will always deny that desire and in fact formulate the desire itself
to be out of place. Built around the drama of recognition and its paradoxical meanings, *Motion Sickness* exemplifies a postmodern literary
challenge to one of the most entrenched epistemological conditions of
the realist novel.

KNOWING BY REPETITION

An analysis of recognition greatly benefits from two of the most
influential studies of the concept—Althusser's theory of interpellation,
which politicized the function of recognition and cast the concept firmly
within the operations of power and social organization; and Barthes's
poststructural semiotics, which pressed us to distrust the conditions of
all that is "readable," "familiar," "stereotypical," and "recognizable."

In Althusser's landmark essay, "Ideology and Ideological Apparatuses" (1971), recognition lies at the heart of his theory of interpellation. Althusser uses the analogy of "hailing" ("hey, you there!") as the
means by which the state identifies and reproduces subject positioning

(as worker, student, family member, or consumer of a specific race, gender, or religion). The individual's response to that hail—the proverbial act of turning around—completes the state's inscription of individuals into "subjects" of ideological apparatus (such as systems of education, religion, family, legal, political, labor, and capitalism). Thus recognition *enables* interpellation, because that automatic response—of turning around to the hail—is naturalized as a self-evident response. Althusser uses a scenario of recognition familiar to all of us: A close friend knocks on my door; I ask, "Who is it?"; she or he responds, "It's me." This answer reveals nothing except the fact that my visitor/hailer and I have an already-familiar relationship. I open the door not because my visitor/hailer identified her or his particular relevance to me (such as "It's Jane"; "It's your sister;" "I'm the plumber") but because I obey the logic of knowing again.

Such is the way, Althusser argues, that the state maintains and reproduces the conditions of production, the positioning of subjects within capitalist relations of exploitation. As we respond to the numerous "hails," we are performing "rituals of ideological recognition" that not only make us subjects of ideological apparatus but that naturalize the very logic of interpellation. "They 'recognize' the existing state of affairs (*das Bestehende*), that 'it really is true that it is so and not otherwise,' and that they must be obedient to God, to their conscience, to the priest, to de Gaulle, to the boss, to the engineer . . ." (Althusser 1971, 123). In the Althusserian theory of interpellation, then, recognition—the logic of acceding to a prior arrangement and relationship—is *already* a misrecognition: "The reality which is necessarily ignored . . . in the very forms of recognition (ideology = misrecognition/ignorance) is indeed, in the last resort, the reproduction of the relations of production and the relations deriving from them" (124).

Although Althusser's thinking on interpellation specifically targets the reproduction of capitalist labor relations, his theory of recognition-as-misrecognition fundamentally informs late twentieth-century political and critical interrogations of (racial, ethnic, sexual, national, etc.) identity and subjecthood. You are not what you say you are: you are what you are hailed. And the ways you are hailed are so familiar, so *repetitive*, that you believe that your response is of your own volition. What is this case but an instance of "a subjected being, who submits to a higher authority, and is therefore stripped of all freedom except that of freely accepting his submission?" (123). What is recognition, then, but an act of ideological submission? At the heart of Althusser's theory of recognition, then, lies a distrust of repetition, the knowing again that accedes to the logic of the familiar, to the repeated.

Likewise, a distrust of repetition underpins Barthes's lifelong study of the semiotic systems. In his study of the signs and codes that span human expressions, from literature, fashion, photography, and advertising to political discourse, Barthes locates repetition as the indispensable logic of knowing by knowing again. His overriding term for signifying the danger of repetition is *doxa*, a term crucial to his interrogation of what constitutes the "familiar," the "recognizable," the "stereotypical," and "stupidity." Most extensively introduced in *Roland Barthes by Roland Barthes*, doxa is "never defined by its content, only by its form, and that invariably wrong form is doubtless: repetition" (Barthes 1977, 70). It isn't that *all* repetition is the wrong form, Barthes clarifies; he distinguishes a "good form," such as an individual's repetition of a point, of a "theme" ("The repetition that comes from the body is good, is right" [71]). The bad form of repetition, or doxa, is the repetition of an unlocatable discourse that comes from nowhere and everywhere— public opinion, cliché, stereotype, commonplace: "Doxa is the wrong object because it is dead repetition, because it comes from *no one's* body—except perhaps, indeed, from the body of the Dead" (71, emphasis in original); "The Doxa is current opinion, meaning repeated as if nothing had happened. It is Medusa, who petrifies those who look at her" (122). As an unlocatable discourse whose omnipresence can translate into the category of the probable, the likely, and the real, dead repetition sits at the heart of knowing by knowing again. What is recognition, hence, but an epistemological operation within the bounds of doxa?[4]

The *form* of repetition, then, links Althusserian formulation of interpellation and Barthsian analysis of doxa. What Althusser identifies as the self-naturalizing logic of knowing again—that "it ["the existing state of affairs"] really is true that it is so and not otherwise" (1971, 123)—finds a parallel in Barthes's identification of doxa's omnipresence: "The Doxa . . . is Public Opinion, the mind of the majority, petit bourgeois Consensus, the Voice of Nature, the Violence of Prejudice" (1977, 47); "The Doxa is not triumphalist; it is content to reign; it diffuses, blurs; it is a legal, a natural dominance; a general layer, spread with the blessing of Power; a universal Discourse" (RB, 153).[5] What Althusser and Barthes bring to the foreground, then, is a fundamental distrust of the condition of knowing again. As they highlight the political work of repetition in the concept of recognition, a suspicion of repetition infiltrates our everyday acts—how we recognize others, how we are recognized, how we announce a certain representation's familiarity or realism, and how we evaluate the probability or likelihood of certain accounts.

Such a suspicion of knowing again infiltrates all aspects of daily life in *Motion Sickness*, whose protagonist-narrator regards acts of recognition with profound unease and distrust. The wandering life of the protagonist is essentially a life of continuous exercise in recognition. A young white American woman who makes a life of traveling across Europe, her itinerant lifestyle is reluctantly funded by her mother, who implores her to return home and "face the music" (Tillman 1991, 88). She moves from one city to another at whim, accountable to no person or schedule; travel acquaintances, friends, and lovers of brief affairs constitute a shifting community. As the most significant testimony of her hermetic status, she is a prolific collector and writer of postcards that she never sends to the intended. The "motion sickness" of the story, then, is the inevitable by-product of an itinerant lifestyle. As Tillman describes in an interview, *Motion Sickness* explores "the anxiety of recognizing how really unstable your identity is. . . . You're not going to achieve a stable existence, but that's not so terrible in a way. It might make you sick, though, once in awhile, because of that motion" (Nicholls 1995, 276).[6]

As the narrator lives the paradoxical condition of permanent travel, her biggest challenge is to exercise proper recognition—of unfamiliar cultural contexts, mores, gestures, and interactions. Each city, with its unfamiliar language, national characteristics, and cultural gestures, presents her with an oblique façade, where even basic social interactions are laden with multiplicity in meaning. In an Istanbul hotel, for instance, what does the silent nod from the hotel manager signify? Is it an indication of minimal courtesy, curiosity, or approval? How does her own "smile and nod and gesture" (Tillman 1991, 10) participate in the interaction? In her uncertainty, mimicry becomes her default response: "The Englishman, when we passed [in the hallway], touched his hand to his head, a kind of salute, and I did likewise, a gesture that has absolutely no meaning to me at all" (ibid.). As she has no means of confirming the "truth" of her understanding, and even less of controlling the meaning of her participation, her interpretations ultimately reveal nothing but her own epistemological framework: "I decide he [the hotel manager] does like me, as I have a need anyway to feel I am liked. No doubt this marks me as an American. I must be full of national characteristics that are hidden from me and are palpable to others" (ibid.). The constructivist nature of her interpretation impresses upon her the predetermined nature of her hermeneutic system—how her American cultural inclination toward amiability, for instance, shapes her practice of recognition: "I may emit naivete and hope in a limited way, the grand *narrative* I'm thrust out of overwhelming my individual predilections and deviations. The mirror over the hotel dresser offers no relief, no clue to my role in the larger story . . . [you] can't take the country out of the girl when the girl is out of the country" (Tillman 1991, 188–89, emphasis added).

When intersubjective recognition takes place within the web of "grand narratives," what comes to the fore but particular plot typologies and characterizations within those grand narratives? Throughout her travels, she watches her individual identity performing various roles in numerous ready-made plots of race, gender, and national identity. In England, when she disputes a fare change made by the train conductor, she sees the predictability of her actions in the responses of her fellow passengers: "From the expressions on their faces, mirrors behind which their opinions sit, I see myself as the ugly, that is, the imperialistic American and, alternatively, the bossy New York woman. Or, less problematically, as just plain rude. Instantly, I'm a set of conditions and positions, a reluctant but undeniable conduit" (Tillman 1991, 35). Instantly she bears the representational weight of a national character or, more specifically, a gendered national character, and she is helpless to resist her utility as a "conduit" in her fellow passengers' interpellation of her. As her visibility, her comprehensibility as a subject, is contingent upon the repetition of a grand narrative regarding "American identity" (i.e., that Americans, especially New Yorkers, are loud and rude), Tillman's protagonist feels herself confined within the dead repetition of doxa—what passes as public opinion, the commonplace, the stereotype.

In a casual train conversation, she reveals to a fellow passenger, a Pakistani man, that she does not wish to be married. "Ahh, he says, scrutinizing me, then may God be with you. I thank him. The rest of the journey he and I are noticeably silent, as if something portentous had occurred. . . . I'm sure he watched me throw my bag into the taxi and shook his head, certain I was meant for tragedy" (73). For the Pakistani man, her revelation is at once descriptive and confirmatory of the tragic plot typology that follows the Western women who eschew the institution of marriage. To Alfred, an English traveler she meets in Italy, she is cast in the mold of an independently wealthy American expatriate: "I have begun to enjoy his fantasy of me, as if I were a projection of his or a twentieth-century American novel. . . . An F. Scott Fitzgerald flapper. Or a Hemingway woman, narrow-hipped, tight-lipped and disappointed in her man" (59). In brief encounters throughout her travels, she collects a myriad of epistemological frameworks trained upon her. Recognition, in these scenes, is nothing but a repetition of preexisting characterizations, plot typologies, and tensions.

Furthermore, Tillman explores the petrified layer of doxa by positioning her protagonist in a location where the grand narratives reign the strongest. Foreign travel—of being outside one's linguistic, national, and cultural context—highlights the large-scale nature of one's interpellation (units of identification). At the intersection of encountering the other's "difference," the act of recognition is simultaneously an act of subsuming "I" into a collective "we," and "you" into a collective "you." To a hotel manager in Venice, the protagonist is a synecdoche of America: "New York, he says, looking at the postmark [of a card she receives], you have a big problem with drugs? I want instantly to resist the you of his question—but agree, yes, we do. He says that he or they have drug problems too" (42). Hence, interpellation is never an exchange between two individuals but between grand narratives—what Althusser identified as the predetermined ideological state apparatuses and what Barthes identified as the omnipresent layer of repetition in language use: "I am indeed behind the door; certainly I should like to pass through, certainly I should like to see what is being said, I too participate in the communal scene; I am constantly listening to what I am excluded from; I am in a stunned state, dazed, cut off from the popularity of language" (RB, 123). Tillman's focus on scenes of foreign encounter highlights intersubjective recognition as being fundamentally oppressive, as being exchanges within a petrified sign system.

WE ARE ALL IN IT

Despite her pressing awareness that she is immersed in grand narratives, Tillman's narrator does not hope to escape her condition. Rather, she lays claim to *her* stock of grand narratives in her interpellation of others and even of herself. In her confinement in the limitations of knowing by knowing again, the protagonist of *Motion Sickness* negates the possibility of the second definition of recognition—of knowing afresh—and simultaneously announces the postmodern epistemological condition of the late twentieth century that questions a foundational premise in the realist novel.

The protagonist's own grand narratives are heavily influenced by the long arm of mass culture, especially by American popular culture—by Hollywood movies, best sellers, game shows, and so on. In an Amsterdam inn, the innkeepers, spanning three generations, remind her of a myriad of American TV shows: "Actually, looking more carefully, they're closer to Western types, on the order of 'Rawhide' or 'Bonanza' or *Seven Brides for Seven Brothers*, and from now on whenever

I see them, either the theme song from 'Bonanza,' or 'I'm a Lonesome Polecat' from *Seven Brides* plays in my mind" (Tillman 1991, 10–11). A café scene in Venice becomes a stage where the patrons enact various well-known scenarios: a scene of an older woman with two younger men suggests the possibilities of an "international intrigue party" involving the CIA and the KGB, or, perhaps, a "gigolo scenario"; as they leave, they are "followed closely by new players," a middle-age woman with a lapdog who courts the attention of an elderly man (43–44). "I wait for someone to appear who's as fascinating as Tadzio in *Death in Venice.* I wait for a little girl, dressed in a red slicker, like the daughter Donald Sutherland searched for in *Don't Look Now*" (45). As she comprehends the foreign setting and people by anchoring them to the plots, scenarios, settings, and characters from her archive of movies, musicals, and books, her mind's wanderings represent a subjectivity dominated by ready-made signs of a postmodern image culture.

The degree of her confinement in the logic of repetition can best be seen in her application of literary codes to herself. Her self-interpellation takes place through well-established, familiar literary characterization and typology. As the narrative begins she is in London, reading *The Portrait of a Lady.* At her narrative's end, she invokes Isabel Archer again, an emblematic female figure of New World innocence hopelessly out of place in the Old World: "Isabel Archer's end in *The Portrait of a Lady* may be worse than mine. It's impossible to tell. I've begun to repeat some stories, but is this the same thing as repeating myself?" (Tillman 1991, 203). As she travels through Tangiers, she mulls over the cultural familiarity of her role through the literary trope of the "wandering woman"—a woman who renounces her Western society for a renegade life of freedom in the desert:

> A long time ago a young woman from France or Germany or Great Britain arrived here on the start of a journey. She left home to travel when travel was hard and when few women traveled alone. I can see her. In a long brown skirt of durable material, a dark jacket, sensible shoes, a broad-brimmed hat and a scarf, she is tall and solid, short and slight, blond, dark. She does not fall in love with anything but adventure. (Tillman 1991, 116)

The descriptive flexibility in this rendition generates a parodic tone, as the specifics of the heroine's nationality, age, or appearance are all deemed interchangeable under the iconic status of a cultural code of the liberated heroine, the white woman who renounces her Western society for a renegade life in the desert (as she later names some names: Freya Stark, Isbelle Eberhardt, Kit Moresby). Like the few, quick sketches of a caricaturist, the narrator's use of the desert adventuress calls upon the most pronounced—the most congealed—features of the cultural code. In the way the narrator holds up the stories as a convention, however, the target of the parody is not so much the heroines and their actions as it is their iconic stature as "untethered" women. The nod of acknowledgment to the feminist import of these stories is countered by mocking their archetypal—their congealed—stature. For the narrator, then, their very familiarity and popularity transform them into just another grand narrative that is used to recognize her—in fact, just as the Pakistani man on the train did. The narrator's immersion in cultural codes, hence, has paradoxical implications; even as she enacts recognition through popular cultural stereotypes and familiar literary tropes, her ironic use of them as caricatures renders them *trite*. Ultimately, the protagonist demonstrates her utter immersion in "the discourse of others," what Barthes calls the pervasive influence of cultural codes (Barthes 1979, 184).

The postmodern condition that the narrator experiences, then, is fundamentally an entrapment in/by recognition. One is known again because the units of knowing (particular interpellation, cultural code, grand narrative) already exist, a condition that Barthes describes thusly: "the name is the exact, irrefutable trace, as solid as a scientific fact, *of a certain already-written, already-read, already-done*; to find the name is to find that already which constitutes the code" (Barthes 1988, 141). Tillman's protagonist compares her congealed state of interpellation to that of her fellow traveler, an Irish man whose ties to the Irish Republican Army determine his self-identification and future:

> Maybe I'm as trapped as Pete. Although I may be in a melodrama, not a tragedy, white middle-class young woman, from yet another dying empire. . . . National identity is like armor. On permanent loan from a museum. It's dull armor that I clink around in. Could I get an operation that would make me oblivious to symbols? Could I be like human Switzerland, always neutral to the partisan demands of birthplace? Get a transnational operation, get placed in a different body politic? (Tillman 1991, 127)

When grand narratives and discourses of others constitute the fundamental units of knowing, recognition can only simply be that—re-cognition.

CONCLUSION

Delimiting recognition to re-cognition, then, *Motion Sickness* challenges two interrelated bases of the realist novel convention—the epistemological promise that both knowing again and knowing afresh may be entertained in one narrative environment and the developmental character whose "progress" parallels the movement from one kind of knowing to the other. *Motion Sickness*'s challenge to the novel convention is a peculiar kind, as its protagonist *covets* what she challenges—the possibility of evading grand narratives and the discourse of others to know afresh. In highlighting the inadequacy of recognition, the protagonist compares re-cognition to the act of reading: "In my hotel room I draw mental pictures. Connect the dots. . . . A hostage to psychology and history. I'm Arlette's reader, for instance, or Jessica's, and I'm my own. I'm almost certain we can't be read like books, though" (Tillman 1991, 175). That is, her kind of recognition is the kind of *reading* that will never attain the epistemological certainty of *knowing* that takes place in books, that will never attain the kind of epistemological certainty offered by proper recognition.

For her, the mirror's reflection symbolizes her confinement in epistemological opaqueness:

> The mirror ought to become a window. To provide the real
> adventure of seeing through oneself. To see through to some-
> thing outside, something beyond. Mirrors are defeating
> because they don't tell you what you look like to someone
> else. As if you could get out of your skin. In a fantasy the
> sublime mirror would . . . permit a true tourism in which
> you would find yourself outside your homeland, and outside
> your body, and see yourself with emotional vividness, as you
> can't, and in the roles you play to others. (Tillman 1991,
> 120–21)

The "true tourism" that she idealizes—reading that may eventually become knowing, a misrecognition that has the hope of becoming a proper recognition—is a depleted promise that only the convention of the realist novel delivers. In contrast, she is a subject who knows that she is consigned to being a reader, never a knower, and that as she is reading through the discourse of others, she is being read just as reductively, partially, and tautologically.

Relatedly, the protagonist's entrapment in recognition inversely highlights what she cannot achieve as a literary convention—the realist novel's character development that is fundamentally a function of the increased ability to know. Her confinement in re-cognition directly translates into her nondevelopmental nature as a character—a subject outside the logic of development, outside the function of development discernible through her ability to correct her misrecognitions or to act upon those corrections, to eventually acquire an ability to know. Like the postcards she writes prolifically and never sends, the protagonist exists in a hermetic circle, reading furiously without the hope of reading afresh, evading the interpellation of home only to be locked in another network of interpellation. Tillman, in an interview, voices a rebuttal to the assessment of the protagonist's immobilized condition: "A sociologist who read *Motion Sickness* in manuscript said he was disgusted by it because the narrator was so passive. And I said what do you mean 'passive'? She thinks all the time" (Nicholls 1995, 278). She certainly thinks all the time; perhaps thinking too much of the time is the inevitable condition of a subject who can only exercise re-cognition. Thinking all the time about the inadequacies of thinking all the time, Tillman's protagonist exists in an epistemological condition that holds no possibility of true tourism.

In *Motion Sickness*, the postmodern suspicion of recognition translates into an epistemological paralysis, as everyday acts are permeated with the dead repetition that is at the heart of Althusserian hailing and Barthesian doxa. However, *Motion Sickness* does more than literalize a postmodern suspicion. It clings to the *memory* of a proper recognition that once was delivered to other characters, like Isabel Archer, a long time ago, in another narrative possibility. As proper recognition becomes simultaneously discredited and desired, *Motion Sickness* articulates a fiction's present that rejects a key convention of the realist novel while still operating under its long shadow. Recognition without repetition, recognition without the congealed discourse of others, recognition that appears as distinctly as a picture on the wall—these are promises reserved only for those creatures inhabiting the narrative environment of the realist novel, that odd epistemological universe where knowing again and knowing afresh can and must exist side by side.

NOTES

1. As my selection of exemplar novels indicates, my analysis of the novel draws from the nineteenth-century Anglo-American novels of realism, a literary moment that dominates the historiography and theory of the novel.

2. A contemporary U.S. writer who teaches at the University at Albany (State University of New York), Tillman situates, as a central exploration, the

role of recognition in her novels. Hence, her protagonists are strongly shaped by epistemological quests, as in *Haunted Houses* (1987), *No Lease on Life* (1998), and, most prominently, in *Motion Sickness* (1991). Other current U.S. writers whose works demonstrate a unique combination of desire and distrust toward recognition include writers such as Lydia Davis, Paul Auster, and Carole Maso. A protagonist in Lydia Davis's short story gives an evocative demonstration of recognition as a depleted source:

> I am thinking about a friend of mine, how she is not only what she believes she is, she is also what friends believe her to be, and what her family believes her to be, and even what she is in the eyes of chance acquaintances and total strangers. . . . Perhaps it must be true that the things about which we all agree are part of what she really is, or what she really would be if there were such a thing as what she really is, because when I look for what she really is, I find only contradictions everywhere. (Davis 1997, 116)

3. Another approach to recognition, especially in the field of political science, grounds the term upon the following definition: "To acknowledge by special notice, approval or sanction; to treat as valid, as having existence or as entitled to consideration; to take notice of (a thing or person) in some way"; "To admit to consideration, or to a status, as being something" (Recognition 2000). An influential study of recognition as the act of acknowledging or distributing goods or rights is philosopher Charles Taylor's (1994) "The Politics of Recognition."

4. *Roland Barthes by Roland Barthes* will hence be cited as RB. Barthes draws on ancient Greek, especially Aristotle's use of *endoxa*, which, in Aristotle's writing, meant "all that is considered true, or at least probable, by a majority of people endowed with reason, or by a specific social group" (Amossy 2002, 369). In theorizing the oppressive nature of the form of repetition, Barthes works in and through Gustave Flaubert's criticism of received ideas. Critics such as Michael Moriarty and Christopher Prendergast have argued that Barthes's use of *endoxa* simplifies what is a more expansive concept in Aristotelian usage. See also the special issue of *Poetics Today* (Pierrot 2002), which is devoted to the topic of doxa in contemporary disciplines.

5. Anne Herschberg-Pierrot (2002), in "Barthes and Doxa," offers an insightful examination of Barthes's use of metaphor (layer, petrification, glutinous, stickiness) in his conceptualization of doxa.

6. Tillman's use of "recognition" in her interview refers to what I have been calling proper recognition, "to perceive clearly, to realize." Furthermore, Tillman's use highlights another dimension of the word—recognition as the acceptance of or resignation to an irreducible fact. Such acceptance or resignation, of course, can only rest upon the second definition of recognition, upon the epistemological certainty of knowing afresh.

208 Fiction's Present

REFERENCES

Althusser, Louis. 1971 [1969]. Ideology and ideological state apparatuses (notes towards an investigation). In *Lenin and philosophy*, 85–126. New York: Monthly Review.

Amossy, Ruth. 2002. Introduction to the study of doxa. *Poetics Today* 23:3: 369–94.

Barthes, Roland. 1977. *Roland Barthes by Roland Barthes*. Translated by Richard Howard. New York: Hill and Wang.

———. 1979 [1970]. *S/Z: An essay*. Translated by Richard Miller. Preface by Richard Howard. New York: Hill and Wang.

———. 1988 [1985]. The sequence of actions. In *The semiotic challenge*. Translated by Richard Howard. 136–150. New York: Hill and Wang.

Davis, Lydia. 1997. A friend of mine. In *Almost no memory*. New York: Farrar, Straus & Giroux.

Herschberg Pierrot, Anne. 2002. Barthes and doxa. *Poetics Today* 23:3:427–42.

James, Henry. 1979. *The portrait of a lady*. New York: Signet Classic.

Moriarty, Michael. 1997. Rhetoric, doxa, and experience in Barthes. *French Studies* 51:2:69–82.

Nicholls, Peter. 1995. A conversation with Lynne Tillman. *Textual Practice* 9:2:269–84.

Prendergast, Christopher. 1986. *The order of mimesis: Balzac, Stendhal, Nerval, Flaubert*. Cambridge: Cambridge University Press.

Recognition. 2000. *The Oxford English dictionary*. Online edition. http://www.dictionary.oed.com/, accessed May 3, 2004.

Taylor, Charles. 1994. The politics of recognition. In *Multiculturalism: Examining the politics of recognition*, ed. Amy Gutmann, 25–74. Princeton, NJ: Princeton University Press.

Tillman, Lynne. 1991. *Motion sickness*. New York: Poseidon Press.

Chapter 15

A Modality

PERCIVAL EVERETT

Ita verba in variis sententiis locis posita, et crebo audita, quarum rerum signa essent, paulatim colligebam, measque jam voluntares, edomito in eis signis ore, per haec enuntiabam.

These words are from Augustine, and they are particularly resonant as I consider how I understand fiction. First, most of us are looking blankly at the Latin, wondering a couple of things. "What does it say?" "Why is it there?" "What is Everett trying to prove by putting it there?" "Does Everett care at all about the content of this sentence?" The fact is, we will all stare, knowing that staring at it will yield no meaning, but hoping that some bit of a single word will appear familiar and lead in some way to some understanding of the something, anything.

It's more than just a puzzle. Without a dictionary and the rules of grammar, this might as well be a barking dog. Perhaps not quite. I will in most circumstances know why my dog is barking, but I can never be sure what he is telling me. Conversely, one might find a Latinist to translate this sentence, but you will never be sure why I have used it.

Consider the Walt Kelly line: "Rabbits are rounder than bandicoots sam."

Here there are recognizable words, but it is nonsense. I can make no meaning of this, though rhythmically it is familiar and I enjoy saying it. I might even enjoy saying it enough that I employ it as a kind of gleeful interjection on occasion. My friend Sweetle Peetles is having tea at my house and tells me of her new crow and, delighted, I say, "Rabbits are rounder than bandicoots sam!" She, knowing my love of the line, amusedly smiles. I have not uttered a sentence that makes sense, but my utterance itself does make sense.

And so I present Sweetle Peetles with a twelve page, single-spaced prose work that has her as a character and offers no resolution, no conflict, and no place. Let's imagine that in it she goes about her daily chores, just Peetling along. She reads it and says, "Why did you write this?"

"Because I am a writer" is not a satisfactory answer. Instead I say, "It's a story." This implies, I suppose, that I am a writer, but it also says something more. It tells her what to expect from the pages in her hand. And what does she expect? What does one expect when one comes to a story? It is different from what one expects from a note magneted to the refrigerator and a loose paper found lying in the gutter.

Nunquam visi caseum in tantis modis diversis paratum.

The above statement says, "I have never seen cheese prepared in so many different ways."

Is this nonsense? Perhaps I am making a point about contextualization and the construction of meaning. Perhaps I am concerned here with some notion of propositional content or at least implication. Or perhaps I am ridiculing my whole endeavor here, and cheese is a code word for something, and I'm either having you on or I'm poking a doll-likeness of myself with a philosophical pin.

Or perhaps, perhaps, perhaps this is just a story, one in which I find myself here writing a twelve-page, though not single-spaced, bit of prose to present to my friend Sweetle Peetles, whose Latin is rusty and who will be frustrated by the opening passage because she could at one time read it but not now, because she has seen it before and because it is at present not available to her or because I am being obtuse.

And what has happened now that I have opened that door?

This is not a work of fiction. Just look me in the eye, sneer and say, "Sit Simplex, Stulte!"

So I will try to keep this simple, and please don't call me "Stupid."

A story is a beetle in a box.

A story is a document that has a beginning and an end, but has no beginning or end.

A story is not a document.

A story is fiction.

But given the existence of the story, the story is a fact, and the elements of the story are in fact not fiction at all, not only within the context of the story but in the totality of reality. If the facts change, then the story is different and is not the same story.

"Sit Simplex, Stulte!"

The aim of fiction is to move from disguised nonsense to disguised nonsense.

There is no such thing as nonsense.

My mission in all of this is not, however, to set up a "physics" of fiction, a new explanation of how things "are fiction." I wish only to suggest that we refocus our gaze from the transcendental connections of meaning(s) toward the obscure and indeterminate surface of fiction. It might be argued that ideation itself begins to appear as a textual effect in the ordinary sense of the text.

But what is the performative force behind the act that I am committing in these brief pages?

Why am I telling this story?

It is, in fact, a story, a work of short fiction for which I have chosen language, fiction, myself, and Sweetle Peetles as characters.

This notion of experiment is interesting. This is not an experimental story. It is not an experimental essay. It is not an extended joke. The corruption of so-called convention, or the recognition of such corruption, exploitation, alteration, whether motivated by aesthetic, political, or commercial (money's not the only currency) interests, is a commitment to generic rules more rigid than an adherence to the so-called accepted conventions.

Immo vero, serio, folks.

This is a work of fiction. This is not an essay. And this is the ending.

Qualche volta è virtu tacere il vero.

Chapter 16

Critifictional Reflections on the Pathetic Condition of the Novel in Our Time

RAYMOND FEDERMAN

The novel is a bourgeois art because it gives itself time to play, and in so doing loses itself in the anguish of its own dreams.

To begin these reflections, I want to quote a passage from one of the great novels of the past: Diderot's *Jacques le Fataliste.*

> Where?—Where? Reader you are of a rather cumbersome curiosity! By the Devil what does it matter? Even if I were to tell you that it was in Pontoise or in Saint-Germain or in Notre-Dame de Lorette or Saint-Jacques de Compostelle would you be better off? If you insist, I will tell you that they were going towards—yes, why not?—towards an immense castle, on the frontispiece of which was written: I belong to no one and I belong to everyone. You were already here before entering, and you will still be here after departing. (*my translation*)

In *Jacques le Fataliste*, Diderot creates a space never before seen in the landscape of the novel: a timeless stage without scenery (not unlike that of the novels and plays of Samuel Beckett), where his characters function more as voices than as full-fledged personalities. Listening to Jacques and his Master talk, one always has the feeling that they are talking from inside a book rather than from reality. I

213

know of no opening of a novel more engaging, more fascinating, and more self-reflexive than that of *Jacques le Fataliste*.

> How did they meet? By chance, like everyone else. What were their names? What do you care. Where were they coming from? The nearest place. Where were they going? Does one really know where one is going? What were they saying? The master said nothing, and Jacques was saying that his captain was saying that everything that happens to us here on earth, good or bad, is written above.

It is certainly the playful self-reflexiveness of *Jacques le Fataliste* that makes of this novel the great fun book that it is, and this because Diderot not only meddles with the text but also offers the reader the possibility of participating in the fiction: "No, no. Of all the different abodes possible, which I have just enumerated, choose the one most appropriate to the present situation." Or even better, the author seduces the reader into the interplay of self-reflexiveness while pretending to be annoyed by the reader's impatience, in the passage I already quoted:

> Where?—Where? Reader, you are of a rather cumbersome curiosity! By the Devil what does it matter?

Clearly, Diderot, like Sterne and numerous other great novelists after him, understood that the novel is very much like the inscription on the frontispiece of the imaginary castle he invents on the spot: the novel belongs to no one, and it belongs to everyone. We (as readers) were here before entering the book, and we will still be here after closing it. This suggests that the process of reading a novel can be measured by the reader's willingness to engage—or let himself or herself be engaged by—the self-reflexiveness of the text. Or as Flann O'Brien puts it in *At Swim-Two-Birds* (another outrageously self-reflexive novel): ". . . a satisfactory novel should be a self-evident sham to which the reader can regulate at will the degree of his credulity." In this respect, readers can be fascinated either by the tale only (which sends them back to their own reality) or by the telling of the tale (which keeps them inside the fiction).

Can it be said then that by denouncing the fraudulence of a novel that tends to totalize existence and misses its multidimensionality, the critical work frees us from the illusion of realism? I rather believe that it encloses us in it. Because the goal remains the same: it is always a question of expressing, of translating something that is already there—

even if to be already there, in this new perspective, consists paradoxically in not being there. In other words, the novel, in a sense, cannot escape the double-headed monster of realism. This mortgage weighs upon it since its origin, since the period when for justifying itself of the suspicion of frivolity, it had to present itself as a means of knowledge—and not only since the nineteenth century. The history of the novel is—one is forced to admit—nothing else but the succession of its efforts to represent—or rather *appresent*—a reality that always evades, always substitutes finer mirrors for vulgar mirrors, more selective mirrors. But, in another sense, the novel is nothing else but a denunciation of its own existence, of the illusion that animates it.

All great novels are critical novels, which, under the pretense of telling a story, of bringing characters to life, of interpreting situations, slide under our eyes the mirage of a tangible form.

All fictitious work forms a block: nothing can be taken away from it, nor can a single word be changed. That is what makes of the novel a lure.

We think we are going to find in the novel the expression of our unity, whereas in fact it only manifests the desire of it. We believe, as we are relating ourselves, that we are going to discover, to uncover that being that we are already. But that being, that somebody, exists in the work only. It is the product of it and not the source. And this is because the essence of a literary discourse—that is to say a discourse fixed once and for all (a discourse that delights in its own form like fire, as Blake put it)—is to find its own point of reference, its own rules of organization in itself, and not in the real or imaginary experience on which it rests.

Through all the detours that one wishes, the subject who writes will never seize himself in the novel—he will only seize the novel that, by definition, excludes him!

> In this matter of writing, resolve as one may to keep to the main road, some bypaths have an enticement not readily to be withstood. The writing wanders into such bypaths, such detours. If the reader is willing to go along, at least he will share in the pleasure which is wickedly said to be in sinning, for a literary sin the divergence will be. (Melville)

To write a novel is a perilous and an absorbing adventure. One never knows in advance where one is going, and if one will reach the good port—as proof of this, the difficulty one has to finish a novel, with the customary necessity of a long interruption (even a regression) along the way.

The need to write a novel arises from a triggering, sometime a musical, mood (mood indigo), a reverie whose inclination follows the course of a moment of historical instability, or of an arbitrary encounter with a landscape—or with a human being.

This act of writing a novel is not without danger: false souvenirs, fake emotions and images that the story will have brought forth, will become henceforth a sterile field of words.

Wild lines of words will cross the sheets of paper obeying only their own furor.

Words will gather together, rush together into certain regions of the paper, small fields of forces will localize themselves—eddies, knots, crests, contours of words, spontaneous designs of signs climbing up and down the pages in mad laughter.

There will be no moment when everything is in place. When the accumulation of words will have reached a point of saturation. When all that remains to be done would be to set the final period. To end it all. To say the story is finished. For in fact there will always be more words. Words! That great pell-mell Babel of words that makes a novel. There is no law, no order that says to the writer, here and Now you must stop. Not a word more! The writer can always go on, but there is always the risk (but that risk was there from the beginning) that one more word may be too much, one more word may destroy it all, may cancel the whole story, may force the whole story down toward an end!

Oh! To end again! (Samuel Beckett lamenting)

The writing of a novel has its particular economy. It answers to a lack—a dissatisfaction that demands to be fulfilled.

The subject of the book inhabits the writer, becomes part of his or her substance, an object of desire rather than a clearly defined project. And it is the tension of the fable in search of its incidents, of its form, of its rhythm, and what remains in suspense (unwritten) above the vacuum of creation that dictates the rest of the story. The entire undertaking relies on intuition. It requires probing and listening to the verbal material.

This mental process is close to alchemical research for which no formula, no phenomenon of incubation, exists. Each new story reinvents its own process. And so the finished book may remotely resemble the original desire without, however, any possibility of ever reconstituting its genesis. The scaffold that sustains the progress of writing is removed during the realization of the novel, including the author himself or herself when revisiting his or her own work.

There was a time when the novelist mobilized all of his defects to produce a work that *concealed him*. The notion of exposing his life to the public probably never occurred to him. We do not imagine Homer or Dante or Shakespeare keeping track of the trifling incidents of their lives in order to bring them to other people's attention.

Perhaps they even preferred giving a false image of what they were. They had that reticence of power that is no longer a property of the deficient, nervous, paranoid, contemporary novelist. Our confessions, our novels, are all characterized by the same aberration: What interest can a mere life afford?

Even the story of a survivor of the Unforgivable Enormity known as the Holocaust, in the context of what is going on in the world today, is banal. What interest is there in books inspired by other books or minds dependent on other minds?

Only the illiterate can give that *frisson* of being, which indicates the presence of truth. Farmers among whom I worked once upon a time impressed me altogether differently than professors among whom I also worked once upon a time. The French intellectuals' theories leave me cold when I contemplate the anguish of the poor, the oppressed, the underprivileged.

I saw beggars in Barcelona, in Pakistan, in India, and in Egypt, and I would have liked to have been their chronicler. They have no need to invent a life for themselves: they *exist*, which does not happen often in our civilization. Why, one wonders, did our ancestors not barricade themselves in their caves?

When the average man lays claim to a destiny, then the average man can describe his own. The belief that psychology reveals our essence necessarily endears our actions to us. We imagine they possess an intrinsic or a symbolic value. Then comes the snobbery of complexes that teaches us to exaggerate our wits, to be dazzled by them, to gratify our ego with faculties and depths with which it is obviously unendowed. The intimate perception of our nothingness, however, is only partially veiled by this process.

We suspect that the novelist who relies on his or her life is only pretending to believe in it, that the novelst has no respect for the secrets discovered there: he or she is not taken in, and we, the readers, are still less so. The characters belong to a second-rate humanity, conscious and contaminated, suspect on account of their artifices, their intrigues. We do not readily conceive of an astute King Lear. . . .

The vulgar, parvenu aspect of the novel determines its characteristics: fatality inhibited, lower-case destiny, romantic agony, pseudo-tragedy déclassée.

Compared to the tragic hero, so rich in the adversity that is his eternal patrimony, the contemporary novel's main character seems like a naive candidate for ruin, horror's cheap-jack, overeager to destroy himself, terrified to fail. He suffers from the very uncertainty of his disaster. There is no necessity for his death. We sense that the author could have saved him, which makes us uncomfortable, spoils our pleasure as readers.

Whereas tragedy occurs on an absolute level, so to speak, the author has no influence over his or her heroes but is only their servant, their instrument. They are the ones in control, and they prompt the author to institute proceedings against themselves. They rule, even in the works for which they serve as a pretext. And these works affect us as realities independent of both the writer and the marionette strings of psychology.

We read contemporary novels in an altogether different way. The novelist is always uppermost in our minds. His or her presence haunts us. We watch him or her struggle with the characters. In the long run, the novelist is the only one who holds our attention. What will be done with the characters? How will the novelist get rid of them? We wonder. Our curiosity is tinged with apprehension. If someone once said that Balzac rewrote Shakespeare using failures, then what can we think of today's novelists, obliged as they are to deal with a humanity that has deteriorated still further? Bereft of cosmic inspiration, the novel's inhabitants cannot manage to counterbalance the dissolving effect of their knowledge, their will to lucidity, their lack of character.

And so they are forced to ask, as the novelist himself or herself is forced to ask: Where now? Who now? When now? Remembering how Samuel Beckett's *The Unnameable* put it at the beginning of his own failed fiction, as he faced the boredom of his fictitious existence to come.

There is only one thing worse than boredom—the fear of boredom. And it is this fear one experiences each time one opens a novel. We have no use for the hero's life, do not attend to it, do not even believe in it, at least those of us who traffic in novels for more than just entertainment or escape.

The genre, having squandered its substance, no longer has an object. The character is dying out, the plot too. It is no accident that the only novels deserving of interest today are precisely those novels in which, once the universe is disbanded, nothing happens. Or if something seems to happen, it is the writing itself reflecting on itself. The only valid novels these days are self-reflexive novels, even if the author is present in the text (often under his or her own name) but seems missing from it.

Deliciously unreadable (and of course unmarketable), with no beginning nor end, these novels could just as well stop with the first sentence as continue for a thousand pages.

And yet . . . we continue to write novels. And some of us continue to read novels.

Not long ago a young woman interviewing me for a magazine confronted me with an interesting question: "Why do you continue to write novels?" she asked. "Why don't you do something else, like making films for instance, or writing for television? Or simply play golf."

As someone fatally committed to the novel, I replied, and I am still pleased with my answer, "I write novels because it is the only place, the last place where one can still write *well.*" And by *well* I did not simply mean that one can write beautiful sentences in a novel for the sake of writing beautiful sentences. By *writing well* I meant also writing correctly in a moral and political sense, I meant writing truthfully, writing what is essential, what is urgent—even with humor or irony if necessary. It is in this sense, I believe, that one should still write novels, should still try to write well, and in so doing make a last stand for the novel. Or, as Beckett put it, *to try and fail better.*

THE FALLEN PROPHET, OR LITERATURE IN CRISIS

I may not be wrong in thinking that this title suggests that in the face of the great social, political, and technological changes that have occurred in the world in the past century, in the face of the great turmoil that the world is today, literature, rather than being in transition with the new century, is in danger—in serious danger—of becoming ineffectual and obsolete, in serious danger of extinction. Therefore, it is essential and urgent for those who still believe in literature, those who still practice literature, those who still produce books, to confront this crisis and this danger and assess the possibilities still available to literature in order for it to survive. In other words, it is urgent for literature to take a stand so that it can continue to *be* in the world and *do* what it has always done: capture the world, represent the world, explain the world, clarify the world, reinvent the world. It is urgent for literature to take a stand, even if it is *The Last Stand of Literature.*

It is a recognized fact that the United States is an anti-intellectual nation, a nation of pop culture, a nation that prefers easy spectacle to self-reflection, entertainment rather than art, and consequently it is difficult for writers not only to be taken seriously but even to have access to the sociopolitical arena. It is easier, in America, for a former football or basketball player, or even a wrestler, easier for a second-rate movie star to become involved in the political process and influence the course of history than it is for a writer or an intellectual. The people of the United States distrust writers, especially when their work refuses to entertain—refuses to tell and retell the same old story the same old way. This raises crucial questions about the role of American writers in the face of the great changes that are taking place in the world today. In this sense one could say that American writers, as far back as the early colonial days, have always been *Fallen Prophets*. Whitman and Melville (certainly the two greatest American writers of the nineteenth century) were indeed Fallen Prophets.

I must emphasize that I am speaking here strictly as a fiction writer and a poet, that I am not a political writer, nor a journalist, nor a pamphletist, nor a philosopher, and certainly not a prophet, but I do think of myself as a serious writer, and I consider my work to have some relevance to what is happening in our world. I should also point out that my work (especially my fiction) has been labeled *avant-garde* and *experimental*, and as such it often has been declared inaccessible (a key term in America these days in the marketplace of books)—inaccessible and unreadable, and therefore useless, irrelevant, and of course unmarketable. One could say that my fiction has been banned from the great supermarkets of books.

But that is also being said of the fiction written by most serious writers. In other words, in America, unless literature *entertains*—entertains in the same sense, let us say, that a Hollywood movie or a television soap opera entertains—it is considered superfluous, as having no raison d'être. That is why literature in America has always been a marginal activity and has never been able to be politically committed.

But this does not mean, of course, that American literature is not concerned with the social and political problems of the world; it simply means that even though serious, intelligent literature continues to be written, too often *it is not made available* to those who still believe in its efficacy.

I learned from my own personal experiences that to be a writer is to live in history, that the writer can never escape his or her time and history, and this because finally history is above all language. It is the writer who fabricates history with language after the events have occurred. That is why the writer bears such responsibility toward his or her work, and especially toward the language he or she uses. If our readers cannot trust our writing (even if it is fiction), then they will not trust the story and the history in which they live.

It is in this sense that literature captures the world, represents it, explains it, reinvents it; in this sense that literature captures the past and the present with words, and even invents future history before it happens.

However, today many writers are retreating from history, and consequently retreating from their responsibility toward language, or rather I should say, many writers finds themselves *forced to retreat* because their work is not taken seriously, because their work is declared useless and irrelevant, or else because their work is found too demanding intellectually, but especially because their work is found not entertaining enough, and therefore nonmarketable, nonpublishable. As a result, many important and innovative books are prevented from being disseminated by publishers, editors, literary agents, critics, librarians, and even professors who refuse to accept serious, intelligent books, refuse to read, publish, promote, distribute, sell, discuss, and teach the current literature, the serious literature being written today.

These are the reasons often given, particularly in America, for rejecting works of contemporary literature, or for relegating these to inaccessible places (such as remote sections of libraries or basements of bookstores) and thus preventing them from being available to those who are still interested in literature.

I must now elaborate on what I have just said. We are now in the new Century, and around us the winds of change are circulating in the world. These winds have swirled into a storm, which is bringing fear, anxiety, insecurity, and doubt to many nations—as reflected especially in the unstable worldwide economy and the return in some parts of the world to extreme right-wing political positions. And so, as we advance into this new millennium, there seems to be a longing for it to be different, a profound desire for this century to be better than the previous one. As we look ahead, we hope that things will improve in the twenty-first century.

But now one must ask, is it possible for literature, for the serious writers of literature, to escape the generalized recuperation that is taking place in the marketplace of books? Is it possible for literature to survive the kind of reduction, the kind of banalization that mass media imposes on contemporary culture? Is it possible for literature to escape the way publicity and advertising ingest and digest culture? Is it possible for literature to survive the hypnosis of marketing, the sweet boredom of consensus, the cellophane wrapping of thinking, the commercialization of desire? In other words, can literature escape conformity and banality and yet play a role and have a place in our society? And finally, are there still people out there in the world willing to turn away from their television screens and find time to read works of literature?

These are the fundamental questions before us today. In the frantic and homogenized landscape of the telematic era in which we live, electronic communication is rendering literature obsolete. As a result, it is becoming a prejudice of the past—a souvenir of another time, when books *really counted* rather than *being counted* by numbers in the supermarkets of books. Literature is in danger of becoming a mere *supplement of culture*, because most works of fiction are written today specifically to be sold to television so that *their story* can be adapted and serialized in that medium for a lot of money. And even those books that are not written directly for television usually function with the same simplistic principle, the same simplified mentality, as television.

However, since I am an incurable optimist, besides being an incurable foreigner, and an incurable word addict, I will propose that rather than retreating before history, rather than retreating in the face of the threat that electronic communication presents, literature must take a stand, even if it is a last stand. But how?

In a recent book entitled, *Métamorphoses*, French thinker Kostas Axelos reflects profoundly on the never-ending end of the world that we seem to have reached, and he writes (I am translating from his French): "It is possible that this era in which we live demands clandestine thinkers to think the world, to traverse that world and transmit signs appropriate to the rhythm of the time. The signs of the past are no longer valid."

And it is true that what passes for literature today in many parts of the world seems unable to transmit signs appropriate to the rhythm of our time—the rhythm of change, of transition, of metamorphosis. Most of the books published today no longer concern themselves with reality but rather with the melodramatized image of reality projected by mass media. Most of these books mimic television, in technique as well as in substance. It is in this sense, I believe, that what passes for literature is simply an insipid secondhand replica of what literature was once upon a time.

This is especially true in America, where *the media have overtaken culture,* but I have a feeling that this is also quickly happening, or will soon happen, in most places in the world where books and television coexist.

For most people, television has become the *real* world, but a world that has only one ideology: commercialized entertainment. Even the reporting of news, that is to say history in the making, must be presented as entertainment, otherwise it does not pass, which really means it does not sell, as we became acutely aware during the Gulf War, which was for us in America a mere television spectacle, a war made for television by television, and presented artistically for consumption as our evening entertainment.

Television has become the real world. A world of spectacle—spectacle as the emblematic sign of a commodity form; lifestyle advertising as its popular psychology; banal seriality as the bond that unites the simulacrum of the show to the audience; electronic images as the only form of social cohesion; media politics as its ideological formula; the buying and selling of abstracted attention as the locus of a marketplace rationale; cynicism, violence, and sexuality as its dominant cultural signs. All these aspects of television culture have invaded what passes for literature today. But if literature, I mean true, serious, intelligent literature, even if it is called *elitist*, is to survive, then it must oppose and even denounce the way television captures the world, the way television presents the world, the way television explains the world.

This does not mean that literature must negate television. Personally, I do not object to it, as some people do, particularly pseudo-intellectuals. On the contrary, I think television is an extremely important medium that has a crucial role to play in our society.

I love television, and I watch it often (*especially football games, American football—after all, the Buffalo Bills, my Buffalo Bills, played in four Superbowls, and they lost four times, but that is not important*).

What is important is that television *cannot replace, must not replace, literature,* and especially *must not dictate to writers how to write their books.*

In order to find its place again, and play a role in the world, literature must resituate itself in relation to the mass media, but not by ignoring or negating television, which is here to stay, but by doing what television cannot do, that is to say present the world and history without interference from economic and commercial forces.

In order for this to happen, writers must regain confidence in literature and assume again responsibility toward language, yes, especially toward language, even if this must be done, as Kostas Axelos suggests, in a clandestine manner, that is to say outside the main stream, outside the literary establishment, on the margins of fame and wealth.

In this triumphant era of mass communication, literature seems ashamed of what it is and what it is doing, and therefore too often readily submits to social and economic compromises. In a world where books have become mere products of consumption and entertainment, it is difficult, if not impossible, to separate the good books from the bad books, the useful books from the useless books, the books that have a purpose from the books that clutter the shelves of bookstores and prevent readers from reaching for literature.

In the big supermarkets of books in America (chain stores usually located in shopping malls), such as Dalton and Walden Bookstores or Barnes & Noble, which sell more T-shirts, calendars, or Stephen King's paraphernalia than books, I recently observed an interesting phenomenon.

In the center of the store are tables piled high with huge quantities of *blockbusters*—best sellers by authors who every six months produce yet another book with the same story, the same plot, changing only the setting and the name of the characters. These are novels that are quickly transformed into second-rate television shows or Hollywood movies. I need not mention the names of these authors; they are well known to us not for their talent but for being very rich, receiving millions of dollars in advance for their next predictable book.

Then I observed that on one side of the store, the entire wall is covered with books designated as *non-fiction*. What this means is that here one finds mostly *how-to books*: books that tell readers how to improve their sex life, how to lose weight, how to become rich fast, how to buy cheap, how to repair cars, how to keep in shape, how to play better golf or tennis, and so on. Or else one finds along that wall the fat, unauthorized, controversial, obscene biographies of celebrities— the rich and the famous.

Along the opposite wall are shelves full of books designated as *fiction*. Most of these are pocketbook editions with sexy, gold-embossed covers—romances, mysteries, adventure novels, spy novels, naive science-fiction or horror stories, soap operas that are waiting there, already packaged, hoping to become television shows.

And then there is another wall at the end of the store, usually the shortest one, because most of these bookstores are like narrow corridors with an open entrance at one end so that people can wander in and out and be seduced by the merchandise lined on the shelves and stacked on the tables.

On that wall, the far wall at the end of the store, one should almost say, at the bottom of the store, there is one shelf with a sign above it that says "Literature" (often written in Gothic letters). Yes, in these bookstores there is still a small space reserved for literature, and in that space one finds hardcover editions of novels by Melville, Faulkner, Tolstoy, Dostoevsky, Balzac, Flaubert, Joyce, Kafka, and even a few contemporary writers such as Saul Bellow, Gabriel García Márquez, Claude Simon, and Samuel Beckett, usually those writers whose work has been authenticated by the Nobel Prize, and therefore recuperated into mainstream commercialization. (Oh yes! It also is on those shelves that one finds books of poetry, but hardly any one ever buys these, except perhaps the poets themselves.)

The problem, however, with this section of the bookstore, is that it is located so far from the entrance, and there are so many obstacles, books, and enticing objects obstructing the shelf where literature awaits to be noticed, that the potential reader rarely manages to reach that wall, except for a few fanatics of literature who still remember where *The Section of the Fallen Prophets* is located.

But let us leave those supermarkets of books and return to our topic: literature in crisis, or rather literature in danger of extinction.

It is quantity and not quality these days that marks the success of a book. That Michael Korda, editor in chief at Simon and Schuster (one of the big commercial publishers in America) should be quoted recently in the *New York Times Book Review* as saying, "We sell books, others sell shoes, what's the difference?" is not surprising from someone who in fact works for Gulf Western Oil. That is the real problem with literature today: it can no longer *mark a difference*, it can no longer be differentiated from other objects of consumption.

Books are now packaged, presented, promoted, and marketed like any other product advertised on television: beer, soap, toilet paper, deodorant, cars, shoes, and so on, without any regard for literary excellence. What's the difference, we are told.

I am, or at least I try to be, a writer. I try to perceive literature today in its failings, its gaps, its disadvantages, and its obscure symptoms as it faces the conflicts, the fears, the demands, and the uneasiness of this new world of ours. But one must look far and attentively to find books in this changing landscape that can still be called literature in the sense that novels by Balzac, Flaubert, Tolstoy, Dostoevsky, Proust, Joyce, and Kafka, and closer to us the late Beckett or Calvino, were called literature and are still called literature—books that respect language, books that work with language in order to capture history rather than merely use or abuse language as a functional tool to present simplistic and simplified secondhand images of reality.

I live in a world where most of us, who write for something other than fame and wealth, or for something other than personal distraction, have stopped reflecting on the purpose of writing—I mean explicitly in the writing itself—and consequently fail to mark the difference that literature makes in the world. Perhaps it is because literature, and especially the novel, has forgotten how to reflect on its *raison d'être*, that is, on what *it is* and what *it does*, that it has been pronounced dead.

Nonetheless, the question remains: How can the writer be part of the world? How can the writer function in this world while writing this world? In a way that question can be stated more directly: How, as a writer, can I be of my time, how can I be a contemporary writer who lives in history and writes in history?

Soon literature will have to explain (even to itself) its place and its role if it wants to survive and be more than just *a supplement of culture*—a vague souvenir of other times and other places. Literature will be able to explain itself, as I suggested earlier, only when it resituates itself in relation to the mass media, and by doing what the mass media cannot do, because by necessity mass media must compromise itself to social and economic forces.

For most people, even those of us who travel in the world, what has happened to our planet in the last few decades of the past century appears almost incomprehensible—the fragmentation of the Soviet Union into a Commonwealth of Republics, the disappearance of the Wall and with it the reunification of the two Germanies, the rise of religious fanaticism in many parts of the world, the quick making and unmaking of political ideologies, the oscillation of democracies from naive liberalism to stifling conservatism, and much more. If all this, all this history in the making, seems confusing and unreal, then it is perhaps because it has come to us via television. History has become a set of easily manipulated images—images that are selected, arranged, packaged, made accessible, simplified, even beautified—and then explained to us by people who claim to be experts.

Meanwhile the writer has deserted his post as witness of history to seek other rewards.

In 1947, Jean-Paul Sartre opened his famous essay "*Qu'est-ce que la littérature?*" ["What is literature?"] with this sentence: "All writers of bourgeois origin have known the temptation of irresponsibility: For more than a century, this temptation has been the norm in literary careers."

What Sartre said, then, is still true today; whether from the East or the West, all writers are of bourgeois origin, and all writers have known the temptation of irresponsibility, especially when facing the demise of literature.

But since the nineteenth century, since the rise of the bourgeoisie, literature has been in a crisis, has been the site of a crisis, and this crisis reflects the constant transformations that take place in the world, or, to put it differently, this crisis of literature is the world—the anguish, the desires, the dreams of those who live in the world, and which the writer captures in his or her writing. Therefore, when literature ceases to represent, to be, to accept this crisis, it becomes entertainment.

In our rapidly changing world, one should be able to say, here are the books I need, and here are the books that are in my way. Having made that choice, I also can decide, as a writer, here is the book I must write, because it is urgent that it be written, and here is the book I will not write, because no one needs it.

THE REAL BEGINS WHERE THE SPECTACLE ENDS

Si la littérature est le silence des significations, c'est en vérité la prison dont tous les occupants veulent s'évader.

—Georges Bataille

What are the forms of representing the world that today parade before us? The cynical or frivolous precipitation of the spectacular, the triviality of trash TV or the obscene tautologies of TV docudrama into which the real subsides without a trace. Now, and without any doubt more than ever, the de-realizing flux of media images runs away with our powers of discernment, our conscience, our lives, and of course our writing. It forces us to surrender to what can only be called, in a strict sense, the *fabulous and seductive grasp of spectacle*. It bars us from a simplified representation of the real. It educates us in the dazed distrust of what is there in front of our eyes—those eyes that have been overfed with icons. But despite our embittered submission to the charm of these icons, despite our willing, overzealous servitude to the spectacle, we know very well that it is all false, that it is nothing but a theater of shadows that exhausts our sense of the real in its emptiness, and teaches us nothing, nothing but a mythology custom-made for a new breed of savages.

But the world is far more complex, far more chaotic, far more confusing, and far more inaccessible than the false images we are offered daily. And the experiences that create the world for us are far more complex, chaotic, confused, and confusing than *THEY* think. By *THEY*, I mean those who falsify *OUR WORLD* for us. *OUR WORLD*—the one we as writers deal with every day—is a static-filled screen, a fuzzy image agitated by emotions a hundred times more voluptuous, but also a hundred times more painful, than those *THEY* are trying to make us feel.

Even the quickest move on the remote control cannot relieve us of the vertiginous bombardment of information to which the world subjects us. Its space is infinitely more profound, more decentered, more polymorphous. And the time we spend in its flow never aligns itself according to the monochrome scenarios that supposedly symbolize its passage.

How to react? How to reply? How to write today the world in which we live? How are we to symbolize differently and more truly (I did not say more realistically but more truly) our experience of the world?

It will most certainly not be in the mode of an easy, facile, positive literature written in an industrial high-tech prose; it will not be a literature that has sold out to the Spectacle whose rich territory it wants to enter by any means, by compromise or by prostitution, but especially through simplistic cynicism, or with an ostentatious kitsch. This pseudo-literature, which is becoming more and more drab, more and more banal and predictable, more and more insignificant, functions beyond the pale of our anguish and desire.

When literature ceases to understand the world and accepts the crisis of representation in which it functions, it becomes mere entertainment, part of the Spectacle.

What is the antidote to this unreflexive and lazy precipitation of what still pretends to be literature? It is the kind of writing that resists the recuperation of itself into distorted or false figures and images. The kind of literature we need now is the kind that will systematically erode and dissipate the setting of the Spectacle, frustrate the expectation of its positive beginning, middle, and end, and cheap resolution. This kind of writing will be at the same time frugal and denuded but rhetorically complex, so that it can seize the world in a new way. This kind of writing must create a space of resistance to the alienated devotion to images—to the refining and undermining of the world by images. This kind of writing should be like an ironic free tense within the opacity of the Spectacle.

If this kind of writing wants to call itself Avant-Pop, or Future Fiction, or Post-Pomo, or Popomo, or Critifiction, or, better yet, I-Don't-Know-What-To-Call-Myself, or New-New-Post, or New-Age, or The-Revolution-of-Writing-Number-70, or simply Writing, or What-The-Hell-Do-I-Know, personally I don't give a damn. It don't bother me. It's fine with me. But enough messing around. [*Stop playing Federman. This is serious.*]

Anyone who persists in *doing literature* without acceding to the fact that doing literature can only be an intraworldly diversion, a career path, a subjective confession, anyone who does not assent to the idea that literature can have no possible social impact, is today urgently confronted with the lacerating questions: What end does it serve? What good is it? What meaning, in the world and for the world, can the pursuit of this activity have?

An activity that society has definitely marginalized, an activity reduced to a sort of deliciously and pleasantly outmoded form of survival, an activity performed beyond the bounds of serious self-reflection.

When literature becomes a surplus of culture, a supplement of culture, it can no longer call itself literature. When fiction becomes a product that can be bought in supermarkets next to the tomatoes, then it no longer deserves to be called literature, or even to be written.

But now one must ask again, is it possible for fiction, for the serious writers of fiction (I assume there are still a few writers among us who think of themselves as serious writers)—is it possible for these writers to escape the generalized recuperation that is taking place in the marketplace of books? The sweet boredom of consensus, the cellophane wrapping of thinking, the commercialization of desire? In other words, can fiction escape conformity and banality, triviality and obscenity, and yet play a role in our society, have a place in our culture? And finally, are there still people out there willing to turn their backs on the SPECTACLE and find time to write and read works of fiction? These are urgent questions that demand immediate answers.

Il n'y a plus moyen d'avancer. Reculer est également hors de question.

Samuel Beckett

Chapter 17

Henry Miller to Henry James

RONALD SUKENICK

Consider things from the point of view of Lady Chatterley's husband. Physically deprived of his passions, all he could do was roll around in that big old house and think, or rather maintain a state of sentience, assuming thinking and feeling are included in the term. With which he seemed quite happy until the gamekeeper started sniffing around his wife. Lawrence believed that anything arising from the passions was well, yes, virtuous. He invented a new, inverted, kind of morality. But in doing so, naive as it seems now, he preserved the very idea of morality for a generation of liberated readers. Or at least that was the effect on me of *Lady Chatterley's Lover*, and of Lawrence's offspring, Henry Miller: the presumptive morality of a life force that undercut traditional morality.

Now in a post-fascist world, it's easy to see the disastrous consequences of a vitalistic morality, just as in a post-Marxist world the malignancy of a purely rational mentality has become obvious. But the history of consciousness staggers, it seems, from doctrine to doctrinaire to correction to overcorrection. One could argue that for a kid growing up in the ultraconventional '50s of Bensonhurst, Brooklyn, the Lawrence-Miller axis was the most liberating path given the going hypocrite/conformist morality.

The '60s, Vietnam and the baby boomers, gave the coup de grace to that conventional mentality. But the loosening up of the psyche in the direction of liberated passions eventually enlisted passions in the service of hypocrite conformity. One could argue optimistically that we are a loop higher in a spiral of liberation. Sexuality, though more exploited, seems to be more free. Relations between parents and children, when there are any at all, seem to be more open and affectionate. Men are more expressive, and women have more drive. One heritage from the Lawrence-Miller mode that seems beneficent is a matter of

231

style—in a word: the extemporaneous. The appeal of the extemporaneous is a combination of the freshness of spontaneity combined with the moral bonus of a presumed honesty. Biographer John Tytell tells us that Miller found his enabling style by writing the way he talked rather than the way he had been writing. The spontaneous quality of speech is what gives Miller's style its power. The case of Lawrence is more subtle regarding speech. He moves in the direction of the incantatory, which is the direction of ritual and magic, hypnotizing the conscious mind to allow more primal understanding to make itself felt.

I use the word "hypnotic" in this connection advisedly, since there are passages in his work whose rhythms appear to be intentionally mesmerizing. So here we have a polarity: Miller's speech patterns leading him to an improvisational freedom, and Lawrence's leading to a kind of releasing compulsion. But there is a problem common to both styles. Lawrence's invocation of the incantatory leads to a numbing repetition, just as Miller's garrulousness leads to a loss of sensitivity, of introspective reflection. If these two writers stylistically are similar in their celebration of passion, then they also are similar in their suppression of thinking. I say "thinking" rather than "thought" because I do not wish to imply intellectual, much less philosophical, formulation. Rather, I mean the normal train of thought of sentient individuals reflecting on the course of things. I mean the kind of monologue that sifts through the mind of Joyce's Bloom, or Conrad's narrators, or most notably through Proust's Marcel.

I once had a job as a night watchman in a factory loft building. I had little to do. It was in that unlikely setting that I came across this sentient strain in the work (and it is possibly no accident that the three aforementioned practitioners are all European) of Henry James—an American, but an American steeped in the ambience of Europe, and therefore a bridge. Reflection does not come easy to a modern American, it having been elbowed out of the way by a simplistic pragmatic tradition. This was especially true of a twenty-year-old night watchman whose shift began with the cleaning of toilets and the mopping of halls and continued with seven hours of staring at walls. But I could read. And maybe it was the very unidimensionality of the job that drove me in the direction of a faceted sensibility such as James's, one that emphasized a hyperactivity of interior life, for above all it was the complex later novels that attracted me, with their endless serpentine sentences and intricate ambiguities. Maybe it was the flat pragmatic character of American culture in the '50s, with its allergy to nuance, its auto -immune reactions to its own subtleties, to which James provided an alternative. In any case, my experience with James was an experience of liberation. The discovery of a style that above all gave one room to think, to speculate, to interpret, was a move quite out of character to one nurtured on Hemingway and Fitzgerald and whose conception of manners was analogous to lying and hypocrisy. Subtlety was for egg-heads. The idea of manners as an extension of the thoughtful had never occurred to me. It is probably no accident that the James vogue of the '50s was spearheaded by Jewish intellectuals whose modus oper-andi was rudeness, incivility, and Marxism, though one suspected, as one got to know them, a kind of reverse snobbism.

It could be argued that the main thrust of American literary mod-ernism, despite Ezra Pound's damnation of the man in the street, was a prejudice in favor of the demotic. The man in the street was an ally, if an ambiguous one, for the Modernists. It may have been the ultimately unsustainable tension between populism and elitism that accounted for the final failure of the Cantos. James, on the other hand, made no concession to the man in the street—at least not in the later novels which, dictated to a secretary, resembled someone thinking out loud. By the time you get to the end of one of those sentences you have com-pletely forgotten how it began, creating the impression, not so much of a stream of consciousness as of a kind of streaming thought without beginning or end. Add the Faulkner of *The Sound and the Fury* with its narrative stream and I would guess you have the kernel of my series, *The Endless Short Story*, as well as other works. So James brought together for me the influence on writing of speech and thought in an amalgam that left ample room for thinking and nuanced feeling, and in fact demanded it. The extemporaneous driven by feeling and the drift of ideas provoked me to consider fiction as a kind of thinking, narrative thinking, as I have described it elsewhere, thinking as enactment.

Henry James was Lady Chatterley's husband. He was the sentient man cut off from his passions, his passions reinvested in the energy of feeling and thought. For us, almost a century away, the release of the passions is both expected and inadequate. For a boy working in a loft building, fiction as an expansion of thinking and nuanced feeling, of speculation and emotional realignment, came as revelation, one that put him outside the going tide of American letters.

Chapter 18

In Their Own Words

The Collective Presents Itself

JEROME KLINKOWITZ

In 1975, during its third year of existence and second of publishing books, the Fiction Collective issued an anthology representative of its work. Called *Statements*, edited by Jonathan Baumbach, and introduced with a "Statement" by Ronald Sukenick, it would be the first of five such volumes assembled during the initial quarter century of the group's life. Since then, readers have been able to track the Collective's evolution through *Statements 2: New Fiction* (1977, edited by Baumbach and Peter Spielberg, with opening comments this time from Robert Coover), *American Made* (1986, edited by Mark Leyner, Curtis White, and Thomas Glynn, with an Introduction by critic Larry McCaffery), *Avant-Pop: Fiction for a Daydream Nation* (1993, with McCaffery entirely in charge), and *In the Slipstream* (1999, edited by Ronald Sukenick and Curtis White, who supplied an Introduction describing the transition to Fiction Collective Two as a complement to Jonathan Baumbach's "Personal History" of the Collective's earlier years).

Together these volumes offer a great resource for scholarship: well over 100 contributions from seventy-eight authors, framed by several thousand words of commentary from Baumbach, Sukenick, Coover, McCaffery, and White. This breakdown itself offers clues for study: the relatively few writers who appear more than once; others, even fewer in number, whose commercial success throughout this period ensured they need never publish a volume of their own with the Collective, yet who lent their authority through appearance here; and, finally, the smallest group of all, those who began their publishing careers with the Collective and were subsequently embraced by conventional houses. That is the individual side of the Collective's efforts. Within the broad sweep of action that these five volumes comprise, there emerge two themes: how the Fiction Collective was developing on its own terms, and how that development fit in (or did not) with the ongoing literary history of fiction in America, three decades of which during the late twentieth century constitute a critically interesting period.

"At the end of the sixties there was an idea in the air that fiction had become impossible," Ronald Sukenick writes in introductory commentary to the first volume. "Fiction was, after all, only a product of the imagination and not the 'real fact' of journalism. In any case, Philip Roth had told us that reality had become more incredible than fiction. One heard a great deal about 'the literature of exhaustion' and 'the death of the novel' " (Baumbach 1975, 8). In 1975, these words would have had an especially familiar ring to them, as they parallel the opening paragraph to Sukenick's "The Death of the Novel" on page 41 of *The Death of the Novel and Other Stories*, published in 1969 by Dial Press and used as an epigraph to the anthology *Innovative Fiction*, over 100,000 copies of which were sold by Dell (Sukenick's paperback publisher at the time) in 1972. "In a curious turnabout," he continues in this recapitulation, "writers in the seventies—those in this volume among them— have learned to profit from what is by definition an impossible situation." In a formulation adopted from his own novella, Sukenick draws the equation that would create the fiction of a new era: "If everything is impossible, then anything becomes possible. What we have now is a fiction of the impossible that thrives on its own impossibility, which is no more or less impossible these days than, say, city life, politics, or peace between the sexes. To paraphrase Beckett, it can't go on it must go on it goes on" (ibid.).

Having quoted the same source to which this cofounder of the Fiction Collective alludes, the editors of *Innovative Fiction* anticipate what he will say in 1975, given the necessity that Sukenick's sense of literary history invokes:

> What you have just read is a statement of the problem the modern writer faces, but it is also the opening to Ronald Sukenick's novella, *The Death of the Novel*, and thus what is a philosophical statement of the problem is conversely a technical reaction to it. Sukenick has written, and we are reading. But are we reading "Literature"? According to the introduction to *The Death of the Novel*, no. It claims literature does not exist in the contemporary world because the reality of our world doesn't exist. Therefore fiction or literature,

which "constitutes a way of looking at the world," cannot exist because there is no world to look at. And yet he writes, and we read, page after page. Why? He says there is no reality, no time, no personality, no God, and even, heaven forbid, no plot. And yet there is something compelling in the way he writes that forces us to read. Is this compulsion, "like eating and making love," merely a way "to pass the time," a way "of maintaining a considered boredom in the face of the abyss"? If it is, it is therefore essential to life. If existence has truly slipped out of artistic reach, literature will of course have to be something more than a way of "looking at the world." In uncertain times, perhaps literature can perform a more primal act. Perhaps it can create a world with a built-in perspective. It can, if literature were in its purest form an epistemological act. This sounds like an innovative idea, and it would be in any society other than those primitive ones that are constantly in the act of creating their world day by day. But to contemporary man, creation must be the very essence of literature, like eating and making love, if literary art is to be of use. (1972, xvi)

Right here is where Sukenick's "Statement" of 1975 picks up the critical thread, providing a translation from his fiction in *The Death of the Novel* to the aesthetics of his new Fiction Collective. "It becomes increasingly apparent that reality is not merely a given but, within limits, to be invented," he asserts. "When reality becomes incredible, fiction, the art of the credible, comes into its own, always starting from the blank page to imagine the unimaginable and to make the impossible seem possible again" (Baumbach 1975, 8).

Sukenick is specific as to the techniques for all this. No "old forms" (7), no familiar plots, little characterization, no reliance at all upon verisimilitude, no inhibitions about staying within the borders that separate fiction, autobiography, and history, plus a new relationship between print and page (including innovative uses of collage)—every one of these literary disruptions described in his *Statements* "Statement" is a technique used in the pieces he had recently collected in *The Death of the Novel and Other Stories*. Indeed, Sukenick's "Statement" could serve just as well as an introduction to that volume. The critical questions to be asked today are whether it served as an accurate introduction to the Collective's 1975 anthology and to what extent it forecast the group's direction over the next twenty-five years. At the very least, it indicates how the Collective was launched with this one rather special writer's mission in mind.

Twenty-seven pieces by as many writers fill the pages of *Statements*. Contributors make their appearances alphabetically, a practice followed in the first three Fiction Collective anthologies. Sukenick's fiction comes near the end, part of *The Endless Short Story* (and thus representing new directions in his work rather than old). Stories by Jonathan Baumbach and Peter Spielberg appear as well, giving the founding fathers full representation, even if their fictive methods are far from as innovative as Sukenick's own (both in his *Endless Short Story* excerpt and introductory "Statement"). What is interesting is who else appears. Of the remaining twenty-four authors, only six fit the bill of "Statement" closely—that is, presenting work that discards old forms and invents new ones meant to "imagine the unimaginable and to make the impossible seem possible again" (Sukenick 1975, 8). These six are Walter Abish, George Chambers, Raymond Federman, Steve Katz, Clarence Major, and Ishmael Reed. Of them, four would publish books with the Collective, including work central to the emerging literary history that Sukenick's "Statement" would forecast: most immediately Chambers with *Null Set* (1977), Federman with *Take It or Leave It* (1976), Katz with *Moving Parts* (1977), and Major with *Reflex and Bone Structure* (1975). It is impossible today to imagine the canon of American fiction without these works. Equally contributive were Abish's novel *Alphabetical Africa* (1974) and his story collections *Minds Meet* (1975) and *In the Future Perfect* (1977), with the same true for Reed's *The Last Days of Louisiana Red* (1974) and *Flight to Canada* (1975), an excerpt from which was appearing in *Statements*. Abish and Reed, however, were being published by New Directions and Random House, respectively—reminiscent of Sukenick's earlier success with Dial Press (an imprint of Dell), Katz's career-starting experience with firms as prestigious as Holt, Rinehart & Winston and Alfred A. Knopf, Federman's fictive debut with the Swallow Press (where Sukenick would join him for one book in 1973, just before the Collective got underway), and even Major's ability to publish volumes of poetry with outstandingly established venues.

Here is the first lesson to be learned from the Collective's endeavor: not that the style of innovative fiction Sukenick championed was impossible to do with commercial houses, but that it had become difficult or impossible *for some writers*. Certainly not for everyone, as the examples of Reed and Abish prove. Significantly, these two others would never do more with the Fiction Collective than support its work via contributions to its anthologies. That in itself is important, for it provides historical evidence for their true allegiance and makes invidious any attempted contrasts of their own innovations as inferior to those who published their books Collectively. Of the others, Major and Katz produced important subsequent volumes within the fold but also would move on to distinguished publication elsewhere. Only Sukenick, Federman (Sukenick's close collaborator on several projects), and Chambers (Federman's dear friend and eventual coauthor) would continue through their careers with the great majority of their novels and story collections coming from the group founded because other outlets were closed to them.

Unmentioned in Sukenick's "Statement" or in the front matter of any subsequent Fiction Collective anthology is the nature of this core group's original success in commercial ranks. Readers are given the implication that publishers had suddenly abandoned fiction that dared to innovate beyond the narrowest of economically trustworthy boundaries. Sukenick's essays of the time, appearing prominently in the *New York Times Book Review* and *Partisan Review*, make explicit arguments along this line, and both the arguments and their histories are recounted by Jonathan Baumbach in his "Personal History," which prefaces the 1999 collection *In the Slipstream*. But how had these authors, including the less formally innovative yet thematically challenging Baumbach himself (whose first novels were published in 1965 and 1968 by trade giants Random House and Harper & Row, respectively), done so well just a few years before, only to be turned down seemingly everywhere now? Was it a government plot, or at the very least the result of a literary establishment's pandering to right-wing forces—"The New Cultural Conservatism," as Sukenick put it in the title of a *Partisan Review* symposium that he helped organize? Had writers' attempts to reinvent reality gone too far for the police, at the very least, for the literary police of publishing, entertainment, and academia, the nexus of which always did and always will exercise a certain amount of control?

At least one fact of publishing history is neglected by the Fiction Collective as it announces its mission and sets out to fulfill it: that Baumbach, Sukenick, Katz, Reed, and so many others allied with its core interests had been able to publish in the American 1960s thanks to a peculiar economy operative in the business world of that time. By the mid-1960s especially, publishers' stocks had become attractive to investors as prime candidates for splits, an early hint of the new investment strategies that would climax (and eventually burst) in the dot-com revolution of the 1990s. With each stock split, a publisher would be richly recapitalized, allowing more editorial and production leeway than usual. In this climate, lists grew in both size and shape, with ample room for acquisitions of comparatively radical work. Thematics pushed new limits, including violence in Jerzy Kosinski's *The Painted Bird* (1965) and sex in *Portnoy's Complaint* (1969) by Philip Roth. Formally, Kosinski

accomplished even more with *Steps* (1968), as did Kurt Vonnegut with the
technically challenging *Slaughterhouse-Five* (1969). All four of these works
appealed to the public, justifying their publishers' investment and paying
out quite well on the risk. But risks were being taken with less promising
authors of the time—writers such as Thomas Pynchon, Richard Brautigan,
and Donald Barthelme, none of whose early editions sold strongly. Still,
the counterculture was booming, and thanks to the irony of a go-go stock
market's willingness to recapitalize, funds to publish its fiction were available. Even an author like Gilbert Sorrentino—a poet working as a trade
editor for Grove Press and bringing out eyebrow-raising acquisitions by
owner Barney Rossett—could start writing novels and see them published by Hill & Wang and Pantheon.

For innovationists, the times had provided a remarkable source of
support. Kurt Vonnegut, whose five novels and twenty-year writer's career had gone nowhere, could be rescued from anonymity (and a des-
perately accepted $6,800-per-year instructorship at the University of Iowa
Writers Workshop) by a three-book contract from Seymour Lawrence
who, by virtue of his agreement with Delacorte Press, had the latitude
to sign on an author just because he had been impressed with the
liveliness of a book review.[1] Simultaneously, Steve Katz (with no more
credentials than an MA from Cornell University and a small press
publication in Italy) would place *The Exagggerations* [sic] *of Peter Prince*
(1968)—a major novel—with Holt, Rinehart & Winston simply by accepting an invitation from editor Aaron Asher at a party—specifically,
as Katz tells it, an offer to publish the novel of whoever would help him
on with his overshoes. There is a note of the apocryphal to Katz's story,
but in principle it is not that far beyond the realities of how Seymour
Lawrence noticed Vonnegut and took him on. Plus Katz did manage to
sell a book of stories to Random House (*Creamy and Delicious*, 1971) and
another novel to Knopf (*Saw*, 1973). Meanwhile, Ronald Sukenick (with
just some little magazine stories and a scholarly book on Wallace Stevens
to his credit) caught the eye of another freewheeling publisher allied
with the Dell empire, Richard Baron, who would put an equally young
trade editor named E. L. Doctorow in charge of seeing *Up* (1968) and
The Death of the Novel and Other Stories (1969) through production.

These are amazing stories from a remarkable time. That they are
true and that the times were actually like this underscore an important
fact not included in the Fiction Collective's initial assessment. Yes, in
1975 American publishers were not encouraging radical innovation in
the genres of short fiction and the novel. But before the early 1960s,
they had not been doing so either. What had happened was that for less
than a decade a coincidence of larger cultural innovation with an

investor-based spike in publishers' profitability created a brave new world for fiction writers willing and eager to expand their discipline's limits. Within this period, a much larger number of them than usual conditions would have allowed produced a breathtaking array of works, from Reed's *The Free-Lance Pallbearers* (1967) and *Yellow Back Radio Broke-Down* (1969) to Sukenick's first volumes and Vonnegut's breakthrough novel, *Slaughterhouse-Five*. As time passed, a new cultural conservatism set in, the momentary flurry of investor interest in publishers' stocks abated, and innovative fiction was back on its own again.

Would it survive? Of course—Vonnegut, Kosinski, Brautigan, Pynchon, Barthelme, and others never associated with the Fiction Collective continued their careers, as did those who had been supportive of the Collective, appearing in the early anthologies but never availing themselves of its self-publishing opportunities: Reed and Abish from *Statements*, Robert Coover from *Statements 2* just two years later. What is interesting are the cases of three other typologies within the Collective's initial roster—what happened to those who either found shelter in or were launched by Collective efforts and were then embraced by commercial houses; to those who had retreated to the Collective from commercial fields and by choice or determination never left it; and to those whose reputations were born and died there.

Katz and Major typify the first group and share several important characteristics in terms of future work as well. Their publications in the 1960s employ that era's most useful innovations—that is, ones that helped put literature on a new course that others could follow. Within the Fiction Collective, they would make equally bold moves: Katz's *Stolen Stories* (1984) and Major's *Emergency Exit* (1979) and *My Amputations* (1986) are as important in literary history as anything they had done before. But in view of their post-Collective careers, something else emerges. In commercially published novels such as *Florry of Washington Heights* (1987) and *Such Was the Season* (1987), Katz and Major become at least superficially more realistic. Not traditionally realistic, of course, no more than a Larry Rivers portrait qualifies as such (in the wake of abstract expressionism's influence) or even a street scene by Richard Estes.[2] Instead, these two writers, so important to the Collective's early efforts, decide that after doing all they can to reject realism's conventions they will now subject them to a fruitful interrogation. Specifically, all those literary features that Ronald Sukenick had banned in his "Statement" from the first *Statements* volume reemerge in the work of two key *Statements* authors—not to be re-embraced but to be examined anew and put to new purposes in light of an era's innovations. As such, they keep pace with the ongoing literary history being enacted by two other writers supportive of the Collective but never publishing books with it, Walter Abish (*How German Is It* [1980] and *Eclipse Fever* [1993]) and Robert Coover (*Gerald's Party* [1986] and *Pinocchio in Venice* [1991]). Many other novels by each of these four writers could be mentioned as well. What is important is not just that two Collectivists who leave the fold join ranks with two supporters who had enjoyed continued commercial success but that this non-Collective style of work parts company with that of their colleagues who remained within the group.

Who else from this first batch left? Maureen Howard, never much of a formal innovator. Who stayed? Jerry Bumpus, a quality, small-press author but commercially unsaleable because of limited appeal rather than radical technique. Who should have never been there in the first place, with no plans for innovative fiction, Collectivist or otherwise? The poet Mark Strand, a friend of Sukenick's, whose stellar reputation (in poetry) dignified the group. Who stayed *and grew* within the Fiction Collective? Beyond Federman and Sukenick, it is hard to plot real growth. Cofounders Peter Spielberg and Jonathan Baumbach kept with it for the rest of their careers, but doing so more in the tradition of the European intellectual novel than of the nativistic, jazz-based, funkily improvisatory fiction of Federman and Sukenick. Indeed, it would be the "avant-pop" nature of this latter pair's work that provided inspiration for Larry McCaffery's fourth anthology in the series, even though Federman and Sukenick are not in it.[3] Not a single contributor to the *Statements* volume appears in *Avant-Pop: Fiction for a Daydream Nation* (1993), suggesting that between 1975 and 1993 the mission described in Sukenick's "Statement" may have lost its way or transformed itself so grossly that only Sukenick and Federman could stay on board.

The truth emerges in the makeup of the Collective's two anthologies that appear in between *Statements* and *Avant-Pop*. Here one sees Federman and Sukenick take a turn toward the fusion of pop culture with avant-garde subversion and innovation that McCaffery would proclaim as the next new thing, while another batch of Collective authors makes feints at the original "Statement" manifesto and then heads off on their own. *Statements 2* begins with its own "Statement," this time made by Robert Coover, who also contributes material from his meganovel, *The Public Burning* (1977a), presently being published to great fanfare by Viking Press. Just as the "Statement" from the Collective's first anthology seemed so much the personal business of Ronald Sukenick, so too does Coover's argument apply most pertinently to his own situation, artistic and otherwise. "America is, at best, a strange place for an artist to work in," he begins, noteworthy for a writer who had just spent much of the past decade living and working abroad (perhaps, if his admission on page xiii of Richard Elman's *Namedropping* [1998] is true, in the employ of the Central Intelligence Agency, albeit with regret). Surveying the American scene to which he had recently returned and contrasting it with the land he had left shortly after publishing *The Universal Baseball Association, Inc., J. Henry Waugh, Proprietor* in 1968 with Random House, another success of commercially innovative fiction, Coover characterizes its economic determinants:

> On the one hand there is the illusion of artistic freedom, constitutionally protected; on the other, there's the operative dogma of the marketplace; will it sell? In America, art—like everything else (knowledge, condoms, religion, etc.)—is a product. The discovery of this is the capstone to the artist's alienation process in America. He knows there is no relation between what is good and what sells, nor between what he's made and how it's used by the market managers. (7)

Constitutionally protected—this would be the principle Coover had to invoke when attorneys warned that *The Public Burning* might libel Richard Nixon. *Will it sell*—the principle Coover worked under when teaching at the University of Iowa Writers Workshop, the most market-driven of all MFA programs. *Knowledge, condoms, religion*—how could Coover's canon, from *The Origin of the Brunists* in 1966 to *The Adventures of Lucky Pierre* in 2002, exist without them? Yes, in the United States everything, from knowledge and religion to condoms, is a commodity, and because he knows that so well, Coover has been able to forge a career as the most typical of McCaffery's avant-popsters. Later on in his "Statement" he repeats Sukenick's saw that commercial publishers have abandoned innovative fiction. But the dictum certainly does not apply to the author of *The Public Burning*, much less of subsequent novels that both celebrate and deconstruct the mythos of everything American, from movies to pornography and the Old West. If the Fiction Collective must exist, then it is for someone other than him.

And so, who is *Statements 2* for? For those who would never venture long or far from its fold, it seems. From the book's contents, one sees important growth in Federman and Sukenick, each beginning to adopt the elements of popular culture and autobiography that would characterize their later work. Among the newcomers, Marianne Hauser and Thomas Glynn would provide works that make statements, but neither would remain Collective-dependent—especially not Glynn, who after a Collective novel and more work both in and for the third anthology would be deemed worthy of support by the high-profile commercial

editor Gordon Lish. Looking ahead to this third volume, one sees
another commercial success emerging: Mark Leyner. But also two other
sides of the original group: Baumbach, Friedman, and Spielberg, taking on few new challenges and contributing to no important canon
other than their own, and Federman, Sukenick, Katz, and Major, all
four of them working in new directions that would take the second pair
into fresh publishing ventures and let the first duo make good on the
Collective's sense of mission, at least in terms of their own growth and
its importance to the ongoing history of American literature.

American Made: New Fiction from the Fiction Collective (1986) makes
good on its subtitle's promise, but in a characteristically 1980s manner.
For the first time, a literary critic rather than Collective author writes
the Introduction. For many of the ten and one-half pages Larry
McCaffery provides, the reader gets a version of old-fashioned jazz record
liner notes, in which every track receives polite mention, even though
discriminating listeners will be hearing an occasional sour selection—
saying that Curtis White's "Howdy Doody Is Dead" is a story that "resembles Hawthorne's foreboding allegories in its complexity, precision
of development, and tone" (10) rivals the classic rationalizations by Ira
Gitler and Nat Hentoff of a jazz group's struggles with some clunky
tune insisted upon by a producer. But the book's editing, by Mark
Leyner, Curtis White, and Thomas Glynn, takes a step beyond that of
the first two anthologies, in that its stories are exclusively by writers who
have published books with the Collective. Farewell, therefore, to Walter
Abish and Jerome Charyn, veterans of the first two volumes—plus no
room for moral supporters such as Robert Coover and Ishmael Reed.
Quite admirably, with a dozen years of existence under its belt, the
Fiction Collective stands on its own.

But can it? McCaffery's Introduction shows how there is still a
need for a mission statement, however that mission may have become
confused. From Sukenick's and Coover's previous efforts come the now-
familiar mantras about publishers' timidities, bookstores' bottom lines,
and editors' independence. The Fiction Collective remains an alternative to this. But the critic warns readers away from assuming "that the
anthology is the product of a unified aesthetic sensibility. Indeed, since
its inception in 1974 the Collective has consistently had to battle the
misconception that it represents a 'Movement' or favors a specific kind
of experimentation" (1986, 2). Of course it had: the virtual identity of
Ronald Sukenick's "Statement" with his own fiction's program guaranteed it. Should Sukenick's words not be heeded? McCaffery repeats
them verbatim regarding publishing conditions, which in the late 1980s
were quite different from those Sukenick had described as being suf-

fered in the economics following the burst of his 1960s bubble. By claiming that these conditions prevent the commercial publication of not just innovative but now any type of "serious fiction" (ibid.) at all, McCaffery justifies the existence of the dozen or so canonically future-less writers who fill out the pages of *American Made*, a group boasting Fulbright appointments, writers-colony fellowships, and all the other predictable awards, plus professorships in small-time creative writing programs. In lieu of commercial success, philanthropic and taxpayer support was keeping these people fed—much better fed, surely, than unaffiliated figures such as Richard Kostelanetz, whose own lack of academic affiliation, grants support, *and* commercial sponsorship had sentenced him to a life lived on less than one-third the income of even a poorly paid creative writing prof. Yet Kostelanetz's theory of "the death of intelligent writing" (ibid.) is cited alongside the allusions to Sukenick's complaints, even though none of this commentary is examined for how it applies half a generation later. Instead, this third volume's Introduction proceeds by praising its contributors' work as " 'non-traditional' or 'experimental' " (11), which would indeed sound like a movement, except that McCaffery has begun by disavowing that the Fiction Collective hosts one.

By 1993, when the next Collective anthology appears, the organization's nature has changed. As described by Ronald Sukenick and Curtis White in their Introduction to the fifth volume, *In the Slipstream*, "We . . . decided to inform the membership that unless we were allowed to re-organize, re-energize and administer the Collective, we would depart, taking the resources with us, and start a new press" (1999, 19). As their resources included those of two large taxpayer-supported universities, Sukenick and White spoke with some clout, making a statement more practically emphatic than any of the front matter of the Collective's first three anthologies. Its fourth would be a product of this power play: the emergence of Black Ice Books as not just Sukenick's personal imprint (shades of Aaron Asher and Seymour Lawrence) but as a vehicle for Movement statements with a vengeance, such as Larry McCaffery's editing of *Avant-Pop: Fiction for a Daydream Nation*.

Fully in control of this book, McCaffery need not find diplomatic words for the work of creative writing profs nor disavow the fact that there is a Movement afoot, as he marshals a new style of writer both within the Collective (Gerald Vizenor, Mark Leyner) and without (William T. Vollmann, Kathy Acker). The innovations of this group are logical extensions of work by Sukenick, Federman, Katz, and Major, all but the last of whom will reappear in the editor's commercial sequel, *After Yesterday's Crash: The Avant-Pop Anthology* (1995). There, McCaffery

will be relatively polite in his analysis. But in the no-holds-barred arena
of Black Ice Books, he fashions an Introduction that reads like a put-
on of an avant-pop narrative, replete with a film-noir characterization
of himself (as Mac, the hard-boiled detective) and a critically fetishized
Kathy Acker who turn a faculty office into something quite different
from the locale that produced the proper literary criticism prefacing
American Made.

> It didn't take me long to get the hang of activities my two-
> dimensional role as a romantic-tough-guy-loner had never given
> me the opportunity to try. While my left hand reached into
> my lap and began masturbating with slow, steady and won-
> drously pleasurable strokes, my right hand reached for my
> lap-top and began typing up the opening to this introduction;
> meanwhile I was dictating an avant-poop porno porn memo
> to my department secretary, who looked surprised only for
> the few moments it took for her to appraise the situation and
> get into the spirit of things by donning Kathy's black leather
> jacket, and vigorously plunging the strap-on she'd triumphantly
> released from its captivity behind my dusty copy of *The Faerie
> Queen* into whatever orifices seemed most readily available
> (and there were plenty of options). Neither she nor Kathy
> seemed particularly embarrassed by the profusion of poppy-
> cock—pop-porn and purple-pickled pecker-juice—pouring
> from my mouth and dick, respectively. (1993, 28–29)

The worst of *Avant-Pop*'s fiction plays out with this sense of knocking
the silk toppers off the heads of the bourgeoisie. The best of it reflects
directions Sukenick, Katz, and Federman were taking in their own work.
Confirmation of this comes from noting the achievements of *Avant-
Pop*'s genuine writers: not the junior high school underground of narratives telling the reader how "I'm waking to the songs of insects fucking
in the decayed hair lining chipped toilet underbellies" (225) or the self-
taken image-mongering of "When the telephone rang at four am, in a
loft cluttered with scores and music notebooks—notebooks seared and
starred with expressive markings like seismographs of restrained psy-
chosis" (103); rather, the rhythms of local culture working their ways to
the surface in texts by Gerald Vizenor and Ricardo Cortez Cruz, or
William T. Vollmann's creation of a credible personal ethic that can
work its way through the detritus of popular culture. What would become brilliant careers would start here. And riding the crest of these
developments are three old folks from the Collective's founding, whose

innovations predate even that key act. None are in *Avant-Pop*, but each reemerges in *After Yesterday's Crash* in full avant-pop form: Katz exploring the exorcist's role he first adopted as a fifteen-year-old boy in Washington Heights, Federman comparing the popular culture phenomenon of *Schindler's List* (1982) with his own list of Holocaust materials, and Sukenick making the first turn toward the embrace of his Jewish American upbringing that would find full issue in *Mosaic Man* (1999).

In the Slipstream is a true omnibus volume, not just presenting fiction from the Collective's latest batch but looking back over three decades of change and development. With opening statements having given way to historical narratives, any sense of mission statement now devolves into that of creation myth. Which is unfortunate, because an honest sense of literary history would admit that the Fiction Collective was founded because a very specific group of innovationists—all New Yorkers with ties to major universities in the Northeast, all veterans of commercial publishing in this same Manhattan that had for a time found resources for the promotion of their work—could find no other ways to continue their careers. Thankfully, the type of fiction they espoused did not become ghettoized. Some authors of it, such as Walter Abish, Robert Coover, and Ishmael Reed, continued their careers without the Collective's help. Others, notably Steve Katz and Clarence Major, sought shelter there for a time, then found their place once more in the commercial mainstream. Most important is the historical fact that Sukenick and Federman, so central to each development within the Collective's history, were not hampered by their allegiance to the group. *In the Slipstream* locates them in a current that includes writers as diverse as Cris Mazza, R. M. Berry, and Diane Glancy, yet all contributing to a canon of American fiction that is no more hampered by the academic politics of creative writing programs than it is by the constraints of best sellerdom. True, the Fiction Collective's rhetoric overstresses the latter (in an awkwardly unexamined way) while pretending the former does not exist. But that does not mean it is not right, in terms of what has mattered in American literary history.

NOTES

1. "The Latest Word," Vonnegut's review of *The Random House Dictionary* for the *New York Times Book Review*, October 30, 1966, reprinted as "New Dictionary" in his first book with Lawrence, *Welcome to the Monkey House* (1968).

2. Photorealism being anything but verisimilitude, for no human eye sees in such an antihierarchal, all-over manner, let alone ever being able to witness a major thoroughfare on Manhattan's Upper West Side totally devoid of people.

3. They do appear in McCaffery's commercial sequel, *After Yesterday's Crash*, brought out with Penguin in 1995.

REFERENCES

Abish, Walter. 1974. *Alphabetical Africa.* New York: New Directions.

———. 1975. *Minds meet.* New York: New Directions.

———. 1977. *In the future perfect.* New York: New Directions.

———. 1980. *How German is it.* New York: New Directions.

———. 1993. *Eclipse fever.* New York: Knopf.

Baumbach, Jonathan. 1965. *A man to conjure with.* New York: Random House.

———. 1968. *What comes next.* New York: Harper & Row.

———. 1999. Who do they think they are? A personal history of the Fiction Collective. In *In the slipstream,* ed. Ronald Sukenick and Curtis White, 9-18. Normal, IL, and Tallahassee, FL: FC2.

Baumbach, Jonathan, ed. 1975. *Statements: New fiction from the Fiction Collective.* New York: Braziller.

Baumbach, Jonathan, and Peter Spielberg, eds. 1977. *Statements 2: New fiction.* New York: Fiction Collective.

Chambers, George. 1977. *Null set.* New York: Fiction Collective.

Coover, Robert. 1966. *The origin of the Brunists.* New York: Putnam.

———. 1968. *The universal baseball association, inc., J. Henry Waugh, proprietor.* New York: Random House.

———. 1977a. *The public burning.* New York: Viking Press.

———. 1977b. Statement. In *Statements 2: New fiction,* ed. Jonathan Baumbach and Peter Spielberg, 7-9. New York: Fiction Collective.

———. 1986. *Gerald's party.* New York: Simon & Schuster.

———. 1991. *Pinocchio in Venice.* New York: Simon & Schuster.

———. 2002. *The adventures of Lucky Pierre.* New York: Grove.

Elman, Richard. 1998. *Namedropping.* Albany: State University of New York Press.

Federman, Raymond. 1976. *Take it or leave it.* New York: Fiction Collective.

Katz, Steve. 1968. *The exagggerations* [sic] *of Peter Prince.* New York: Holt, Rinehart & Winston.

———. 1971. *Creamy and delicious.* New York: Random House.

———. 1973. *Saw.* New York: Knopf.

———. 1977. *Moving parts.* New York: Fiction Collective.

———. 1984. *Stolen stories.* New York: Fiction Collective. In *Innovative fiction,* ed. Jerome Klinkowitz and John Somer, 158–160. New York: Dell, 1972.

———. 1987. *Florry of Washington Heights.* Los Angeles: Sun & Moon.

Keneally, Thomas. 1982. *Schindler's list.* New York: Simon & Schuster.

Klinkowitz, Jerome, and John Somer, eds. 1972. *Innovative fiction.* New York: Dell.

Kosinski, Jerzy. 1965. *The painted bird.* Boston: Houghton Mifflin.

———. 1968. *Steps.* New York: Random House.

Leyner, Mark, Curtis White, and Thomas Glynn, eds. 1986. *American made: New fiction from the Fiction Collective.* New York: Fiction Collective.

McCaffery, Larry. 1986. Introduction. In *American made,* ed. Leyner et al., 1–11. New York: Fiction Collective.

———, ed. 1995. *After yesterday's crash: The avant-pop anthology.* New York: Penguin.

———, ed. 1993. *Avant-pop: Fiction for a daydream nation.* Boulder, CO and Normal, IL: Black Ice Books.

Major, Clarence. 1975. *Reflex and bone structure.* New York: Fiction Collective.

———. 1979. *Emergency exit.* New York: Fiction Collective.

———. 1986. *My amputations.* New York and Boulder, CO: Fiction Collective.

———. 1987. *Such was the season.* San Francisco: Mercury House.

Reed, Ishmael. 1967. *The free-lance pallbearers.* New York: Doubleday.

———. 1969. *Yellow back radio broke-down.* New York: Doubleday.

———. 1974. *The last days of Louisiana Red.* New York: Random House.

———. 1975. *Flight to Canada.* New York: Random House.

Roth, Philip. 1969. *Portnoy's complaint.* New York: Random House.

Sukenick, Ronald. 1968. *Up.* New York: Dial Press.

———. 1969. *The death of the novel and other stories.* New York: Dial Press.

———. 1975. Statement. In *Statements,* ed. Jonathan Baumbach, 7–8. New York: Braziller.

———. 1985. *In form: Digressions on the act of fiction.* Carbondale: Southern Illinois University Press.

———. 1999. *Mosaic man.* Normal, IL: FC2.

Sukenick, Ronald, and Curtis White, eds. 1999. *In the slipstream: An FC2 reader.* Normal, IL and Tallahassee, FL: FC2.

Vonnegut, Kurt. 1968. *Welcome to the monkey house.* New York: Delacorte Press/ Seymour Lawrence.

———. 1969. *Slaughterhouse-five.* New York: Delacorte Press/Seymour Lawrence.

Chapter 19

World Book

CAROLE MASO

"It is no longer possible to think in our day other than in the void left by man's disappearance. For this void does not create a deficiency; it does not constitute a lacuna that must be filled. It is nothing more, and nothing less, than the unfolding of a space in which it is once more possible to think" (Foucault 1973, 342).

This quotation from Michel Foucault's *The Order of Things* seems for me to get to the heart of where we are now going. World events in the past two years press the novel with astonishing speed into its next phase, and in some way the place it has been tending toward for 100 years. "Orts, scraps and fragments, she quoted what she remembered of the vanishing play," wrote Virginia Woolf in her war-torn and broken-hearted *Between the Acts* (1990, 133). As the novel breaks apart, becoming shards, a debris field, without a real audience or raison d'etre, it free falls into the space of pure radiance, a place of unimaginable intellectual and emotional freedom—cut off from the quaint scaffoldings of narrative and character—for this no longer makes any sense except as a sentimental record of human folly, we write now whole-heartedly into our own obsolescence, our own obscurity—a place at once tender and absurd and fierce. We chronicle figments, and it is as if we have already disappeared, and our shadow words are trailing us, leaving their extraordinary, flickering residue.

It shall be a record of our vanishing that one of the voices offers. It shall be a book of scraps. Last messages left on answering machines, trace elements, in the Unfinished Book of Hope—a sort of reliquary, a dome, a memory of bread, a dormer, a basket, a rabbit path. It shall be a cradle that holds time. A prayer. More and more a prayer. It shall speak to what mattered most—as much as it was possible to do so. It shall be a pageant, a celebration, a mourning grove, a history of our

251

suffering at once intimate and epic, the progress of our regret, the passage of yearning. My mother's voice, the swing swung, the way you looked that night. The bells. Birds, migration, peace in our time. A philosophy of wings will emerge.

It shall be our lives—eclipsing the darkness—our lives passing brightly before the darkness and obscuring it for a moment.

She was busy, should she be asked. She was midstream. She was standing in front of the illuminated manuscripts in that ancient Italian city. She was alive. We were working, should she be asked on an erotic song cycle. It shall be a record of heartbreak. The dust in her hair— what is left now of those two tremendous towers and their daylight inhabitants. What is left. Remnant of a beautiful, blue morning—New York City—just the words once before we fall back into forgetfulness: surrendered, evaporated, dissolved, perfects. That fragment of flame that was my life. Trailing daylight.

To see the sky one more time through those towers, the view they arrange. The light as it made its way across their skin. They were your friends—you always called them that. The boy you loved who had worked at their summit carrying cool, blue drinks. Windows on the World.

Things that maybe you did not know. I loved rain, snow, anything that purely, recklessly and without harm fell from the sky to grace this earth.

I used to find my self on Sullivan Street, where from one angle I could see the gorgeous Empire State Building and then by turning, by pivoting without lifting a foot, I could see the World Trade Center. I must have done it a thousand times.

The pivot now made silently in the dust. A habit I know.

A record of our resourcefulness and longing and our folly.

There were things I wanted you to know.

There's a list I've been keeping.

What did you think was beautiful there?

My father bee laden among the roses. Peace eludes us, I can scarcely believe.

Crossing the color fields, figures pass before her—she remembered a world of pure vibrancy and form—miniscule now they pixelate and blur. No one says it, and there is no need to, for it is abundantly clear. . . . The living and the dead, the bodied and the disembodied inextricably linked, the mingling of a thousand dusts. Small voices: a voice calls, a voice screams, some voice somewhere sings, another asks for help, begs for water, asks for a story, especially a story, and if there were a story like that I would be the first in line. . . . A story with assertions, a story with solutions, pointless now.

We write now into our extinction with surprising reserves of energy, perversely embracing the motion toward our disappearance. From the erasures, from the negations, from the violence and assaults and trespasses and betrayal, from the love for all that passes, the novel in new forms will persist; it alone has the potential of coming closer than any other human document to the poignancy and terror of the moment.

REFERENCES

Foucault, Michael. 1973. *The order of things: An archaeology of the human sciences.* New York: Vintage Books.

Woolf, Virginia. 1990. *Between the acts.* London: Hogarth Press.

Afterword

Two Presents

BRIAN MCHALE

I disappear around the bend.
So long. End of story.

—Ronald Sukenick, *The Death of the Novel*

To begin at the beginning: shouldn't this book's title be plural?

Reflection suggests, and the contributions to this volume confirm, that there are really two "presents" to be distinguished when we talk about "Fiction's Present." The first is what we might call (somewhat inadequately, and for lack of a better term) the *phenomenological present.* This is the present of immediate experience: human consciousness in its complex, moment-to-moment negotiation with the world outside itself and with its own processes (memory, association, anticipation, fantasy). Capturing the phenomenological present—registering what it feels like to be inside someone's skin, someone's mind—has been on fiction's agenda since at least the invention of the Richardsonian epistolary novel in the eighteenth century. The high-water mark of this phenomenological project, however, was reached in the modernist period, when the formal innovations of Henry James, Joyce, Proust, Woolf, Faulkner, and others yielded a simulation of immediate experience unattainable in earlier eras:

> Mr Bloom stood at the corner, his eyes wandering over the multicoloured hoardings. Cantrell and Cochrane's Ginger Ale (Aromatic). Clery's summer sale. No, he's going on straight. Hello. *Leah* tonight: Mrs Bandman Palmer. Like to see her in

255

that again. *Hamlet* she played last night. Male impersonator. Perhaps he was a woman. Why Ophelia committed suicide? Poor papa! How he used to talk about Kate Bateman in that! Outside the Adelphi in London waited all the afternoon to get in. Year before I was born that was: sixty-five.[1]

A typical moment of consciousness in Mr. Bloom's day: he registers the visual surface of the urban landscape, meanwhile monitoring the approach of the irritating C. P. M'Coy ("No, he's going on straight"). An advertising canvasser himself, he is especially attentive to advertising signs; his Dublin, like Melville's New York, is a "textual City of Words" (as Joseph Tabbi puts it in this volume). Bloom recalls having seen Mrs. Bandman Palmer in *Leah* before and projects a scenario (a possible world) in which he would see her in it again. Reflecting on *Hamlet*, he speculates about Ophelia's motives for suicide (another possible world), which in turn triggers painful associations with his own father's suicide. Memories of his father's stories open a window into the deeper past— the state of affairs "before [he] was born." Perception, anticipation, speculation, association, and memory (both firsthand and secondhand) all converge to yield a convincing image of the experience of present-ness, of presence: fiction's present.

   This is the sort of presentness that Alan Singer has in mind when he describes the self-deceiving consciousness that, if not an invention of the modernists, certainly comes into its own in modernist-era fiction. Tabbi detects it already in Melville, whose *Benito Cereno* achieves "an exemplary production of presence in fiction." Ronald Sukenick discovers it in the "streaming thought" of Joyce's Bloom, Faulkner's Compson brothers, Proust's Marcel, and, movingly, in Lady Chatterley's husband (whose physical immobility mirrored Sukenick's own, in the latter stages of his illness). But this simulation of presentness comes at a high cost. It depends upon the elaborate devices that are modernism's great contribution to fiction's repertoire of techniques: the perspectivist apparatus that Singer describes in Flaubert's *Comices Agricoles* scene; collage poetics, as evoked here by Lance Olsen; the device of stream of consciousness itself, anticipated by Melville (according to Tabbi), and visible in all its artificiality in my previous quote from *Ulysses*. "Stream of consciousness," writes Robert Caserio in this volume, "is a supreme illusion invented by fiction to represent interior life." Yes, precisely: a supreme illusion, an invention, *not* a mirror held up to the present of interiority. Or, if it *is* a mirror, it is one that calls attention to its own mirroring apparatus as much as it does to the thing (the "stream") captured in the mirror.

The paradoxical economy of fiction's phenomenological present is such that the more *immediate* its illusion of presentness the more that illusion depends on devices of *mediation*. To achieve the effect of consciousness's moment-to-moment negotiations with the world and itself, fiction calls upon highly artificial devices that far from being "second nature" to anyone must be *learned*, mastered by writers and readers alike. But insofar as we notice such devices (and we cannot help but notice them), we are no longer "within" the present, alongside the character, looking out through his or her eyes or over his or her shoulder, but "outside," contemplating the writer's ingenuity. The irreducible tension here between immediacy and mediation is precisely the same as the one, familiar from digital culture, between *immersion* (another version of presentness) and *interactivity*.[2]

In this situation in which immediacy and mediation are deadlocked, one possible way forward would be to shift the site of immediacy from the interior of the fictional world (the character's experience) to the interface between the text and its reader—in other words, to relocate the phenomenological present in the *reader's* experience. To put it differently, a solution might be found in treating interactivity itself as a kind of immersion—in *immersing* the reader in interactivity. This solution is already anticipated by *Benito Cereno*, where (if we follow Tabbi) the agonizing delay of Captain Delano's recognition and the collapsing syntax of the recognition itself implicate the reader in the character's consciousness. Immersive interactivity emerges more fully in high modernism, where the characters' difficulties in negotiating their worlds—say, the governess's in *The Turn of the Screw*, or Quentin's and Shreve's in *Absalom, Absalom!*—are transferred (perhaps even in the Freudian sense of "transference") to the reader. Our difficulties mirror their difficulties, and vice versa.

Already a discernible tendency in modernism, this transfer of the locus of experience from character to reader becomes a cornerstone of postmodernist poetics—programmatically, and maybe a bit literal-mindedly, in texts such as Calvino's *If on a Winter's Night a Traveler* or Sukenick's "The Death of the Novel," but also in Beckett's fiction, in Pynchon's *Gravity's Rainbow*, and McElroy's *Women & Men*, in the novels of Christine Brooke-Rose and Kathy Acker, and so on. Here is Sukenick, for example:

> Another call. And still another. Three calls in succession all pointing to financial catastrophe. This is what happens when you try to finish a story you been working on for two weeks in one hour. Nobody ever calls me here. Few people know

my number. I set myself the hour, I start composing, and
there you are. All plans shattered. Fuck it. I think I'll have
a drink. I mean another drink. Angel milk. Everything's blow-
ing up, falling to pieces. Art dissolves back into life. Chaos.
It's not the way I planned it. Just burned my desk badly with
a cigarette. What else can happen? The house can burn
down. Finish my half pint, Golden Days. A little Jimmy Reed
on the phonograph. I'm at my best when everything ex-
plodes. I thrive on chaos. I have feeling for it, a blues mentality, if you know what I mean. I have a feeling for it. Actually
I'm quite happy. Didn't wanna work next year anyway, not
really. What a relief. And the review of my Stevens book, just
got a good review in *The New York Review* one of the calls told
me. That was one of the two books I was working on. Did
anybody ever write a story like this? *I wanna roll you baby/roll
you all over town.* Unfortunately it'll never be published. *Some
time you have to cry/some time you have to lie/you can make it if
you try.* But I'm not even gonna try, fuck it, I'm just gonna
sit here and finish my half pint. *Feeling lowdown.*[3]

Sukenick's consciousness, like Bloom's, streams. Like Bloom's, too,
it absorbs inputs from the world outside it (telephone calls, Jimmy
Reed's blues), registers activities in the present ("Just burned my desk
badly with a cigarette"), recalls the past ("one of the two books I was
working on"), and projects alternative possible futures ("The house can
burn down," "Didn't wanna work next year anyway," "It'll never be
published"). Finally, Sukenick's present unfolds, like Bloom's, at about
the same rate as the reader's reading of the passage; the two durations,
character's and reader's, are roughly commensurate. But unlike Bloom's,
Sukenick's present is also the moment of composition—the scene of
writing ("I set myself the hour, I start composing, and there you are").
The present of writing and the present of reading, one "inside" the
world of the text and the other "outside" it, mirror one another;
Sukenick's phenomenological present is transferred to the reader, across
the text/world interface. "Art dissolves back into life" (in a different
sense than Sukenick probably intended).
    "Did anybody ever write a story like this?" Yes, Beckett did, for
one, in *Texts for Nothing* and elsewhere; Steve Katz did, the year before,
in *The Exagggerations* [sic] *of Peter Prince;* Raymond Federman would, a
little later, in *The Voice in the Closet;* later still, so would intransigently
anti-illusionistic novelists such as Kathy Acker, whom Tabbi associates
with a contemporary "apocalyptic" mode in fiction. Other postmodernist

novelists, employing other methods, also would displace phenomenological presentness from the level of the character to the level of the
reader. Singer traces this displacement of presentness from character to
reader in his chapter in this volume, and, unless I am mistaken, it also
is the focus of Leslie Scalapino's and Lidia Yuknavitch's chapters, perhaps also of Brian Evenson's. Scalapino, for instance, characterizes her
text *Defoe* as "a fiction which is 'within' its language" but also one that
"was not to be a virtual reality"—not a virtual reality, not a simulated
experience because, I infer, it constitutes an *actual* experience for the
reader. Yuknavitch writes:

> my writer self began to loop into her selves until the charac-
> ter self in my novel, plus the writer self looking in toward
> her, and the self writing this text all became indistinguish-
> able from the words. I thought this will confuse readers.
> They will lose their place.

Precisely. Readers "lose their place" and acquire a new one, a place
(and time) "indistinguishable from the words." "A production of presence in the prose itself," Tabbi calls it: fiction's present.

The second of fiction's two presents is its *historical present.* To inquire into fiction's present in this sense is to raise the question of
fiction's responsibility to its historical moment. It is to consider how
fiction takes stock of its own situation (which is also our collective
situation) in time and space, in the light of its (and our) past and its
(and our) possible futures. Alternatively, to inquire into fiction's historical present might also be to ask how the historical moment shapes,
enables, and constrains fiction. Or, finally, to inquire into fiction's historical present might be to reflect on the means by which historicity,
the experience of history, comes to be incorporated into fiction. All
three of these projects are represented in this volume.

Fiction's responsibility to its historical moment, its attempt to grasp
its own historical situatedness, is akin to what Fredric Jameson famously
called *cognitive mapping.* Timothy Murphy calls it that, too, in his chapter in this volume, adopting Jameson's definition: cognitive mapping is
the individual's situated representation of "that vaster and properly
unrepresentable totality which is the ensemble of society's structures as
a whole."[4] *Postmodernism,* in this context, is either a name for a particular cognitive mapping of the contemporary world or a name for what
impedes and inhibits our achieving such a cognitive mapping (or both
at once, conceivably). Murphy thinks it is the latter, an impediment to

cognitive mapping. Robert McLaughlin also thinks so, but he detects a renewal of responsibility toward the historical present in some varieties of *post*-postmodernist fiction (Jonathan Franzen, David Foster Wallace). In a similar vein, Christina Milletti counters the charge that fiction has failed to capture our historical moment—specifically, our post-9/11 moment—by citing innovative fictions by Gertrude Stein, Kathy Acker, and Christine Brooke-Rose that do engage the present, but that do so *through*, not *despite*, their formal innovations. Tabbi imagines a genre (or anti-genre) of "world-fictions" that would be adequate to the "world-system" that is in the process of overwhelming and displacing national states and their national literatures. He thinks he has glimpsed the forerunners of this emergent world-fiction in Tolstoy, Melville, Gaddis, Pynchon, and Vollmann.[5]

How does the historical present shape, enable, and constrain fiction? This seems to be the question that mainly animates R. M. Berry's and Jeffrey Di Leo's "Twelve Theses," though they also raise questions about fiction's responsibility to and engagement with its present. Fiction's place in our historical moment, in particular its situation in relation to a contemporary mediascape dominated by speedier, higher-resolution virtual realities, is taken up by Samuel Delany, Raymond Federman, and Tabbi. Jerome Klinkowitz addresses the same issue in a more concrete and narrowly focused way in his case study of the Fiction Collective's changing relationship to the publishing industry and the commercial marketplace in the last quarter of the twentieth century.

Finally, the issue of fiction's historical present can be viewed in light of "historical fiction," in an extended sense. How does the novel incorporate the experience of history? How does it reflect historicity? Robert Caserio approaches this concretely, proposing a number of devices by which the historical is inserted or embedded in the novel, literally folded into it, including inset narratives and the figure of *mise-en-abyme* (though he does not use that term). Joseph McElroy is more speculative. Surveying a number of more or less likely candidates (Ford's *The Fifth Queen*, Coetzee's *The Master of Petersburg*, Leonid Tsypkin's *Summer in Baden-Baden*), he seeks "a novel whose ground is a history intersection, its mind not brio of invention but, on the one hand, contained inside a factual spirit while, on the other, acknowledging how it [the factual spirit, presumably] got there." If such a novel existed (as perhaps it does), then it too would constitute a version of fiction's historical presentness, though not necessarily a cognitive mapping of its immediate situation.

So if about half of this volume's contributors are concerned with fiction's phenomenological present—in some cases, the characters'

phenomenological present, in other cases, the reader's, and in still
others, both—while the other half are concerned with some version of
its historical present, then are they all just talking at cross purposes?
Well, maybe—though it might be more generous (and probably more
accurate) to say that they are talking not at cross purposes exactly but
at various angles to each other. Still, it would be easier to reconcile
them all if there were some unproblematical way to integrate phenomenological presentness and historical presentness in a sort of "unified
field theory" of fiction's present. Unfortunately, such a unified picture
is hard to come by—perhaps impossible. "Fiction," Tabbi writes, "needs
to create in readers an *experience of presence,* bringing to consciousness
the experience of living in 'an integrated zone of activity and institutions which obey certain system rules' " (the quoted phrase is Immanuel
Wallerstein's). Phenomenological presence and historical presentness
need to be brought together. Yes, but how exactly?

On the one hand, it clearly will not do just to imagine that because historical presentness is a *collective* experience, one that all of us
who occupy the same time and space share, then all we need to do is
add up all the individual phenomenological presents reflected in all our
contemporaries' fictions in order to achieve a kind of cumulative historical present of fiction generally. The historical present *is not* merely
additive or cumulative; it is not just a matter of piling up individual
experiences until we get a tall enough pile to qualify as "our historical
moment." The whole is greater, and different, than the sum of its parts.
At some point, structure intervenes—precisely that "ensemble of society's
structures as a whole" that is so hard for the individual subject to grasp,
and that necessitates cognitive mapping.

An alternative approach, then, might be to develop some model of
integration where one present fits inside the other more or less snugly,
like *matrushka* dolls—some kind of concentric model, where fiction's
phenomenological present appears as inscribed within, circumscribed by,
the collective historical present, circle within circle. Perhaps the historical present could be seen as constituting the phenomenological present's
horizon of expectations (see Murphy's chapter), establishing the conditions
for its coming to be in the first place, and the outer limits of its possibilities. Attractive though this may be as a way of integrating the two presents
in the abstract, it does not help us much when it comes to bridging in
concrete terms the gap between, say, Sukenick's phenomenological present
(which also is ours, his readers') near the end of "The Death of the
Novel" and the collective historical present of 1969 or 2006.

If abstract models fail us, then perhaps we should look for places
where the phenomenological present and the historical present coincide

or converge in some illuminating way. One such place of intersection and overlap might be the sphere of *doxa*, as Sue-Im Lee describes it here in her chapter on Lynne Tillman's fiction. Doxa is the discourse of the collective—the stereotypical, the clichéd, the taken-for-granted, common knowledge; what goes without saying; what "everybody knows." It is, of course, historical through and through; it is utterly determined by its historical moment—the "voice," in some sense, of its time and place, the mirror of its historical present. But doxa also makes up a large portion of the interior discourse of fictional characters (and of their readers, for that matter). Mr. Bloom's interior discourse, for instance, is saturated with the language of received wisdom and unexamined platitudes, of doxa ("Perhaps [Hamlet] was a woman. Why Ophelia committed suicide?"), but so is Sukenick's in "The Death of the Novel" ("I thrive on chaos. I have feeling for it, a blues mentality, if you know what I mean"). Here, then, is one place where the phenomenological present is literally, demonstrably informed by the historical present—where the historical present, at least in part, *constitutes* the phenomenological present.

Doxa is general, like the snow all over Ireland; like oxygen, it is everywhere. But fiction's two presents, phenomenological and historical, also may converge at certain specific points, specific moments. One such moment might be the shattering recognition of race and violence undergone by Melville's Captain Delano, in Tabbi's account, in which both cognitive structure and the world-system are implicated. Another such moment is the one Carole Maso evokes in her contribution to this volume. On the one hand, what happened in New York City on September 11, 2001, undoubtedly belongs to the order of world-historical events; it looms monstrously large in our sense of our own, and fiction's, historical present. On the other hand, the events of that morning also formed part of our own individual phenomenological presents, and those of some fictions (more and more of them, with the passage of time: William Gibson's *Pattern Recognition*, Jonathan Safran Foer's *Extremely Loud and Incredibly Close*, Ian McEwan's *Saturday*, Jay McInerney's *The Good Life*, Ron Sukenick's *Last Fall*, etc.; see Christina Milletti's chapter). We experienced those events—most of us, thankfully, mediately, not immediately, through the mediation of televised images—and incorporated them in our moments of consciousness on that day, to be recovered at later moments as more or less traumatic memories. Fiction's historical and phenomenological presents converge on 9/11, and Carole Maso, reflecting on fiction's present, boldly appropriates one of the repressed and forbidden images of that day—the image of the falling man, of falling people[6]—to capture her sense of what the novel must become now in the present in which it finds itself. "As the novel breaks apart," she writes,

> becoming shards, a debris field, without a real audience or raison d'etre, it free falls into the space of pure radiance, a place of unimaginable intellectual and emotional freedom.

I am struck by the resonances between this haunting image and one of Lidia Yuknavitch's, in her own chapter here:

> This made me feel briefly like an untethered astronaut. . . . I became as free floating as a word or image let loose from its meaning-making.

Is this the ultimate image of fiction's present that we should take away from this volume: fiction after 9/11 free-falling into its own present, its own two presents? And which is it, free-*falling* or free-*floating*? Is there a difference?

NOTES

1. James Joyce, *Ulysses* (1934, 75).
2. See Ryan (2001). Another relevant pair of terms is Charles Bernstein's opposition of absorption versus artifice in his poem-essay, "Artifice of Absorption" (1992).
3. Ronald Sukenick, *The death of the novel and other stories* (1969, 100–101).
4. Frederic Jameson, *Postmodernism, or, The Cultural Logic of Late Captialism* (1990, 51), quoted in Murphy's chapter. See also Jameson's "Cognitive Mapping" (1988).
5. I take it that Tabbi's world-fiction is akin to what Franco Moretti has called "world-texts" (1996).
6. I'm indebted for my understanding of the imagery of 9/11, and in particular of Richard Drew's photograph of one falling man, widely seen and then abruptly and utterly repressed, to Peggy Phelan's moving lecture, "Performance Photography: Narrating the Present Tense" (2004).

REFERENCES

Bernstein, Charles. 1992. Artifice of absorption. In *A poetics*, 9–89. Cambridge MA: Harvard University Press.

Jameson, Frederic. 1990. *Postmodernism, or, the cultural logic of late capitalism.* Durham: Duke University Press.

————. 1988. Cognitive mapping. In *Marxism and the Interpretation of Culture*, eds. Cary Nelson and Lawrence Grossberg, 347–357. Urbana and Chicago: University of Illinois Press.

Joyce, James. 1934. *Ulysses*. New York: Random House.

Moretti, Franco. 1996. *Modern epic: The world-system from Goethe to García Márquez*. London and New York: Verso.

Phelan, Peggy. 2004. Performance photography: narrating the present tense. Paper presented at the Annual Meeting of the Society for the Study of Narrative Literature, Burlington, Vermont.

Ryan, Marie-Laure. 2001. *Narrative as virtual reality: Immersion and interactivity in literature and electronic media*. Baltimore: Johns Hopkins University Press.

Sukenick, Ronald. 1969. *The death of the novel and other stories*. New York: Dial Press, 1969.

About the Contributors

R. M. Berry, professor of English at Florida State University, is the author of the novel *Leonardo's Horse* and the story collection *Dictionary of Modern Anguish*. His literary criticism has appeared in *Philosophy and Literature*, *Narrative*, *The Journal of Beckett Studies*, and various anthologies.

Robert L. Caserio, author of *The Novel in England 1900–1950*, is professor of English at Pennsylvania State University, University Park. His recent writing on fiction appears in *A Concise Companion to Contemporary British Fiction* and in *The Cambridge History of Twentieth-Century English Literature*.

Samuel R. Delany is the author of *Hogg, Dhalgren, Phallos*, and, most recently, *About Writing*. He teaches at Temple University.

Jeffrey R. Di Leo is dean of the School of Arts and Sciences at the University of Houston-Victoria. He is editor and founder of the journal *symplokē* and editor and publisher of the *American Book Review*. His most recent publications include *Affiliations: Identity in Academic Culture, On Anthologies: Politics and Pedagogy*, and *From Socrates to Cinema: An Introduction to Philosophy*.

Brian Evenson is the author of eight books of fiction, most recently *The Open Curtain*. He is a senior editor for *Conjunctions* magazine. He also is the director of the Literary Arts Program at Brown University, where he teaches fiction writing.

Percival Everett is professor of English at the University of Southern California. His novels include *Glyph, Erasure*, and *American Desert*, among others.

Raymond Federman's latest novel, *Return to Manure*, was recently published in both French and English versions. Also published recently was *Le Livre de Sam*, a memoir of Federman's friendship with Samuel Beckett.

Jerome Klinkowitz helps edit *The Norton Anthology of American Literature*. Among his forty books are *Keeping Literary Company*, *You've Got to Be Carefully Taught*, and *The Vonnegut Effect*.

Sue-Im Lee is assistant professor of English at Temple University. In addition to essays in contemporary U.S. fiction and Asian American literature, Lee is the coeditor of *Literary Gestures: The Aesthetic in Asian American Writing*. She is currently at work on the book *A Body of Individuals: The Paradox of Community in Contemporary Fiction*.

Michael Martone's new book is *Michael Martone*, a memoir, composed of fifty different contributors' notes.

Carole Maso is the author of nine books, including the novels *Ava* and *Defiance*, a book of essays, *Break Every Rule*, a memoir, *The Room Lit by Roses*, and the prose poems, *Beauty is Convulsive*. She teaches at Brown University.

Joseph McElroy is the author of the following nine novels: *A Smuggler's Bible*, *Hind's Kidnap*, *Ancient History*, *Lookout Cartridge*, *Plus*, *Women and Men*, *The Letter Left to Me*, *Actress in the House*, and the forthcoming *Cannonball*. He has received the Award in Literature from the American Academy of Arts and Letters.

Brian McHale is Distinguished Humanities Professor in English at Ohio State University. He is the author of *Postmodernist Fiction*, *Constructing Postmodernism*, and *The Obligation toward the Difficult Whole: Postmodernist Long Poems*. He also is the coeditor, with Randall Stevenson, of *The Edinburgh Companion to Twentieth-Century Literatures in English*.

Robert L. McLaughlin is professor of English at Illinois State University and writes frequently on postmodern fiction and culture. He wrote with Sally E. Parry *We'll Always Have the Movies: American Cinema during World War II*.

Christina Milletti is assistant professor of English at the University at Buffalo, State University of New York, where she teaches fiction writing and the twentieth-century novel. Her collection of short stories, *The Religious and Other Fictions*, was recently published.

Timothy S. Murphy, associate professor of English at the University of Oklahoma, is the author of *Wising Up to the Marks: The Amodern William Burroughs,* the general editor of the journal *Genre: Forms of Discourse and Culture,* and the translator of books and articles by Deleuze, Derrida, and Negri.

Lance Olsen, chair of the board of directors at FC2, has authored many books of and about innovative fiction, including, most recently, *Anxious Pleasures, Nietzsche's Kisses,* and *10:01.*

Leslie Scalapino has written twenty-five books of poetry, fiction, essays, and plays. The most recent is *Dahlia's Iris—Secret Autobiography and Fiction.* Also recent is *Zither & Autobiography.*

Alan Singer, professor of English at Temple University, writes on literary theory, aesthetics, and the visual arts. His most recent book is *Aesthetic Reason: Artworks and the Deliberative Ethos.* He has published four novels, most recently *Dirtmouth.* He is currently completing the new novel *The Inquisitor's Tongue* and a critical work tentatively titled *The Self-Deceiving Muse.*

Ronald Sukenick was publisher and founder of the *American Book Review* and board chair and founding member of Fiction Collective Two until his death in the summer of 2004. He authored more than a dozen books, including the classic novel of the 1960s, *98.6.* He was the recipient of the American Book Award and the Morton Dauwen Zabel Award from the American Academy of Arts and Letters.

Joseph Tabbi is the author of *Cognitive Fictions,* founding editor of *ebr,* and professor of English at the University of Illinois at Chicago.

Lidia Yuknavitch is the author of three works of short fiction, including *Real to Reel,* as well as the author of a sociocritical book on narrative and violence. She is the editor of *Chiasmus Press.*

Index

Cornell, Joseph, 34
Cornell University, 240
corporation, 36, 39, 102–103
Correction (Bernhard), 152–155
Corrections, The (Franzen), 109, 111
Cortázar, Julio, 187
Cortez Cruz, Ricardo, 246
Corvo, Baron, 13
  Hadrian the VII, 13
cosmopolitanism, 96–97
Cottom, Daniel, 42n. 3
counter-globalization, 36–43
  See also anti-globalization; global-
    ization; globalization studies
Count Zero (Gibson), 42n. 3
Cradle Will Rock, The (Robbins), 11
Creamy and Delicious (Katz), 240
creative writing See under writing
Credits Included (Toufic), 59
crime, 22, 71, 113, 123
Critical Inquiry, 17
criticism, 3–4, 6–7, 17, 30, 75, 82,
    87, 89, 91, 185
  disciplinary, 82
  literary, 3, 87, 165, 246
  materialist, 82
  See also critics
critics, 3–9, 14, 29–31, 40, 73, 89,
    91, 104, 111, 164, 166, 221, 244
  academic, 76, 180
  literary, 132
  See also criticism
critifiction, 19, 185, 188, 228
Cruise, Tom, 18
culture, 19, 38, 72, 74, 76, 79, 85,
    87–88, 90, 95, 102, 108–109,
    111, 113, 116, 154, 185, 221,
    229
  American, 232
  business, 2
  common, 74–75
  consumer, 110, 115
  contemporary, 3, 29, 111, 221
  corporate, 78
  digital, 257

industry, 37–39
instant messaging, 19
local, 246
mass, 17
material, 84–85
media, 84–85
of counter-globalization, 40–41 (see
    also globalization)
of globalization, 97
of irony, 113
pop, 106, 110, 219, 242–243, 246–
    247
postmodern, 111
supplement of, 223, 226, 228
surplus of, 228
televisual, 114, 223
cultural studies, 30, 76, 81
cyberpunk, 34
  movement, 34
  See also fiction: cyberpunk

Dante, 148, 217
Davenport, Guy, 14
DaVinci Code, The (Brown), 18, 20–
    21
Davis, Lydia, 108
De Man, Paul, 14
Dean, James, 503
death, 20, 50–53, 77, 79, 82, 114,
    125–126, 152–153, 186
Death in Venice (Mann), 203
Death of the Novel and Other Stories, The
    (Sukenick), 236–237, 240, 255
Death, Sleep, and the Traveler
    (Hawkes), 143
deconstruction, 57, 81
Defoe (Scalapino), 53, 55–64
Delacorte Press, 240
  See also press
Delany, Samuel, 260
Delay, Tom, 71
Delbanco, Andrew, 73, 89, 92–97
  Melville, 97
Deleuze, Gilles, 48–49, 54, 154–155,
    156n. 2

economy, 36, 39, 41, 83–85, 221
  of attention, 130
  of fiction's present, 257
  of writing a novel, 216
*Edinborough Companion to Twentieth-
  Century Literatures in English*, 84
electronic book review (ebr), 73–74
Eliot, T. S., 34, 42n. 2, 97, 101, 187
  Waste Land, The, 101
Ellis, Brett Easton, 73, 94
Elman, Richard, 243
  Namedropping, 243
Emergency Exit (Major), 241
Emerson, Ralph Waldo, 73, 82, 91
emotion, 49–50, 56, 58, 114
empire, 36, 74, 76–77, 79, 83, 85–86,
  177, 180, 204
Empire (Hardt and Negri), 36, 43n.
  18, 73–74, 77–78
Empire of the Senseless (Acker), 77–80
Empire's New Clothes, The
  (Harootunian), 98n. 1
Endless Short Story, The (Sukenick),
  238
Engels, Friedrich, 33, 71
  Communist Manifesto (with Karl
  Marx), 33
  See also Marx, Karl and Marxism
English studies, 159, 161
Enlightenment, 134–135
entertainment, 18, 20, 218, 222–224,
  226, 228, 240
environment, 79, 86, 90, 150
  activism for, 39
  electronic, 96
  historical, 161
  narrative, 197, 205–206
  of author, 96
  of city, 96
  of information, 75, 92
  of media, 89–90, 97
  textual, 96
  threats to, 1
  See also ecology; nature
epic, 1, 172

Ernst, Max, 189
  Hundred-Headed Woman, 189
escapism, 20
Esquire, 18
essays, 1, 9
Estes, Richard, 241
eternal recurrence, 53–54
ethnicity, 35, 85
Europe, 5–6, 34, 83, 165, 200, 232
Evenson, Brian, 259
event, 49, 51–62
Everett, Percival, 209
evidence, 129–137
  See also self-deceiver
Exagggerations of Peter Prince, The
  (Katz), 240, 258
exchange value, 38
Excitable Speech (Butler), 22
experimental fiction *See under* fiction
experimentation, 14, 110, 142, 244
extended haiku, 12–13
Extremely Loud and Incredibly Close
  (Foer), 262

Farrell, Stephen, 84
fascism, 165
Fathers and Crows (Vollmann), 172–180
Faulkner, William, 34, 224, 233, 255–
  256
  Absalom, Absalom!, 257
  Sound and the Fury, The, 233
Federman, Raymond, 228, 238–239,
  242, 244–247, 258, 260
  Take It or Leave It, 238
  Voice in the Closet, The, 258
Female Man, The (Russ), 43n. 16
Fiction Collective, 235–247
  See also FC2
FC2 (Fiction Collective Two), 235–247
  See also Fiction Collective
fiction, 1–10, 11–15, 17–21, 25–26,
  34, 40, 47–54, 59, 63, 67–68, 73,
  76–79, 82–83, 86, 92, 97, 102–
  104, 107, 109–111, 114, 116,
  128, 132, 140, 145, 147–148,